AN OBSERVER'S GUIDE

First Steps in Upholstery

Traditional Handmade

Observer's Guides

Home and Garden

The Herb Grower's Guide
Car Care

Art and Craft

Pencil Drawing
Drawing with Ink
Using Pastels
Beginning Watercolour
Materials and Techniques of Oil Painting
Materials and Techniques of Watercolour
Materials and Techniques of Acrylic Painting
Materials and Techniques of Collage
Let's Make Pottery
First Steps in Upholstery—Traditional Handmade

Where Is It?

British Paintings—Hogarth to Turner
European Paintings of the 18th Century
Twentieth Century Paintings—Bonnard to Rothko
Italian, French and Spanish Paintings of the 17th Century
British Paintings of the 19th Century
Paintings and Sculptures of the 15th Century
Nineteenth Century Continental Painters
European Paintings of the 19th Century
Dutch and Flemish Paintings of the 17th Century

AN OBSERVER'S GUIDE

First Steps in Upholstery

Traditional Handmade

Hilary Clare

Line drawings by Dinah Cohen

FREDERICK WARNE

Published by Frederick Warne (Publishers) Ltd, London, 1981

The author would like to thank Pam Wood for her assistance in reading the draft manuscript and proofs.

Imperial and metric measurements are used throughout the book. Where measurements are given as a guide to working the metric equivalents are shown in accurate proportion to the imperial measurements.

ISBN 0 7232 2761 6

Printed and bound in Great Britain by
Butler & Tanner Ltd, Frome and London
1618.681

Contents

Introduction

Upholsterers skilled in traditional handmade work are regrettably a dying breed as young people are unwilling to undertake the long apprenticeship involved. When they can be found today, their prices are high due to the time the work takes and the increasing cost of the basic materials. This is disappointing to people who, like myself, are fascinated by old chairs, whether they are furnishing a home or have an heirloom in need of attention.

However, judging from the popularity of adult education upholstery classes and short residential courses, more and more people are becoming interested in learning this craft. This makes sense as, apart from renewing the cover when it becomes dirty or worn, a well-executed, traditional handmade upholstered chair has a life of at least twenty years.

An antique chair cannot be upholstered successfully by modern methods and, due to the inevitable disintegration of foam, would in any case have a much shorter life. Hence all the methods described apply to traditional handmade upholstery with no reference being made to modern foam techniques.

This book is written for the amateur and I would strongly urge, as it is only short, that you take the time to read through the early chapters before attempting any practical work. The chapter on terminology is of particular importance as the terms mentioned apply to all upholstery work and subsequently they are frequently referred to on the assumption that you are familiar with them.

A piece of advice: choose a dining chair or stool as your first job. This will give you valuable experience for more difficult work and, as it will not take too long to finish, your enthusiasm for the craft will be maintained.

Although upholstery is time-consuming, the results are most rewarding. I hope that this book will pass on to you some of the satisfaction and enjoyment which I gain from the craft.

Tools

Not many tools are required for upholstery and they are not too expensive—an investment of a few pounds will cover their cost and this may be reduced further by raiding the household toolbox. However, as with any craft, the bad workman will not be able to blame his tools if the correct ones are used (Figure 1).

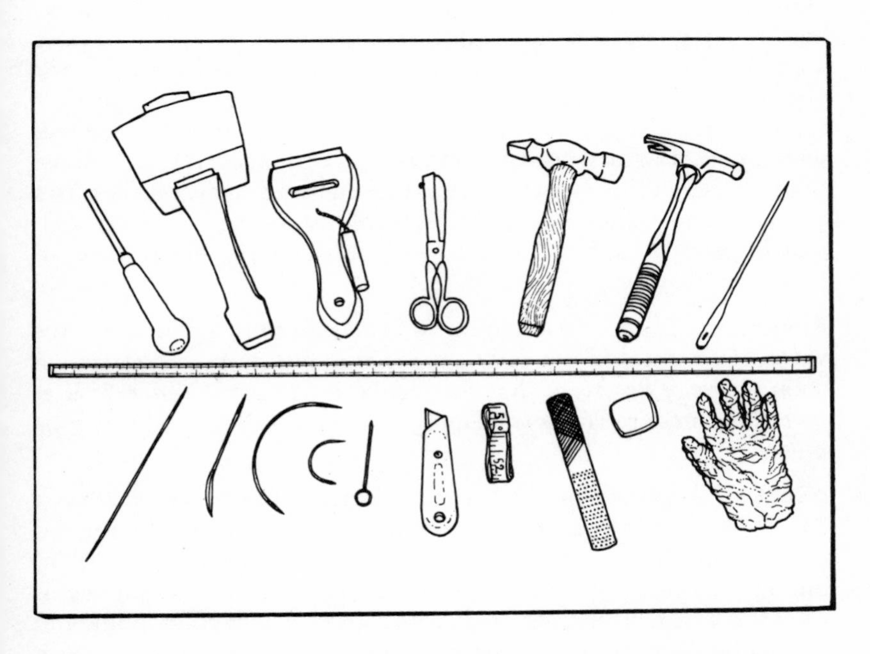

Figure 1 ripping chisel; mallet; webbing stretcher; scissors; webbing hammer; upholsterer's hammer; regulator; mattress needle; spring needle; twine needle; sewing needle; skewer; craft knife; metre stick; tape measure; wood rasp; tailor's chalk; old leather glove

Hand tools

Ripping chisel This is used in conjunction with the mallet for lifting out tacks when taking off the old upholstery from a chair.

Mallet 10 cm (4 in) or 11.5 cm (4½ in) wooden mallet is used to hit the end of the wooden handle of the ripping chisel to lift out tacks when taking off old upholstery. A hammer should not be used for this purpose as the impact of the metal head is too severe on the chair frame.

Webbing stretcher Although there are various types of webbing stretcher, the one illustrated is the one most commonly used.

Scissors 22.5 cm (9 in) in overall length. The scissors illustrated are ideal for all upholstery work and using them with the blunt nose on the bottom prevents cutting any layer of material other than the one intended.

Hammers Two hammers are required. The first is used for tacking webbing only—a household hammer with a heavy head is suitable. The second is an upholsterer's hammer which has, at one end, a claw for lifting out tacks and, at the other, a 13 mm (½ in) tacking head. The upholsterer's hammer is beautifully weighted, which makes light work of hammering in the tacks. Today, most of these hammers have a magnetic tacking head, which has its uses but can also inflict injury on the upholstery novice. It is well worthwhile trying to purchase an upholsterer's hammer without magnetic head.

Regulator 25 cm (10 in) long. When beginning upholstery, the value of this tool is not fully appreciated but, with experience, it soon becomes apparent that the regulator has many different uses including manipulating stuffings, easing material and forming pleats.

Needles A variety of needles is required in upholstery and each has its special job, but they are not expensive. The double pointed mattress needle is available in various lengths, but a 25 cm (10 in) one will do most jobs. The spring needle, as the name implies, is used for sewing in springs; it is curved and has a bayonet point and should be 12.5 cm (5 in) in length. The curved needle for use with twine has one pointed end and should also measure 12.5 cm (5 in). The small, fine, curved needle, threaded with carpet thread, is used whenever any sewing is required on the covering material.

Skewers 10 cm (4 in) long with a looped circular end, these skewers are unique to upholstery. They replace pins in dressmaking, so buy at least two dozen.

Other items You will almost certainly already have some of the following at home: sharp-bladed craft knife, wooden metre stick, cloth tape measure, coarse wood rasp, tailor's chalk and an old leather glove (right hand if you are right handed).

Work surface

The best work surface is a carpenter's bench because it is the right height and heavy enough not to move when work is in progress. In addition its vices are useful for holding drop-in seats when taking off old upholstery. Many people work on a pair of trestles. The tops of the trestles need to be lipped on both sides and both ends to prevent the chair legs from sliding off. Alternatively, a board 175 cm (5 ft) by 87 cm (2½ ft) can be laid on top of the trestles. However, whatever you choose or have available, do work on a surface at table top height, as upholstery is easier and less tiring to do standing up.

Before deciding upon the location of your work surface, bear in mind that taking off old upholstery is a dusty, dirty job.

Sewing machine

Upholstery requires a sewing machine capable of sewing through four and sometimes five thicknesses of upholstery covering material—for instance when sewing piping into a seam. For this reason, an industrial sewing machine is the most suitable type, but since few people are likely to own one, I recommend that you use an older, heavier machine rather than a modern, lightweight one, as these are not generally engineered for such work. Use a thick gauge needle and always machine with button thread, as dressweight cottons are not strong enough. You will also need two sewing feet for your machine—a straight stitch foot and a piping/zipper foot.

Upholstery supplies

When obtaining supplies, there is less wastage when a greater quantity is purchased. However, how much of each item you buy will depend on the amount of upholstery you intend doing and the outlay you want to make.

Webbing Generally 5 cm (2 in) wide, webbing is of two types: Old English black and white, which is the stronger, and Elephant brand brown jute webbing. It is sold by the metre or by the roll.

Hessian Available in various weights. Tarpaulin or mangled hessian is required for covering webbing and springs where strength is needed and 305 g (10 oz) hessian is used on the outside back and outside arms of chairs. It is usually 183 cm (72 in) wide.

Scrim Jute and linen scrims are available. The jute variety, 183 cm (72 in) wide, is the cheaper and is suitable for all purposes. However, where fine work is required the linen scrim, 102 cm (40 in) wide, is easier to work.

Calico Lightweight unbleached calico, 185 cm (73 in) wide, is used for undercovering. However, if the chair is to have a loose cover, then a heavier calico is more suitable. Black calico/black lining, 79 cm (31 in) or 122 cm (48 in) wide, is tacked on the underside of the work to make a neat finish by covering the tacks and the raw edges of the covering material.

Horsehair Horsehair is taken from the mane and tail. It is washed, twisted into ropes and the curl set by steaming and boiling. When dry, the ropes are untwisted and teased. It is very expensive to buy new and even then will probably not be pure horsehair but a mixture, the greater percentage being hogshair which is too soft and has short, straight hairs. The best horsehair is long and curly, giving spring and resilience to the upholstery. Ask your friends if they have an old horsehair mattress they no longer need, or advertise for one in a corner shop. If you can obtain one, it will need to be unpicked and then cleaned. The cleaning is best done through a carding machine which has a vacuum for extracting the dust and a carding attachment which combs and loosens the hair. Your local upholsterer may have a carding machine and be prepared to do this for you or he may know someone who has such a machine. Otherwise, the horsehair can be put into an old pillowcase, securely tying the opening with twine, and washed in the bath. This will certainly get the horsehair clean but, when it is dry, it will need to be carefully teased out by hand which takes time and never leaves the hair as loose and fluffy as when it has been machine carded.

Fibre Horsehair can be used for both the first and second stuffings in upholstery but, as it is so expensive, it is usually used only for the second stuffing. Fibre is therefore used for the first stuffing and this can be of two kinds: Algerian grass and coir. Algerian grass is curled and dried shredded palm leaves and can be green or black in colour; coir is coconut fibre and tan coloured. I personally find that Algerian grass is easier to work.

Wadding This is put on top of the second stuffing to prevent horsehair working its way through the covering material. Again there are two types: lintafelt and skin wadding. Lintafelt, 67 cm (27 in) wide, is cotton waste felted together to form a thick layer. A single thickness is used on seats of easy chair size and larger and when deep buttoning. Skin wadding, 45 cm (18 in) wide, is used in a double layer on smaller seats and on the inside back and inside arms of chairs—one layer only being necessary on the outside back and outside arms where there is no horsehair. When using skin wadding, tear off the fold on both sides of the length to make a soft edge.

Piping cord (Figure 2a) Different thicknesses of cotton piping cord can be purchased and the diameter required depends on the size of the chair and on the covering material used. A fabric with a pile requires a small diameter cord because the pile stands up and this makes the piping seem wide, whereas a finely woven material needs a thicker cord to produce the same effect.

Twine Upholstery twine (Figure 2b–d) is made from jute or hemp and is very strong—ordinary string is no substitute. Twine is available in various thicknesses with the stoutest, no. 1 (2b), being used for tying springs to webbing and the finest, no. 3 (2d), for stitching. However, to begin with, buy one ball of medium, no. 2 (2c),

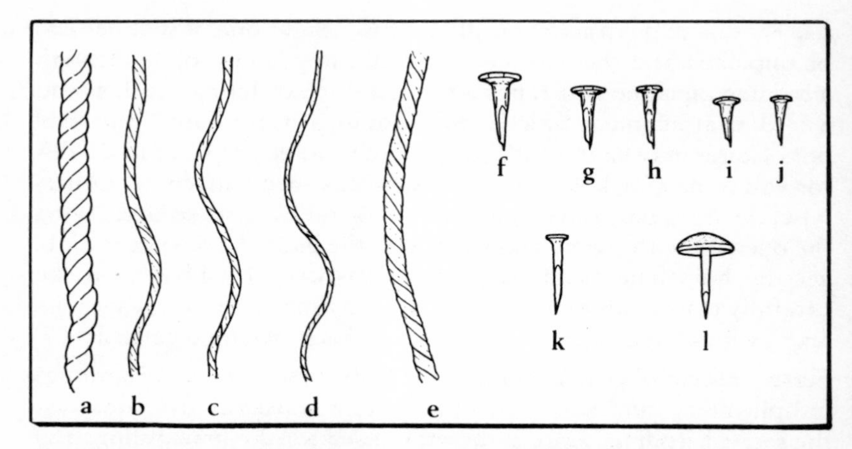

Figure 2 a piping cord; **b, c, d** twines nos. 1, 2 and 3; **e** laid cord; tacks—**f** 16 mm (5/8 in) improved; **g** 13 mm (1/2 in) improved; **h** 13 mm (1/2 in) fine; **i** 10 mm (3/8 in) improved; **j** 10 mm (3/8 in) fine; **k** 13 mm (1/2 in) gimp pin; **l** 13 mm (1/2 in brass nail

upholstery twine, which should meet all requirements as it is both fine enough to stitch with and sufficiently stout to tie in the springs. Always draw the twine from the centre of the ball. It is advisable to put the ball in a container with a hole in the lid for the twine to pass through, as this will prevent the twine from becoming knotted when the ball disintegrates.

Laid cord Laid cord (Figure 2e) is very thick and is used for tying the springs. It is sold in 500 g (1 lb) balls.

Thread It is not necessary for the colour of the thread to match the fabric as none of the stitching will show. A neutral fawn colour will be suitable for most work. Button thread should always be used when machining. For slip stitching, however, it is best to use carpet thread.

Tacks A tip for the newcomer to this craft—upholsterers use tacks and not nails! The difference is in the fine tip on the upholsterer's blued tack (Figure 2f–j) which enables the worker to position the tack with thumb pressure before hitting it with the hammer. Tacks have heads which are improved or fine. The improved heads are larger and are used when fixing open-weave materials, ie webbing, hessian and scrim. Fine-headed tacks are used for fixing close-weave fabrics, ie calico and covering materials. However, if the wood is very hard or the tacking recess is narrow, then use fine-headed tacks where normally improved tacks would be required.

These will be easier to hammer in and will not split the wood. Longer tacks are used for fixing materials which give strength to the upholstery, eg webbing and mangled hessian.

The following sizes of tacks will be required: 16 mm ($\frac{5}{8}$ in) improved (2f), 13 mm ($\frac{1}{2}$ in) improved (2g) and fine (2h), and 10 mm ($\frac{3}{8}$ in) improved (2i) and fine (2j). They are sold in 500 g (1 lb) boxes. Keep each type separate and labelled in screw-top jars or tins.

Gimp pins 13 mm ($\frac{1}{2}$ in) are used for fixing braid (Figure 2h). They are available in various colours.

Adhesives A latex adhesive is used to attach the braid. The only other glue used in traditional handmade upholstery is for repairing the wooden frame. Animal glue, bought in pellets and dissolved in water in a glue-pot over a gas jet, has the advantage of being a flexible adhesive and is reversible—water being the solvent. However, woodworkers' modern synthetic glues are more easily applied.

Springs The springs used in traditional handmade upholstery are called hour-glass springs (Figure 3). They are made of copper-plated wire, are double cone in form and copper or black in colour.

Figure 3 Double cone 'hour-glass' spring

Various gauge wire is used, ie 8 gauge (the strongest), 9, 10, 12 and 14 (the finest and softest). A guide to the uses of the different gauges is as follows:

8 gauge	settee seats and large armchair seats
9 gauge	smaller armchair seats and nursing chair seats
10 gauge	dining chair seats, inside backs of armchairs and on the spring edge of settee seats and large armchair seats
12/14 gauge	settee arms and large armchair arms (the selection of gauge depends upon the softness required)

Springs vary in length from 10 cm (4 in) to 35 cm (14 in). It is best to measure the springs previously used in the chair and to take one of each type with you to the shop. If you have a bare frame, then the proportions of the chair must always be borne in mind allowing for the fact that springs when tied in will be compressed 25 mm (1 in).

Covering materials The essential factor in a covering material is that it must have 'stretch', otherwise it will be impossible to fit the material tightly to the upholstery. For this reason velvets, linens, tweeds and tapestry materials are excellent. It is important to have a strong material from the point of view of wear and for fitting, as a thin material will tear too easily. If you choose a velvet, make sure that it is upholstery weight and that it contains some synthetic fibre. Pure cotton velvet 'bruises' when sat on and it is impossible to restore the pile. The velvets with synthetic fibre can also be cleaned readily with one of the patent upholstery cleaners. Hide as a covering material is regaining popularity, but it is expensive and requires great skill to fit. I do not, therefore, recommend it to beginners. However, leather-grained PVC (polyvinyl chloride) fabrics, with woven or knitted backing, are an artificial leather suitable for upholstery. They are available in a wide range of colours, have good stretch properties and can be cleaned with a damp cloth. The usual width of covering material is 130 cm (51–52 in).

Pile fabrics, eg velvets, are smooth to the touch in one direction of the length but when the hand is taken in the opposite direction the pile is brushed up. It is essential with these fabrics that the pile runs smoothly from the back to the front of the seat and from the top to the bottom of the back, wings, arms and border. This is so that dust does not settle into the pile and so that when someone edges forward on a seat, he moves with the pile and not against it.

When using a patterned covering material, it is important that the pattern is centred on the inside back and seat and also that the pattern matches on the two inside arms. Centring of the pattern on the outside arms and outside back is less vital but advisable, provided that not too much covering material is wasted. Extra material will be needed with a patterned cover, but how much will depend upon the size and repeat of the pattern. When the material is striped, it will be necessary to line up the stripes on the seat with those on the inside back, and the stripes on the inside arms must match. Again extra material may be required.

Braid Braid is used to trim chairs covered in a fabric. Upholstery braid is usually 15 mm ($\frac{1}{2}$ in) wide and is heavier and more closely woven than the braid used for soft furnishings.

Brass nailing Close nailing gives an attractive finish to hide and PVC fabric covered chairs. The best nails to buy have solid brass domed heads which are 10 mm ($\frac{3}{8}$ in) in diameter and steel shanks 13 mm ($\frac{1}{2}$ in) in length (Figure 2l).

Ripping off and upholstery repairs

Having dealt with the tools and supplies used in upholstery, we are now ready for the practical work. Before you start work on your chair, however, do have a good look at it. That seems an obvious statement but, for example, does the shape of the chair look right or has some unskilled handyman done the last upholstery? If this is the case, there may not be much you can gain at this stage until the old upholstery has been removed. However, you will often find on an old chair that the upholstery was done by a skilled craftsman and it could be that the original upholstery is still on the chair. The writing of notes when taking off the old upholstery will help when the re-upholstery is begun. An alternative to making notes is to take a few photographs at various stages when removing the old upholstery.

Other points to note before starting work are: is the chair comfortable? If you feel that the arms need to be a little thinner or the back a little fatter, then note by how much. Is the seat the right height from the ground? Dining chairs should be 42.5 cm to 45 cm (17 to 18 in) from the top of the seat to the floor and easy chairs should be 32.5 cm to 35 cm (13 to 14 in).

However, when noting all these points, do remember that the chair frame dictates to the worker the way in which it should be upholstered. In this sense, upholstery is not a creative craft.

Ripping off

The removal of old upholstery is known as ripping off. This is done in the reverse order to upholstery and therefore the place to begin is on the bottom of the chair by removing the black lining. With ripping chisel and wooden mallet remove each tack in the same

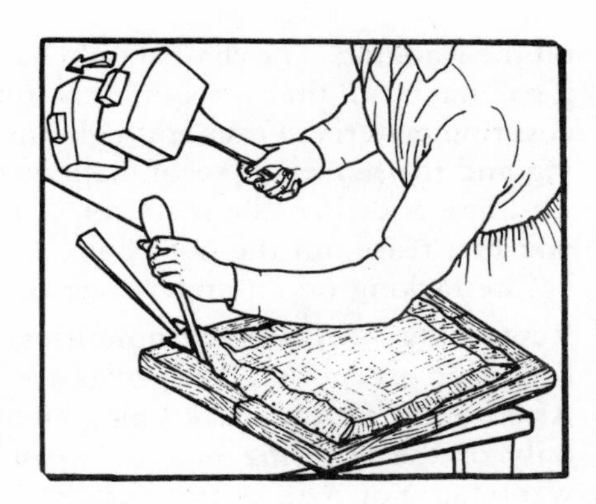

Figure 4 Ripping off—away from the corners and with the grain of the wood

direction as the grain of the wood. It is very important to work with the grain of the wood in order to avoid splitting chunks of wood off the frame. If you do accidentally knock pieces off the frame, keep them, as they must be glued back later. Hold the chisel in the left hand (if you are right handed) at an angle of 45 degrees to the tack head and hit the end of the handle of the ripping chisel with the mallet. This blow will enable you to get the end of the ripping chisel, by lowering the angle, slightly under the tack head. Then give several more blows with the mallet until the tack flies out. Because the tacks do fly out, always work sideways or away from you, never towards you. Figure 4 shows the angle of the ripping chisel; notice also the grain of the wood. When all the tacks have been removed from the bottom, stand or lay the chair on the bench and rip off the other layers. Newcomers are always surprised at the number of tacks which were used on the old upholstery and vow never to put as many back, but I am sure they do—and more!

Upholstery repairs

Although you will find that most chairs need to be entirely re-upholstered and therefore all the old materials will have to be ripped off the frame, some repairs can be done without having to re-upholster completely. However, you will need to refer to techniques mentioned in later chapters in order to understand fully some of the terms which follow.

Re-covering By ripping off in the reverse order to upholstery, you have the opportunity to assess the job as you go along. You may consider that the upholstery is still sound and that the chair only needs re-covering, in which case remove the old cover and just lift off the wadding. The chair should have a calico undercovering and, if so, maybe all that is required is some new wadding and the new covering material. Often, though, the calico undercovering is missing and the horsehair second stuffing has been covered only with wadding and then the material. If this is the case, I suggest that you first tease out the horsehair, adding a little more if required, before tacking on an undercover of calico.

Rewebbing Perhaps the upholstery on the chair is still in good condition except that the springs are bulging through the webbing. After taking off the black lining and the tacks holding the bottom only of the covering material, you are then able to renew the webbing. You will notice that each spring has been tied to the webbing with twine in three places. Cut and remove this twine. I find that this sort of job is best done by removing one old web at a time, starting with one of the centre ones and replacing it with a new piece of webbing before moving on to the adjacent webs (Figure 5). Then start on the centre web in the other direction, remembering to weave. When rewebbing, it is very important to pull the webbing tight and you will find that the springs make this task difficult. It is helpful if someone can push down on the springs whilst you attach the web but if this is not possible, let the springs come around and above the webbing so that you can fasten it and then push the springs back under afterwards. When all the webbing has been renewed the springs need to be sewn to it again, with thick twine and a spring needle. It is of course more difficult to do this when working from the bottom as you have to reach behind the webbing in order to return the needle. Lastly, retack the bottom of the cover and put back the black lining.

Figure 5 Rewebbing a sprung chair

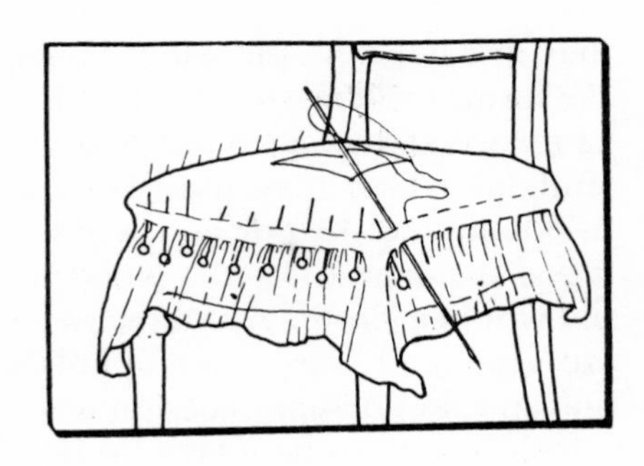

Figure 6 Skewers holding new scrim around roll edge

Retaining the first stuffing If the webbing which needs replacing has previously been put on top of the seat frame, it will be necessary to rip off all the old seat upholstery. However, the stitched edge on the first stuffing may be in a good condition; indeed to be worth saving, it must be. If this is the case, rip off the tacks on the chamfered edge holding the scrim, cut the bridle ties in the centre and any other twine loops and remove the pad carefully. When the chair has been rewebbed and the new hessian tacked on, then lay the first stuffing back onto the seat. Measure and cut a new piece of scrim which is large enough to cover completely and fold under the first stuffing on all four sides. Centre this piece of scrim on top of the first stuffing and put in a temporary tack on the back, front and side rails. Next put bridle ties in the centre of the seat sewing through the webbing, hessian, first stuffing, old and new scrim. Now, starting at the back, smooth the new scrim over the roll edge and hold with skewers. Do the same on the front edge and then skewer the sides (Figure 6). With twine and mattress needle, sew a running or tacking stitch through the scrim and roll. This makes the new scrim a part of the first stuffing and, by adding a little more fibre under the edges if necessary, the scrim can be folded under and tacked to the frame. The first stuffing can also be retained in this way on the back and arms of chairs if, again, it is in a good condition.

What can be saved?

When you start ripping off the old upholstery and discover all the dust and dirt, you may think there is nothing that could be worth saving. By and large this is true, with the exception of the horsehair which does not deteriorate with age. Some people will say that springs, if they are still standing straight, can be re-used, but I feel that this is penny-pinching. However, you will want to measure the springs and retain one of each kind so that you have some guide as to size and gauge when you buy new ones. There are different stuffings which may have been used: seaweed, which will have dried out and the salt in it will have rusted the springs and tacks; wood shavings known as wood wool; rag flock, which is combed, old woollen clothing; and the two fibres still used currently, Algerian grass and coir. Some upholsterers will recard Algerian grass and coir, but on one occasion when I had this done with some fibre which looked to be worth saving, I found that, when it had been through the machine, it was brittle and turned to dust.

Although the horsehair might be the only part of the upholstery worth saving, you may, during the ripping off, find other interesting items which have perhaps slipped down into the chair and been lost for years. For example, an old regulator was found by one student—black marks for that upholsterer! Under three layers of cover I once found a beautiful Berlin woolwork tapestry which I restored and was able to put back onto the chair. Look out also for the frame-maker's name and possibly a date which may be written or embossed into the wood.

Renovation of the chair frame

Repairs to the frame

When all the old upholstery has been ripped off, the chair frame can be examined to see if any repairs are necessary before the re-upholstery is started. Now is the time to stick back any pieces of wood which came off the frame during ripping off. It is not necessary to fill the holes made by the tacks as, unless the frame has been upholstered many times, the wood will take the next lot of tacks—I have never known it not to.

Regluing of joints Test the joints of the arms by standing in front of the chair, holding both arms and moving them sideways. Test the seat joints by putting one knee on the front of the frame, holding the back and moving your arms backwards and forwards. If there are joints which are loose then it is best to open them up. This can be done by gently slipping a ripping chisel into the joint gap on the inside of the frame and tapping it with a mallet. Remember that if it is, say, a back leg joint, then both back leg joints will need to be opened. The joints will usually be dowel (Figure 7a) or mortise and tenon (Figure 7b). The mortise and tenon may

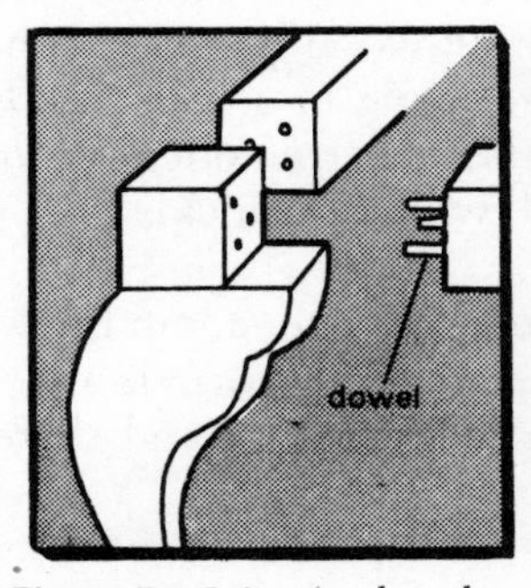

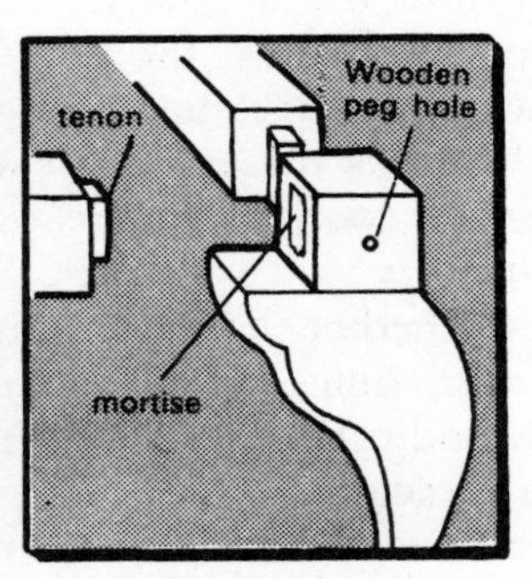

Figure 7 Joints: a dowel b mortise and tenon

have a peg through it which will need to be removed before the joint will separate. A dowel may be broken, in which case it will need drilling out and replacing with a new one—usually 10 mm ($\frac{3}{8}$ in). If a tenon is broken, the repair is more complicated.

The joints must be thoroughly cleaned with glass-paper to remove all the old glue, because otherwise the joint will not fit well and in any event fresh glue will not stick to old glue. The gluing of joints on a seat frame should not be started until the whole is ready to be assembled because modern woodworkers' adhesives allow only a few minutes 'working time' before they begin to set. Line up the sash cramps which will be required to hold the joints and adjust them to the approximate size required. Make sure you are working on a flat surface. Then glue both surfaces of all the joints, quickly assemble and position the sash cramps to hold the joints, placing a thick pad of old rag between the metal of the cramp and any polished wood on the frame to protect the wood. Do not overtighten the cramps. Now check that the chair is standing flat on the bench and does not wobble. Wipe off any excess glue and leave the chair for as long as possible, preferably 24 hours. If the chair has corner brackets or wedges between the seat rails, these should be put back into position, as they not only help to strengthen the joints but also keep the rails square.

More involved repairs Personally, as I am not a carpenter, I do not attempt any repairs more difficult than those already mentioned. It is best to have more complicated work done by a carpenter skilled in antique restoration.

Woodworm Woodworm beetles attack walnut, pine, deal, birch and beech, and their presence is shown by 1 mm circular flight holes. Although mahogany, teak and rosewood are not usually prone to woodworm, the non-show-wood portions—the unpolished parts—of such furniture are made in a soft wood and the beetles do attack these areas. The beetles from one piece of wormy furniture in a room, if not treated, will very quickly pass to all the other furniture.

To test whether the woodworm is still active, tap the wood and if a fine dust comes out of the holes then the worm is alive. A clean hole also indicates that it is a new flight hole and therefore the beetle is present.

To treat a chair for woodworm, the upholstery should of course first be ripped off. With the nozzle supplied, you then liberally apply a proprietary brand of woodworm killer into all the holes and cracks. Bear in mind that woodworm beetles make and fly out of the holes in May to mate, returning to them immediately to lay their eggs. These hatch into grubs which burrow through the wood. The grubs are poisoned directly by the insecticide and by eating the insecticide-soaked wood, and therefore I would advise you to give several applications of the killer to the chair in order to be as certain as possible that all the grubs will be affected. Allow the wood to dry for a couple of days before beginning the upholstery.

If a part of the chair frame has been attacked with woodworm to the extent that it is crumbling away, then it will be necessary to replace that piece of wood completely.

Restoring the show-wood

With the frame bare and all the necessary repairs completed, the show-wood, ie the polished wood, can be restored, either now or later when the calico undercovering is on the chair. Certainly if it is done before you begin the upholstery, the show-wood is more accessible. On the other hand, care must be taken to ensure that the wood does not get knocked later.

As a general rule, the less that is done to the finish of an antique, the better it is. With years of use, the wood will have gained a patina which must be preserved and any minor blemishes are considered attributes that give it 'character'. Cleaning is all that is required unless the wood has been varnished or painted. In this case, you will need to strip off the old finish, restain and french polish.

Cleaning the wood Over the years dust will have become embedded in the layers of polish which have been applied, the effect of which will be particularly noticeable on any horizontal surfaces where it will be seen that the colour is much darker. Treat all the show-wood, and particularly these areas, by applying a good wax polish with no. 000 steel wool. This grade of steel wool is almost as soft as cotton wool but nevertheless has a sufficiently abrasive effect to remove the dirt without marking the wood. At the same time, the wax polish gives a good finish. Buff up the wood with a soft duster from time to time. If there is carving or decoration on the chair, this will be more difficult to clean. However, the task is made easier by wrapping a little steel wool around an old toothbrush. Seeing the true colour and grain of the wood gradually appear gives great satisfaction.

If you have had to insert any new wood to repair the show-wood, now, when the wood is clean, is the time to stain it so that the colour can be matched accurately.

Although wax polish can be purchased readily, you may prefer to make your own. Here is a simple recipe. Shred beeswax (obtainable from a hardware store) into turpentine and let it dissolve. This is a very slow process which can be speeded up by immersing the container in hot water. However, as the wax is highly inflammable, do not put the container directly over a flame. Adjust the consistency by adding more beeswax or turpentine until it resembles soft butter when set.

Stripping off the old finish If the chair has been varnished or painted, the only solution is to strip off the finish and start again. Preferably, the stripping should be done out-of-doors as it is a messy job and in addition the smell of the stripper can be overpowering. Apply a paint or varnish stripper with a brush, leave it to soften the finish (the time depends upon the stripper used, but it is usually about ten minutes) and wipe off with a rough cloth, eg an offcut of hessian. Repeat until the old finish is completely removed. It is best to strip each part of the chair in turn rather than trying to do the whole at once. For any carved or grooved areas, apply the stripper with an old toothbrush.

Staining Apply a spirit stain with a piece of cotton rag or wadding. Always try out the stain on the inside of a chair leg, or some other place where it will not show, to make sure that the colour is right. Spirit stain is obtainable in many colours named after the various types of wood, but unfortunately the designations do not in fact match the true colour of that wood, eg one named American Walnut gives a good mahogany colour. You will often need to mix a number of different coloured stains together to obtain the desired colour. This mixing of stains is certainly required when a repair in new wood has been made which has to be stained to match the rest of the frame. Remember that it is easy to stain the wood darker by making further applications, but that it is difficult to remove stain to make it lighter. Let the wood dry out overnight before you begin to french polish.

French polishing To french polish a flat surface, such as a table top, is an extremely skilled craft. However, although the form of a chair is not so exacting, the polishing must be done in a dust-free atmosphere.

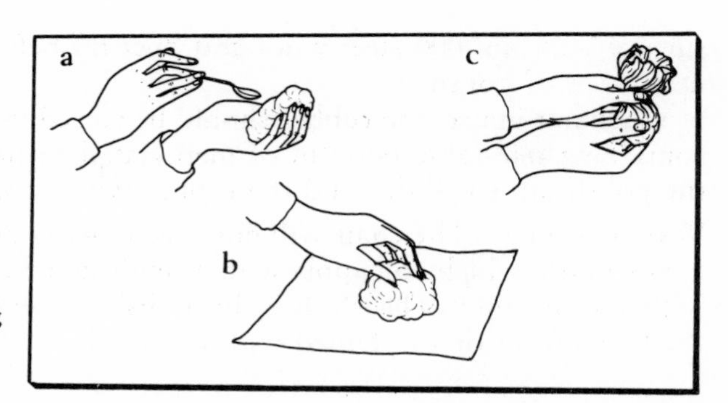

Figure 8 Loading and making a 'rubber'

French or button polish, which contains shellac, can be purchased from a hardware store in shades ranging from a light yellowy-brown to dark brown. If you are satisfied with the present colour of the stained wood, then use the lightest shade. The polish is applied with a 'rubber' which is made from a 25 cm (10 in) square piece of fine cotton (eg an old handkerchief). On to a soft ball of cotton wool about the size of a tangerine pour one teaspoonful of shellac (french) polish (Figure 8a). Place this ball of cotton wool, polish side down, into the centre of the cotton square (Figure 8b). Draw up the corners of the cotton square around the cotton wool, twist them and hold the twist in one hand (Figure 8c). Bang the rubber on to the palm of the other hand and, when the shellac polish begins to come through, the pad is ready for use. Apply the polish by making long straight strokes or small circular movements with the rubber and keep it moving all the time. If the rubber stops on the wood, it will stick and leave a nasty mark. When the rubber requires reloading with polish, untwist the cotton square and apply a little more polish directly on to the cotton wool ball. Do use the polish sparingly, as it is better to apply several thin coats rather than one thick one.

When the chair has had one coat of polish, leave it to dry for 24 hours before applying the next layer. At least two coats of the shellac polish will be required to seal the wood. The french polish builds up only a preliminary shine; it is the subsequent wax polishing which gives a full-bodied shine. However, if a more glossy finish is required, then continue with the coats of shellac polish, allowing each layer to dry properly, until the required sheen is achieved. If dust particles become embedded into the polished surface, let the shellac polish dry and then lightly rub over the surface with no. 000 steel wool and dust off before applying the next layer of polish.

When not in use, the rubber should be stored in a screw-top jar containing one tablespoonful of methylated spirits, as otherwise the polish on it will dry and the rubber will become hard.

Wax polishing The chair will now need plenty of polishing with a wax polish which you apply with a small shoe brush and buff off with another similar brush. It is this polishing which distinguishes the finish from that obtained with a varnish.

Other blemishes

Scorch marks Fortunately, chairs are not susceptible to ink stains, glass marks and cigarette burns on the wood in the way that tables are, but they do become scorched either by having been placed too close to a fire or in too strong and hot sunlight. In either case, the result is that the polish melts and forms bubbles which burst, giving a crazed surface. If the surface is not too badly damaged, you may be able to restore it with no. 000 steel wool and wax polish but do not rub through the stain. On the other hand, if the scorching is severe, the affected area will need to be stripped, restained and polished.

Deep scratches and other surface holes Scratches and holes caused by counter-sunk screws etc, can be filled with melted candlewax to which an appropriate spirit stain has been added. Fill the hole whilst the wax is still soft and, when it has hardened, polish over the whole area. Such holes can also be filled with a wood filler so long as it is one which will take the stain when dry.

Upholstery terms

The following terms, in alphabetical order, concern all upholstery work. It is important that they are fully understood and applied to all jobs including those detailed in the following chapters.

Setting the material This applies to the hessian, scrim, calico and covering material layers.

Before commencing any upholstery, mark the middle of each chair rail with biro, felt-tipped pen or tailor's chalk. When each symmetrical material piece has been cut, find the centre of the top and bottom by folding the material and mark these points also, with biro on hessian, scrim and calico but with tailor's chalk on the covering material.

Setting the material involves matching up the centre marks top and bottom on the material with those on the frame and fixing with one temporary tack in each place (Figure 9). Then smooth the material to the sides, ensuring that the weave is straight, and fix a temporary tack in the middle of each side rail. This procedure ensures that the material is correctly positioned before tacking begins and, more importantly, it keeps the weave of the material straight.

Before beginning to tack along each rail, remove the 'setting' temporary tack, check on the straightness of the weave and tension the material as required.

Straight of the weave Your upholstery work will be highly successful if you remember one golden rule—always work on the straight of the weave of all upholstery materials. By doing this, you avoid endless problems by ensuring that the fabric will fit well at the same time as gaining maximum strength from the material.

The 'straight of the weave' rule applies firstly to the cutting of material pieces. The selvedges are always straight so they present no problem. On the width of hessian and scrim, pull a thread right

Figure 9 Material 'set' on the straight of the weave

across the top of the width and trim the material to this thread. With lightweight calico, it is easier to 'square' the width by making a cut in the selvedge and then tearing across. On plain covering materials, fray the edge until one thread runs right across or, if the weft threads are well pronounced, cut straight across the width on one of these threads.

With the material 'straight', the measurements for the fabric piece required can then be marked out. With hessian, scrim and calico, measure down the length and across the width of the material making cuts at each point. On the hessian and scrim, pull out a thread from the fabric at the cuts and cut along the line of the drawn threads. The calico can be torn from both cuts. With covering materials, it is necessary to draw out the size of piece required on the right side of the material using a wooden metre stick and tailor's chalk.

Material pieces are always cut square or rectangular. Thus the shape is worked on the chair from the symmetrical pieces of fabric. You will appreciate that, when the material is 'set' on the chair, the straight of the weave is maintained (refer again to Figure 9). In this respect, when actually tacking the material onto the chair, continually check to ensure that the warp and weft threads are running straight from back to front (or top to bottom) and from side to side.

There is only one exception to cutting on the straight of the weave. This concerns printed covering materials, eg printed linen. In this case, because the pattern has to be centred and because the printed pattern does not often coincide with the weave, the material must be cut straight according to the printed pattern.

Tack drags/tack ties/cats' teeth Known by various names, these terms denote a fault made when tacking covering materials. If the covering material is tacked too tightly or through wadding, the resulting pull on the material will create a line which runs from each tack into the upholstery. The remedy, where this happens, is to lift each tack, release the tension and reposition pulling the covering material sideways between tacks, or cut back the wadding.

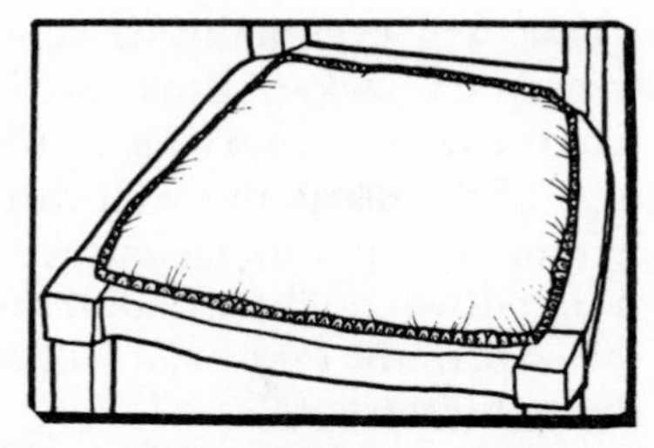

Figure 10 Tack drags on a pin-cushion seat

Tack drags are particularly noticeable on pin-cushion upholstery (Figure 10) and when brocade materials are used.

Do not be fooled into thinking that when the upholstery has flattened a little with use the tack drags will disappear, because this does not happen.

Tacking order The order of tacking all upholstery materials on a chair is back (or bottom), front (or top) and then sides. This is because if there is a straight rail it will be the back (or bottom) rail and by beginning there the problem of keeping the weave straight is eased.

As the corners of each layer of material are always tacked last, temporary tack along the rails to within 5 cm (2 in) of the corners only.

Temporary tacking All pieces of upholstery material may require quite a bit of adjustment before the tacks are in the correct position—this is especially true at the corners. In order to make repositioning easier, the tacks are only half-sunk or 'temporary tacked' into the wood (Figure 11) which means that they can easily be taken out, if required, with the claw on the hammer.

It is advisable to adopt the habit of temporary tacking all upholstery fabrics as it saves much time in the long run, causes less damage to the frame and there is less risk of tearing the material.

Initially, four temporary tacks are used for 'setting the material'.

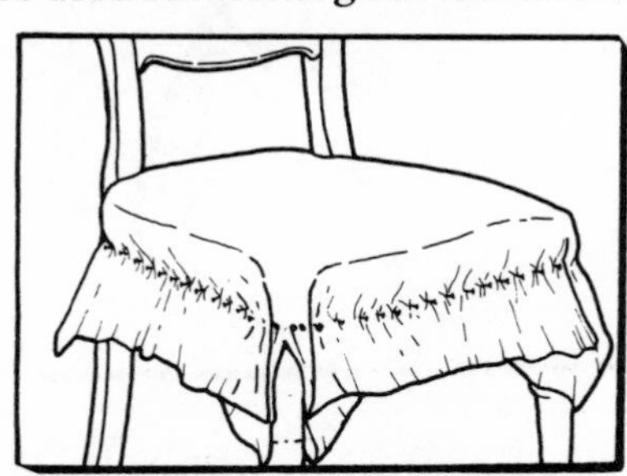

Figure 11 Temporary tacking

These will eventually be removed in turn when the material is temporary tacked along each rail. When the corners have been fixed with temporary tacks and you have checked on the straightness of the warp and weft threads again, then all the tacks can be hammered right in. Do ensure when tacking off that the tack heads lie flat down on the wood. If the tack goes into the wood crookedly, the edge of the tack head will cut into the materials thus weakening the upholstery.

Upholsterer's knot This knot, which is a slip-knot with a difference, is the one most used in upholstery. Make a single knot at the end of a piece of twine and with a curved needle thread the twine through where the upholsterer's knot is required. Then drop the needle and hold the two pieces of twine between thumb and finger 7.5 cm (3 in) away from the single knot (Figure 12a). Pick up the single knot in the other hand and pass it over the two pieces of twine and through the loop (Figure 12b). Still holding the knot,

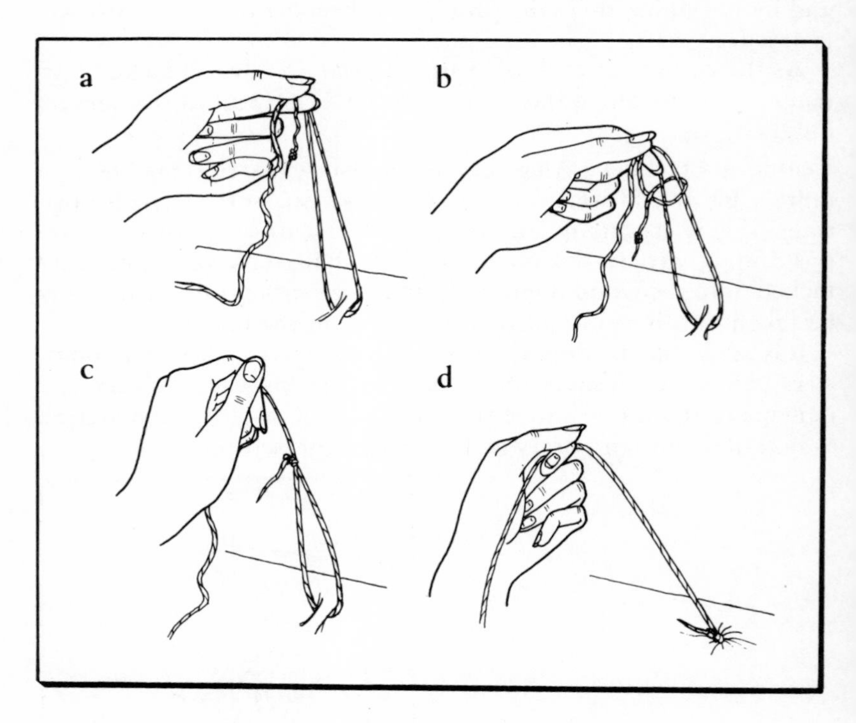

Figure 12 Upholsterer's knot

pull the long piece of twine with the other hand at the same time easing the loop down so that it rests against the knot (Figure 12c). Then pull until the knot rests against the fabric (Figure 12d) and the upholsterer's knot is complete.

Depending where the knot is required, it can be made through fabric, as described above, or around the shank of a half-sunk tack.

Webbing stretcher The webbing is stretched across the frame with a webbing stretcher. Beginners to upholstery often have difficulty in trying to remember how to hold it. Hold the handle upwards with the mechanics facing you (Figure 13a). Feed a fold of the webbing through the slot and insert the bar into the fold (Figure 13b). Then adjust the webbing by rolling it around the bar so that the webbing is pulled tight when the stretcher is held against the frame (Figure 13c). Hold the spare end of the webbing in the hand which holds the stretcher. The required tightness of the webs

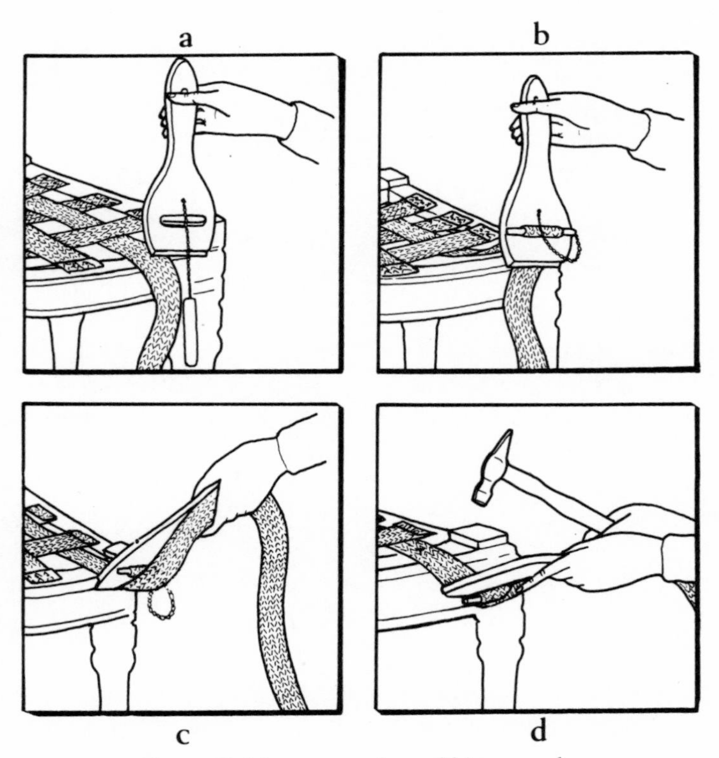

Figure 13 How to use the webbing stretcher

depends on the strength of the frame. If the webs are too tight on a delicate corner chair, the wood will split. At the other extreme, the webs on a settee will need to be very taut. You can test the tautness of the webbing by holding it stretched across the frame and then twanging both sides of the webbing in the middle of the frame. The differing degrees of tightness will give different sounds—a higher pitch when the webbing is tight.

Drop-in seat

Figure 14

A drop-in seat (Figure 14), also called a loose seat, is certainly the best type of seat to begin on for anyone new to upholstery.

Ripping off The vice on a carpenter's bench is useful to hold the seat when ripping off the old upholstery. Otherwise the frame can be held on the work surface with a G-cramp. Remember to work with the grain of the wood and inwards from the corners. Check that the joints are firm.

Webbing A drop-in seat, unless it requires springs, which is rare, is webbed from the top of the frame which is denoted by a bevelled edge. Bearing in mind that the webbing is 5 cm (2 in) wide and that there must not be more than 5 cm (2 in) between webs or from web to frame, mark out on the wood the position of the webs in tailor's chalk. These seats generally require three webs in each direction, but if the frame is small two by two will be sufficient, whereas the larger frame of a carving chair will require four by four. As most seats are wider at the front, the back to front webs

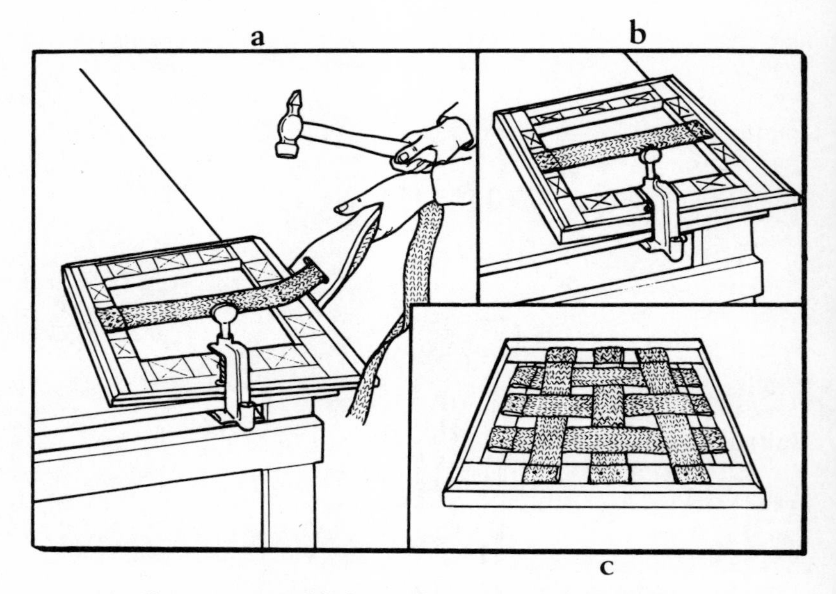

Figure 15 **a** and **b** fixing of webbing; **c** webs interlaced

will need to fan out slightly in order to spread them evenly across the front width.

Fold over 25 mm (1 in) of webbing with the fold uppermost and, using the large hammer, secure with five 13 mm ($\frac{1}{2}$ in) improved tacks as shown in Figure 15a. Stretching the webbing to the opposite rail will be easier if the frame is cramped to the work surface. You will remember that the way to use the webbing stretcher was explained in the previous chapter. Before relaxing the tension on the webbing, hammer in three tacks (Figure 15a). Cut the webbing off 25 mm (1 in) from the tacks, fold the surplus over and fasten it down with two further tacks (Figure 15b). Do not overstrain the webbing on a drop-in seat as it can easily twist the frame. Note that the tacks are positioned in the centre of the rail, to ensure that the webbing is fixed for maximum strength and to allow for subsequent tacking on the outer edge of the frame.

Before starting to tack the webbing between the side rails, remember to interlace the webs (Figure 15c), so that they will support each other. This must be done before the first end is tacked.

You will notice that at both ends the fold in the webbing is uppermost. This is done so that if the tack heads wear through the webbing, they will penetrate the spare piece on top, and the main strength of the webbing will not therefore be affected.

Hessian Measure from mid-rail to mid-rail on the length and width at the widest part of the frame, add 5 cm (2 in) to each measurement and cut out a piece of mangled hessian or tarpaulin.

Set the material (refer again to Figure 9). Then, starting on the back rail, make a 25 mm (1 in) fold upwards along a thread and fix with 10 mm (⅜ in) improved tacks 25 mm (1 in) apart along the middle of the rail to within 5 cm (2 in) of the corners. Keeping the weave straight, stretch the hessian tightly to the front rail and secure singly with tacks 5 cm (2 in) apart (Figure 16a) and hammer them in. Fold over the surplus hessian on the front rail and fix a tack every 5 cm (2 in) in between those under the fold (Figure 16b). Initially the hessian is tacked singly on this rail as it is impossible to pull a folded edge tightly. Tack the first side folded as for the back rail and stretch tightly to the second side, tacking as explained for the front rail. As maximum strength is required from the hessian, it is never cut at the corners or around uprights. Simply fold the hessian neatly at the corners (as can be seen in Figure 17a) and, pulling tightly, tack off. Trim the edges of the hessian, if necessary, leaving 5 cm (2 in) surplus all round.

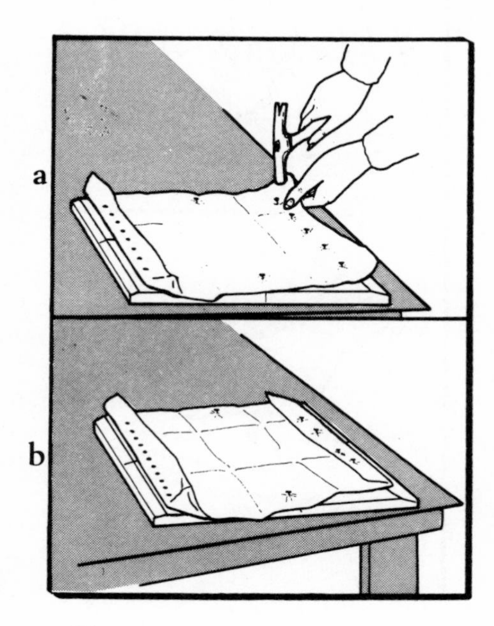

Figure 16 Tacking of hessian

As there is little depth to the upholstery on these chairs, the hessian layer has the important function of spreading the weight-load evenly across the webbing.

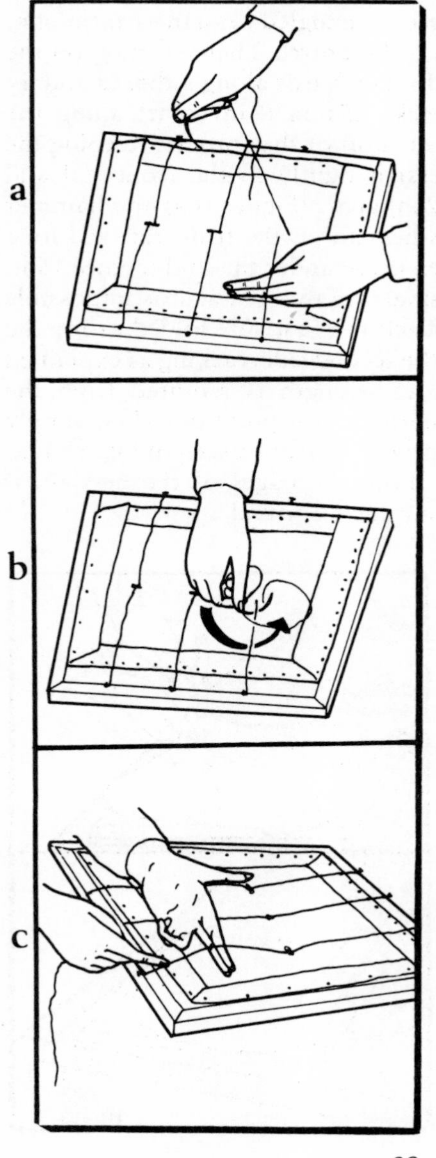

Stuffing loops These loops hold and regulate the amount of horsehair which is required.

Evenly space three 10 mm (⅜ in) half-sunk improved tacks along the outer edge of the back rail and three further tacks opposite them on the outer edge of the front rail. With a curved twine needle threaded with no. 2 or 3 twine, make an upholsterer's knot around the middle tack on the back rail and hammer the tack in. Make a 15 mm (½ in) stitch through the hessian in the middle of the seat. Passing the twine over the index and middle fingers held sideways mid-way between the back tack and the stitch (Figure 17a), tie the stitch with a half-hitch (single knot) (Figure 17b). Between that stitch and the front tack, again pass the twine over the same two fingers. Wrap the twine three times around the front tack (Figure 17c), hammer it in and cut off the twine. Make similar loops between the other two pairs of tacks.

Figure 17 Stuffing loops on a drop-in seat

Horsehair Horsehair is teased out and fed under each loop (Figure 18a) to the depth of the loop across the whole frame. As there is only one stuffing layer on a drop-in seat, the horsehair needs to be closely packed but not so much that it loses its resilience. To regulate the horsehair, use the finger tips of both hands to gently comb through the hair, starting at the front and working backwards (Figure 18b). This will have the effect of packing the hair down at the same time as ensuring that the whole surface is evenly covered with hair—pay particular attention to the edges and corners. Finally, a little extra hair is placed around the centre of the frame (Figure 18c) to give a slight dome.

If your drop-in seat is one of a set, then before putting the calico over the hair, it is a good idea to remove and weigh the horsehair you have used in order that the same amount can be put on the other seats.

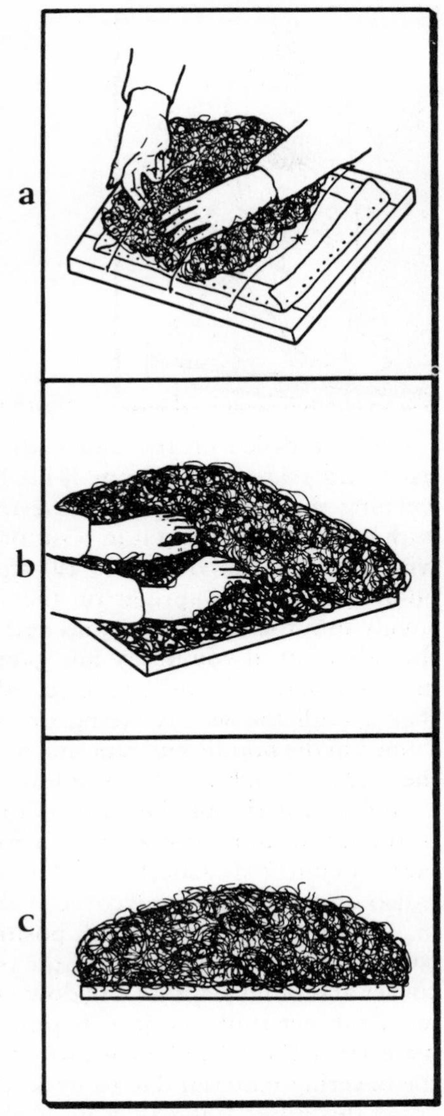

Figure 18 Horsehair stuffing

Calico As the undercovering of calico is tacked on the underside of the frame, measure over the hair on the length and width at the widest part of the frame allowing sufficient to tack underneath on all sides.

Figure 19 Tensioning calico

'Set' the calico on the underside of the frame and tack at the back underside with 10 mm ($\frac{3}{8}$ in) fine tacks 25 mm (1 in) apart. Keeping the weave straight, ease the calico firmly over the hair with one hand, holding it in position on the underside of the front with the other hand (Figure 19) and tack. It is easier to do this holding the frame upright on the work surface. As the seat fits snugly into the chair frame, no hair must be allowed to overhang the sides, but, if you notice any gaps on the top edge, then a little more horsehair should be added. When tacking the calico, check that overall the seat is taking on the shape required, ie slightly domed in the middle and tapering to the sides and corners. Keeping the weave straight, tack the sides.

At the corners, pull the centre of the calico tautly to the underside of the frame and put one tack 15 mm ($\frac{1}{2}$ in) back from the corner point (Figure 20a). Check that there is the same amount of surplus calico on each side of the corner before hammering the tack right in. With the surplus material, position a pleat on one side of the corner, aided by the flat end of the regulator, laying it towards the corner and pulling across and down tightly (Figure 20b). The pleat must run vertically as near as possible to the corner. As surplus material will need to be cut away from the inside of the pleat on the covering material due to its thickness, it is as well to practise doing this now. Make a cut up to the centre tack from the corner of the calico. Then, holding the pleat between finger and thumb, cut up under the pleat 15 mm ($\frac{1}{2}$ in) from the fold to the centre tack (Figure 20c). You will have cut away a piece of material the shape of an inverted 'V'. Now tack the pleat down before making

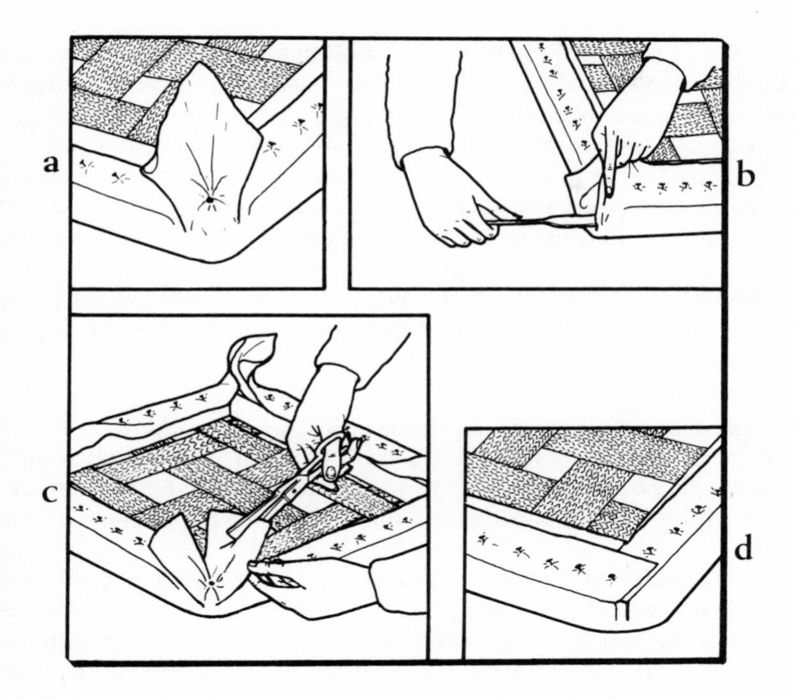

Figure 20 Corner pleats on drop-in seat

a similar pleat on the other side of the corner (Figure 20d). Finally trim off the calico 5 mm (¼ in) from the tacks when all the corners have been tacked down.

Fixing the calico is good practice for putting on the covering material as exactly the same method is used. However, calico stretches more easily and is less bulky than covering material. Thus pleats made with the covering material will need to be pulled more tightly in order for them to be neat and vertical.

The calico needs to be pulled firmly over the hair so that it does not wrinkle under the covering material and so that the tension is shared between the calico and the covering material. However it should not be pulled so tightly that the seat becomes hard.

Wadding Measure and cut two separate pieces of skin wadding the size of the top of the seat and lay them over the calico.

Covering material This is also tacked to the underside of the frame 15 mm (½ in) back from the edge with 10 mm (⅜ in) fine tacks. Take the measurements for the cover on the length and width over the widest part of the seat to the underneath of the frame. Before beginning to tack along each rail, trim back the wadding to ensure that it does not overhang the top edge.

Although the covering material is attached in the same way as the calico, it is even more important that the straight of the weave from back to front and side to side is followed or, if the material has a pattern, that the motif is exactly centred on the seat to ensure that a first class result is achieved.

The pleats on the corners (refer again to Figure 20), if done neatly and pulled down tightly, will not be visible when the seat is dropped into the chair frame.

Trim the material 15 mm (½ in) from the tacks.

Black lining Cut a piece of black lining large enough to cover all the tacks and raw edges with 25 mm (1 in) turn-under all round. This is tacked on with 10 mm (⅜ in) fine tacks. The corners are neatly folded under and spare lining cut away if the corners are too bulky.

Some chairs have pegs which sink into holes on the drop-in seat frame. It is necessary to have these holes free only on the underside of the frame but it is not always possible to avoid tacking material over them. If this is the case, then after the black lining has been tacked on, arrange a continuous ring of tacks around each hole. The material covering the hole can then be cut away with sharp pointed scissors as the ring of tacks will prevent the material from fraying.

Pin-cushion work

Pin-cushion work is a flat upholstery found on Regency and Edwardian chairs (see Figure 10). A pin-cushion seat is upholstered from the top of the seat and the methods used are the same as those for a drop-in seat. Often these chairs have a very narrow recess or rabbet on to which all the upholstery materials must be tacked. Thus it is advisable to use only fine headed tacks to avoid splitting the wood. Leave a 5 mm (¼ in) gap between the webbing folds and the show-wood frame so that the covering material can be tacked down flat. Black lining is not really necessary on this type of seat, but if you prefer to have the webbing and hessian hidden, then the black lining must be tacked on before the webbing.

The treatment of an upholstered panel on the back of a chair is often similar to that of a pin-cushion seat. However, the outside back covering material sometimes has to be tacked on first with a

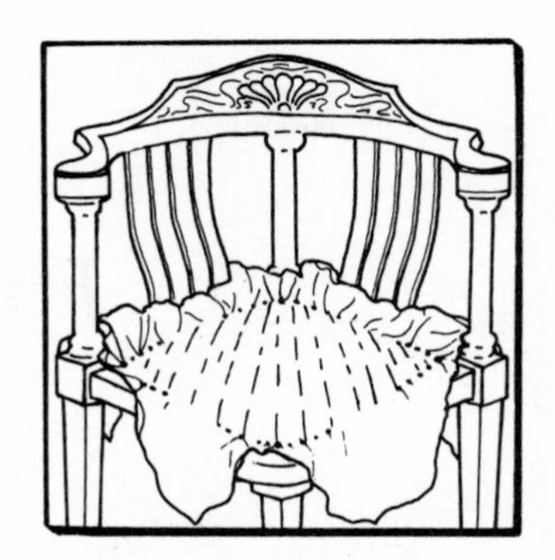

Figure 21 Attaching covering material on a corner chair with diamond-shaped pin-cushion seat

layer of skin wadding placed on top of it to prevent the horsehair penetrating the back cover.

Although some corner chairs have round pin-cushion seats, a word should be said about those with diamond-shaped seats. The pin-cushion upholstery is done on the top of the frame as if working on a square seat until the covering material stage. Then, to measure for the cover, take the corner to corner lengths plus 5 cm (2 in). The mid-point of the top and bottom edges of the cover should be 'set' to the top and bottom corners with the mid-points of the other two sides being 'set' to the side corners. Keeping an eye on the straightness of the weave, temporary tack away from the back corner to half-way along both back rails. Adjust the tack at the front corner and tack to the middle of both front rails. Work in a similar way from both sides' corners (Figure 21). It is a tricky job to fix a cover on the diagonal, but so long as the weave is kept straight in both directions the work will be successful.

Footstool

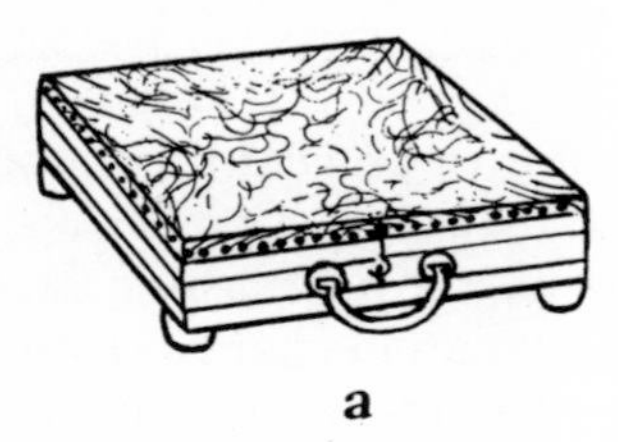

a

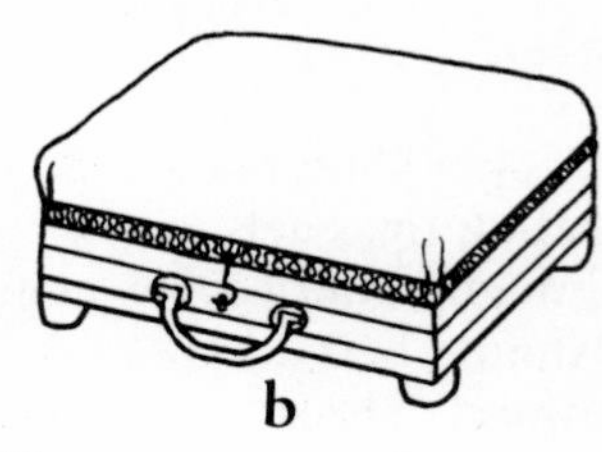

b

Figure 22

Figure 22a shows a Victorian carriage foot warmer covered with carpet. With a little upholstery, this makes an attractive footstool (Figure 22b).

Ripping off Carefully rip off the old materials and clean the showwood with no. 000 steel wool and wax polish.

Outside back cover As the underneath of the top upholstery will be visible from inside the stool, a piece of covering material must be tacked, wrong side up, with 10 mm ($\frac{3}{8}$ in) fine tacks to the top of the stool first. Cover this with one layer of skin wadding.

Webbing One web across the middle of the width will be sufficient. Use 10 mm ($\frac{3}{8}$ in) improved tacks.

Hessian Tack the hessian with 10 mm ($\frac{3}{8}$ in) improved tacks.

Tack roll As only little depth is required to the upholstery, this is an ideal occasion on which to use the tack roll.

Cut strips of mangled hessian 10 cm (4 in) wide and long enough to go around the top edge of the stool. With 10 mm ($\frac{3}{8}$ in) improved tacks 25 mm (1 in) apart, tack the strips to the very outside edge of the frame as shown in Figure 23a. Allow extra fullness, by pleating, so that there is sufficient hessian to go around the outside of the corners. A new piece of hessian should not be joined on a corner. It is better to do this along a straight edge and allow a 5 cm (2 in)

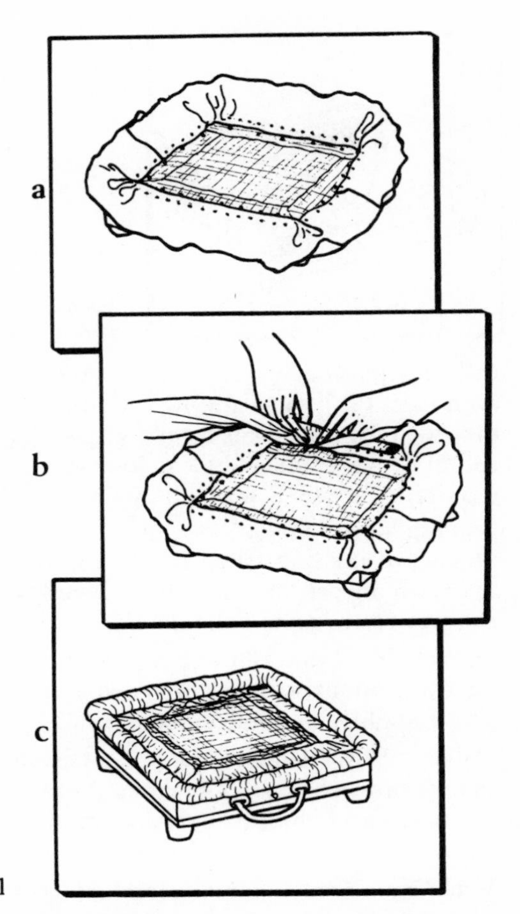

Figure 23 Making a tack roll

overlap. Then lay half a width (ie 22.5 cm (9 in)) of skin wadding rolled up as tightly as possible along the edge of the wood and bring the hessian over it tautly (Figure 23b). As the finished roll needs to be slightly proud of the hard edge, as shown in Figure 23c, and this is particularly true at the corners where it is important to cover the sharpness of the wood, the hessian brought over the wadding is held tightly with the fingers of both hands and then the fingers are slipped slightly back towards the edge moving the hessian and wadding roll at the same time. This final little movement tightens the hessian around the wadding roll and ensures that the roll will cover the hard edge of the wood. Tack the hessian down with 10 mm ($\frac{3}{8}$ in) improved tacks as close as possible to the wadding

Figure 24 Positioning of stuffing loops with a roll

roll. It will be necessary to tighten the roll of wadding before fixing each tack. Push the wadding roll firmly into the corners and ensure that the tack roll forms a right angle. Trim the end of the wadding roll in order to make a close join when a new piece of wadding is required and avoid making this join on a corner.

Stuffing loops Two loops only are required. Figure 24 shows the placing of the first stitch on the top outside edge of the tack roll, over two fingers (depth of the tack roll) and tied off on the opposite top outside edge of the roll.

Horsehair Tease out and feed horsehair under the loops regulating the amount with the finger tips. Add a little extra horsehair to give a slightly domed centre.

Calico With 10 mm (⅜ in) fine tacks, fit the calico as explained in the previous chapter. The tacks should be fixed 5 mm (¼ in) above the bottom of the lid. Make a small pleat on both sides of each corner.

Wadding Two separate pieces of skin wadding large enough to cover the horsehair and tack roll are required.

Covering material The material is tacked to the bottom of the sides of the lid with 10 mm (⅜ in) fine tacks. Again make two pleats on each corner remembering to have the pleat vertical and lying towards the corner (refer again to Figure 20). Using scissors, trim the covering material flush with the bottom of the lid.

Braid Latex adhesive, if bought in a small bottle, has a brush attached to the lid which is useful for gluing braid. Starting at the middle of the back of the footstool, apply a thin layer of adhesive 10 cm (4 in) down the length of the braid and position the braid over the tacks. To ensure that the braid holds fast, tap along with the head of a hammer (Figure 25a). It is best to apply adhesive to

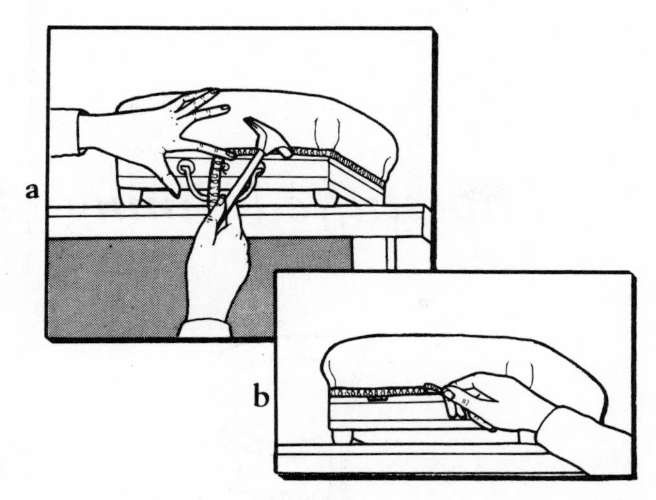

Figure 25
Attaching braid

short lengths only. End off by turning under 15 mm (½ in) of braid to overlap the start by 15 mm (½ in) (Figure 25b). It should not be necessary to tack gimp pins to hold the braid except, possibly, at the end.

Inside of the stool Measure and cut covering material for the sides allowing 15 mm (½ in) for seaming in each corner and an additional 25 mm (1 in) on the width. Machine at each corner omitting 5 mm (¼ in) at the top and 20 mm (¾ in) at the bottom and trim and open out the seams. Position the side pieces over one layer of skin wadding and tack the top edge on the rabbet with 10 mm (⅜ in) fine tacks. With latex adhesive, stick the bottom of the side material to the bottom. Measure and cut a piece of stiff card the size of the bottom. Measure and cut covering material to cover this card with 25 mm (1 in) turn-under all round. With a layer of skin wadding laid on the top of the card, stick the material to the card with latex adhesive on the underside only, stretching tautly and cutting away excess fabric at the corners. Fit the material covered card into the bottom. Trim over the tacks with braid.

Tack rolls

As tack rolls are generally employed where a shallow depth is required to the upholstery, they can be used on many types of stools, the backs of writing chairs, on wings and on loose seats where the chair frame needs a deeper upholstery than that detailed in the previous chapter.

Top-stuffed dining chair

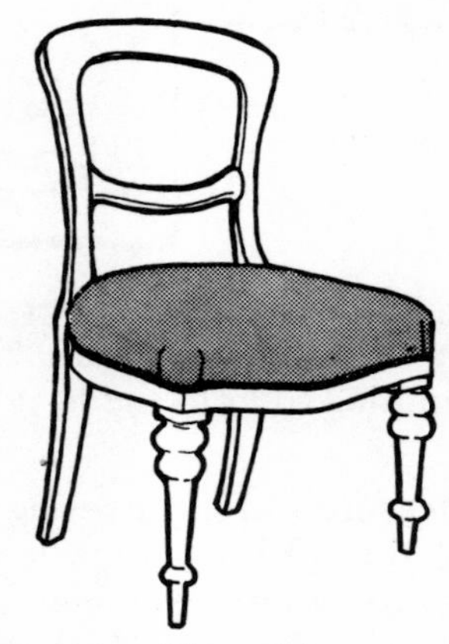

Figure 26

Top-stuffed means that all the upholstery is worked on the top of the frame. As dining chairs are not sat on for more than an hour or two at a time, it is usually not necessary for the seats to be sprung.

Ripping off Take off the old upholstery in the usual way. Before commencing the re-upholstery, check that the top outer edges of the seat rails are bevelled. The tacks holding the scrim will be attached to these edges and the chamfer will prevent them from splitting the wood. If there is no bevel, rub down the sharp edge with a wood rasp (Figure 27).

Webbing Depending upon the size of the seat, mark out and tack with 13 mm (½ in) improved tacks three or four webs in each direction.

Hessian Tack the hessian with 13 mm (½ in) improved tacks by the same method as for a drop-in seat. Fold the hessian across the

Figure 27 Rasping seat rail to make a chamfer

back corners and tack down; tack it on top of the top part of the front legs at the front corners.

Stuffing loops for fibre Three stuffing loops are required along the front rail, three down each side and two on the back rail. With a curved needle threaded with no. 2 or 3 twine, take a stitch 8.5 cm ($3\frac{1}{2}$ in) in from the outer edge of the front rail and the same distance in from the outer edge of a side rail. Make an upholsterer's knot. Half-sink a 10 mm ($\frac{3}{8}$ in) improved tack on the chamfered edge

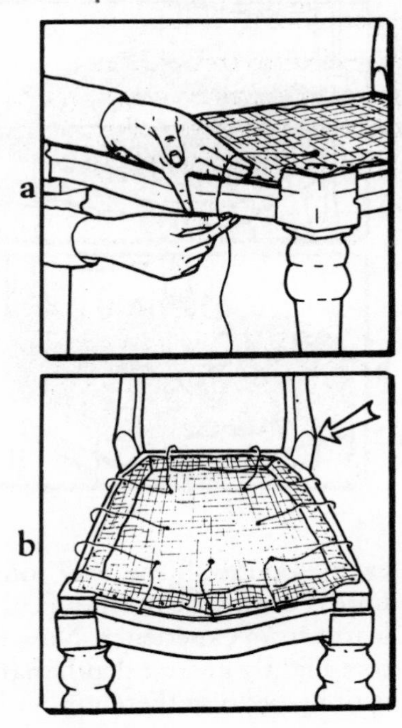

Figure 28 Stuffing loops for fibre

opposite the stitch on the front rail. Bring the twine over three fingers held vertically on the edge (Figure 28a), wrap it three times around the tack's shank and, when the tack is hammered right in, the loop is complete and the twine can be cut off. The other loops, all identical in size, are positioned as shown in Figure 28b. The number of fingers under the loop depends upon the depth of stuffing required on the seat. On this chair, which has a waisted back, the point where the bottom of the waist (indicated by an arrow in Figure 28b) goes into the leg upright gives the depth of the upholstery. On a non-waisted chair, the previous upholstery indicates the depth required and this can be seen on the back leg upright where the wood will not have been bleached or polished where the upholstery has been. This will also coincide with the bottom edge of any carving or decoration there may be on the upright.

Fibre Tease and put Algerian grass under the loops. These need to be well packed (Figure 29a) but at the same time the fibre must not become solid. Aim for the sensation of having a good handful of springy fibre as you feel the edges and make sure that there is an

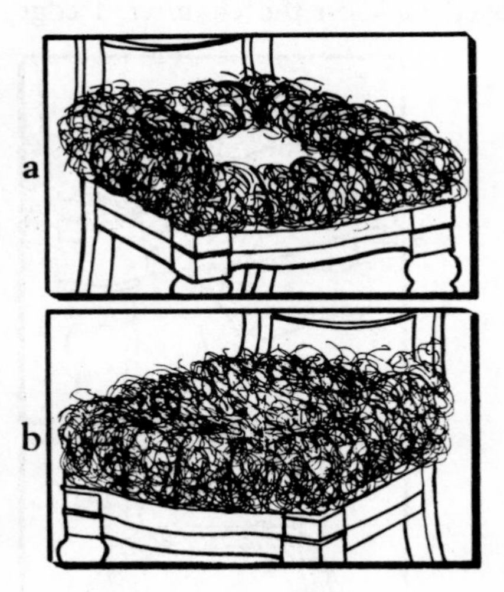

Figure 29 Fibre stuffing

even amount all the way round. Knowing how well to pack the fibre is one of the most difficult tasks in upholstery and can only be learnt from experience. Now fill in the centre of the seat with fibre to a slightly greater depth than that at the edges (Figure 29b). This is done because there are no loops to hold it down.

Scrim Measure with a tape measure over the top and down the sides of the fibre and allow 10 cm (4 in) turn-under on both measurements remembering to measure the width at the front, ie the widest part. Set the scrim on the chair.

Bridle ties Before tacking down the scrim, bridle ties must be sewn in the centre of the seat. The stuffing loops hold the fibre around the edges and the bridle ties hold the fibre in the centre of the seat and keep the scrim in position when sewing the roll later.

With a mattress needle threaded with no. 2 twine at the end of which there is a simple knot, plunge vertically down through all layers of the upholstery in the back left area of the centre portion of the seat. Return the needle through the upholstery about 15 mm (½ in) from where the twine went through the first time and tie an upholsterer's knot, pulling until the knot just makes a small indentation in the scrim (Figure 30a). Carry the thread across to the back right area of the centre, plunge down and come up again and, making no knot, do the same stitch in the front right area and front left area, ending up with the last bridle tie in the centre of the seat. Before tying-off the twine with a double knot in the centre of the seat, check that the stuffing is held evenly by each tie by adjusting the twine between stitches (Figure 30b).

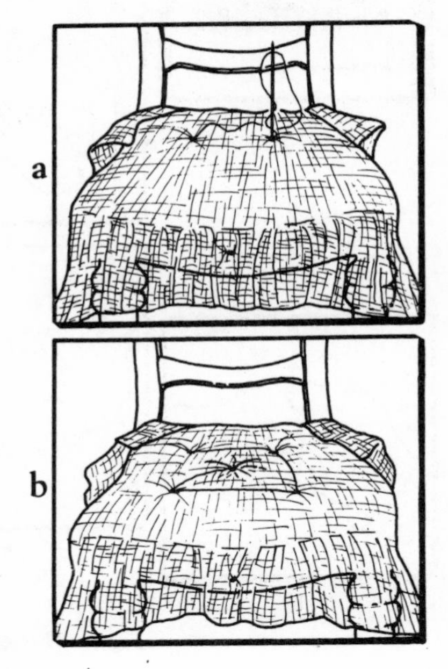

Figure 30 Bridle ties

Tacking down the scrim Now we can concentrate on the scrim again. With the back of the chair towards you, remove the temporary tack, fold up the scrim and lift the fibre on the edge upwards. As shown in Figure 31a, you will find that there are gaps. Stuff extra fibre along the bottom edge (particularly in the corners) before tucking the surplus scrim under the fibre (Figure 31b). With the aid of the regulator, hold several threads of the scrim at the mid-point at the right tautness (Figure 31c) and tack the scrim to the chamfer in the middle of the rail with a 10 mm ($\frac{3}{8}$ in) improved tack.

To obtain the correct tautness of the scrim is also a difficult job. It has to be loose enough in order that the roll, which is sewn later on all four sides, stands slightly proud of the edge, but it also has to be tight enough so that there is no spare scrim. I usually find that if the scrim makes a right angle (measured by the angle between

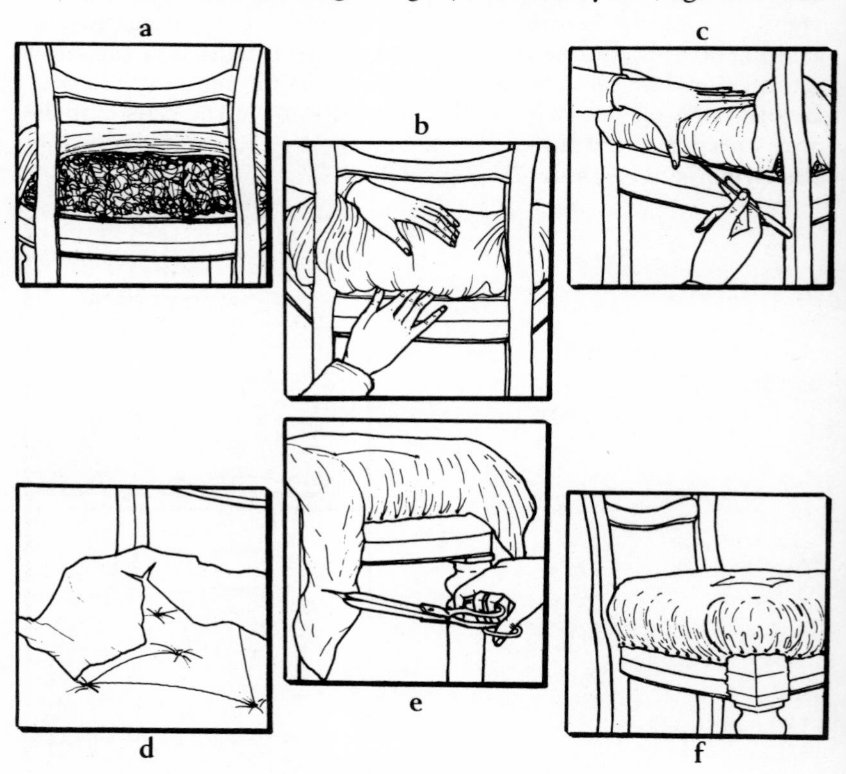

Figure 31 Attaching scrim

the thumb and index finger) between the top of the seat and the side rail as shown in Figure 31c, then it is tight enough. However, do err on the side of slackness as a little spare scrim can be 'lost' down the side when stitching, but if the scrim is too tight there is no way that you can make a satisfactory roll.

Continue tacking along the bevel of the back rail with the tacks 25 mm (1 in) apart. If the back rail is straight, you will be able to follow a thread in the scrim. Add extra fibre along each edge and particularly in the corners. Do make sure that the weave of the scrim is straight from back to front before tacking along the front rail and from side to side when tacking the sides. It will not be possible to follow a scrim thread along the side rails or on the front rail, unless it is straight.

The scrim is tucked under the fibre so that it completely envelops the fibre and thus prevents it working through a gap between the edge of the scrim and the rail, which would happen if the scrim were just turned up.

Starting with the back leg corners, bring the scrim up and lay it flat on the seat. Then cut in from the corner of the scrim diagonally towards the mid-point between the front and side of the back upright stopping the depth of the fibre from the upright. Make a 15 mm (½ in) V-shaped cut (Figure 31d), so that the material will not tear, and ease the scrim down to each rail with the help of the regulator. The scrim now has to be folded and tucked under the fibre. There will be some surplus scrim, as shown in Figure 31e, which can be cut away at these corners to make the tuck under less bulky. You will find that you will not be able to follow the back scrim thread as more scrim needs to be tucked under at the corners.

It is important to make sure that the front corners contain plenty of fibre because, at these points, fibre is required to make the roll on the side and on the front. Tuck the surplus scrim under the fibre at each corner. There will seem to be plenty of fullness and this needs to be tacked in little folds on the chamfer (Figure 31f). The tacks can be placed much closer together. The fullness should be anchored in lots of little folds rather than by larger pleating in order to ensure that the scrim is held firmly for the edge stitching. With the second front corner completed, hammer in all the tacks.

Blind stitch The purpose of this stitch is to insert a loop of twine around the stuffing which when pulled tight draws the stuffing towards the outside of the frame to give support to the edge of the upholstery.

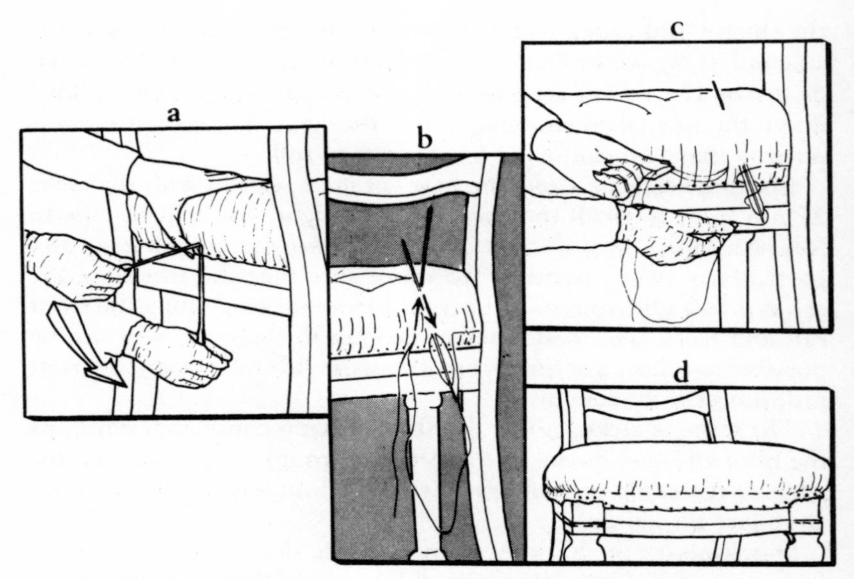

Figure 32 a, **b** and c blind stitch; **d** blind stitch completed

Unless your hands are tough, it is advisable to wear an old leather glove as, after some time, it can be painful to keep pulling the twine sufficiently tight.

Being right handed, I find it easier to work from right to left. Before each stitch, the stuffing must be brought to the edge of the frame using the regulator as shown in Figure 32a. Thread the mattress needle with no. 2 twine and, with the back of the chair towards you, insert the needle 15 mm (½ in) up from the tacks and 25 mm (1 in) from the leg in an upwards and backwards direction. The needle point should come through the scrim about 10 cm (4 in) away from the tacking rail. Pull the needle up but, just before the eye comes through the scrim, return the needle so that it exits through the scrim against the leg 15 mm (½ in) up from the tacks. Tie an upholsterer's knot and pull tight. This is the starting off stitch and it is used each time a new length of twine is needed.

Now regulate the stuffing and insert the needle upwards and backwards on a line horizontal with the first stitch but 5 cm (2 in) to the left (Figure 32b). Without taking the eye right through the scrim, return the needle halfway between the present and first stitch but, before extracting the needle, make two turns around the needle with the right-hand length of twine, ie the twine leaving the first stitch (Figure 32c). Pull the needle out and draw the twine tight. Repeat this stitch along the back to finish at the other back leg, making sure that the stitching line is 15 mm (½ in) up from the tacks. Cut the twine off and start again on the side, continuing along the front and along the other side (Figure 32d). Remember to regulate before each stitch. As wrapping the twine twice around the needle makes a double knot which does not slip once tightened, all you need do is to cut the twine 25 mm (1 in) from the knot.

Roll stitch The roll which is formed by this stitch gives the upholstery its shape and durability and therefore it is very important that the roll is evenly filled, even in size, at an even height around the frame and evenly proud of the frame. To obtain this uniformity of shape, the stuffing between each stitch has to be carefully regulated with the regulator in the direction shown in Figure 33a.

The roll stitch is sewn 15 mm (½ in) above the row of blind stitching with a mattress needle and no. 2 twine. Again it is best to wear a glove.

Begin along the back rail; with the left hand holding, between thumb and first two fingers, the stuffing and scrim to be included

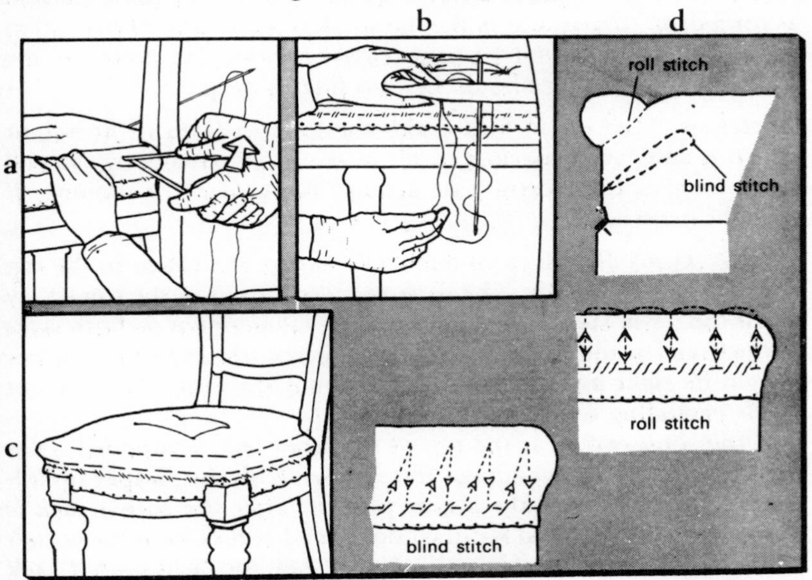

Figure 33 a and b roll stitch; c roll stitching completed; d profile and diagrams of blind stitch and roll stitch

in the roll, insert the needle straight up 16 mm ($\frac{5}{8}$ in) deep into the roll and 25 mm (1 in) from the upright. Pull the needle right through and return it against the upright through the same thickness of roll to exit 15 mm ($\frac{1}{2}$ in) above the row of blind stitching. Make an upholsterer's knot and pull tightly.

Regulate the stuffing immediately to the left of the first stitch, hold the roll and insert the needle 25 mm (1 in) along from the previous stitch up through the roll (Figure 33b). Return the needle through the roll 25 mm (1 in) to the right through the same place as the left-hand part of the first stitch. Before pulling the needle out, make two loops around the needle with the piece of twine on the right, ie the piece leaving the first stitch. Then bring out the needle and pull the twine tight. Continue along the back and cut off at the upright. Start again along the side, continue along the front and along the other side (Figure 33c).

You will see that the roll stitch is similar to the blind stitch except that in the roll stitch the needle is taken right through the scrim and there is no gap between the stitches (Figure 33d).

Stuffing loops for horsehair Three rows of stuffing loops from back to front are required to hold the hair. Follow the same method as for a drop-in seat, but make the stitches on the top of the roll at the beginning and end of each row of loops (as done on the footstool). The loops should be two fingers deep.

Horsehair Tease and feed under the loops a layer of horsehair which is sufficiently packed to fill in the groove made by the roll stitch. Add a little extra hair around the centre for doming, if thought necessary.

Calico Using 10 mm ($\frac{3}{8}$ in) fine tacks, secure the calico to the top of the sides of the rails. The back corners are cut in the same way as for the scrim layer. When the calico is taken down on both sides of the back leg and pulled, the material across the top of the corner should be tight and smooth. If this is not the case, then the cut needs extending a little.

If the show-wood at the top of the front legs is rounded, then make a pleat on either side of the corner. With this deeper upholstery, it is easier to make a neat pleat if, after the corner tack is positioned, the material is pulled down and across from the corner in the direction of the arrow in Figure 34a and held with a tack 25 mm (1 in) away from the corner. As this tightens the material across the top of the leg, cut the calico up to the centre tack before

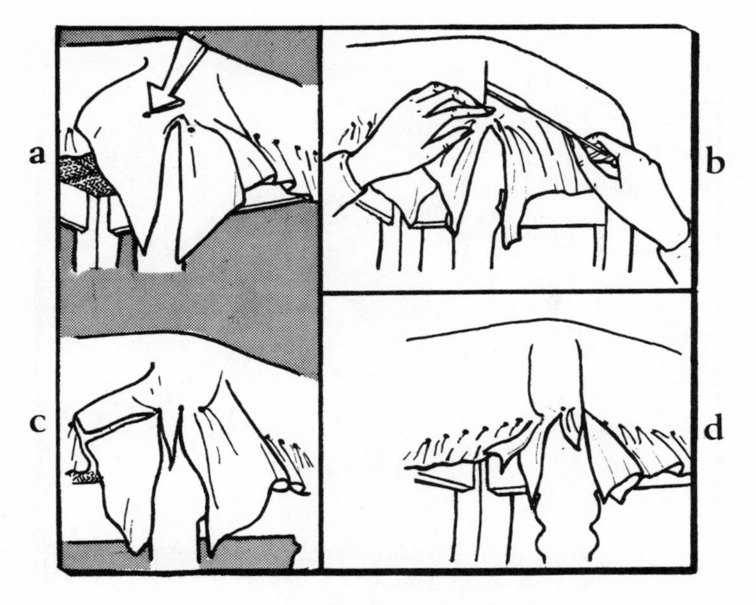

Figure 34 Pleating a rounded corner

stretching the material in the same way to the other side of the corner. Next, as shown in Figures 34b, 34c and 34d, position the pleats, cut away the excess thickness and tack down. You will find the pleats easier to make with the chair lying on its back.

On the other hand, if the wood at the top of the leg is square, then it looks better to have a single pleat on the front rail. To do this, continue tacking the calico on the side rail up to and 25 mm (1 in) around the corner on the front rail, pulling the calico down and across the corner (Figure 35a). If the calico is not tight enough over the corner, then folds will appear under the pleat when it is pulled down. Stretching the calico across the front rail, hold and position the pleat, which must be vertical and on the corner. The flat end of the regulator will help you form the pleat (Figure 35b). Pull the calico down very strongly when setting the pleat, then holding the pleat in one hand and allowing 15 mm (½ in) fold-under, cut up under the fold to the tack (Figure 35c). Cut in again from the bottom edge of the material to join the first cut 5 mm (¼ in) away from the tack. Now tack down the pleat (Figure 35d).

Wadding Two separate layers of skin wadding which extend across the top and halfway down the side upholstery are required.

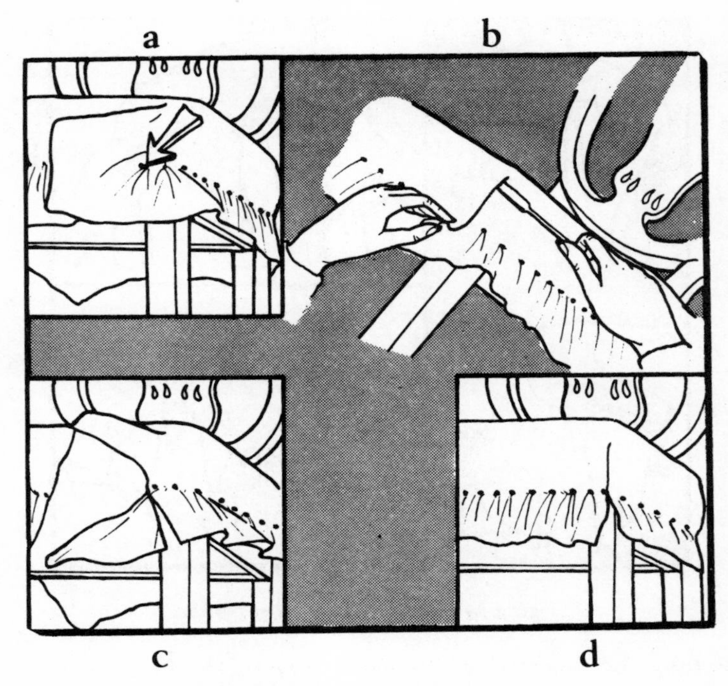

Figure 35 Pleating a squared corner

Covering material There is usually show-wood along the bottom of the rails of a dining chair so that the covering material is tacked flat just above the show-wood with 10 mm ($\frac{3}{8}$ in) fine tacks in exactly the way in which the calico was fixed. If there is no show-wood on the bottom of the rail, the material is taken to the underside of the frame.

As the covering material is the most expensive item in upholstery, do plan any cut before attempting to make it. And remember to err on the side of caution as a cut can always be extended if it has not been made deep enough. Don't forget the final V-shaped cuts to prevent the material tearing when cutting for the back corners.

The pleats on the front corners of this chair must be tight and remember to have them lying vertically. You practised on the calico layer, but calico stretches more than covering materials and is thus easier to work. As long as you have kept the weave of the material straight when fixing the cover, the corners will lie correctly. Take your time positioning the pleats and do not be afraid to pull the material really tightly. Refer again to Figures 34 and 35. Use a sharp-bladed craft knife to trim off the material just above the show-wood.

Black lining Attach the lining to the underside of the chair with 10 mm ($\frac{3}{8}$ in) fine tacks. Make a straight cut from the corner of the lining at each leg, cut away any excess, fold under and tack.

Braid Stick and fold under 15 mm ($\frac{1}{2}$ in) at the end of the braid and start attaching the braid at a back upright. At the top of the front legs on some chairs, the braid will have to be mitred, not cut, around the show-wood. It may be necessary to hold the mitres with gimp pins. However, just before the final hit on the pin, lift over a thread of the braid with the regulator so that the gimp pin will be hidden as much as possible when tacked off.

Victorian mahogany-framed armchair

Figure 36

The arms and backs of easy chairs are always upholstered before the seat, because it is easier to build up the seat to fit the space between the back and arms than vice versa. The chair in Figure 36 has a show-wood back and care must therefore be taken not to damage the wood when hammering the tacks. Additionally, as the rabbet on this back is narrow, only fine headed tacks will be used for all upholstery layers.

UPHOLSTERY

Ripping off Before ripping off the old upholstery, take the measurements for the amount of covering material which will be required. These measurements will not be completely accurate but will suffice as a rough guide to the amount of covering material needed.

Arm pads

In order that both arm pads are as near as possible the same shape and size, it is as well to work the two at the same time, cutting the same size upholstery materials for each.

Stuffing loops for fibre Check that the top edge of the sides and front of the arms is chamfered. Make three stuffing loops from side to side on the bevel, each loop being four fingers deep in the centre of the arm.

Fibre The loops need to be well stuffed with teased Algerian grass.

Scrim As a fine roll has to be worked on three sides of the arm, you may find it preferable to use linen scrim. Add extra fibre along the edges before tacking down the scrim with 10 mm (⅜ in) improved tacks (or 10 mm (⅜ in) fine tacks if using linen scrim), allowing sufficient scrim for sewing the roll on the sides and front; the back can be taken down more tightly.

Blind stitch and roll stitch On the sides and front sew the blind stitch just above the tacks. The roll sewn 15 mm (½ in) above the blind stitching should be finer than usual, ie only 15 mm (½ in) deep (Figure 37). When sewing the roll down the first side, do make sure that you are leaving sufficient scrim and fibre to do a similar roll on the other side. Due to the wooden base on the arm, it is

Figure 37 Stitched arm pad

impossible to sew bridle ties and thus it is easy for these small arm pads to become lopsided. You can prevent this by hammering in three 35 mm (1½ in) nails just far enough to hold the scrim down the centre of the arm. The nails should of course be removed when the roll is complete.

Stuffing loops for horsehair Sew one loop from the back to a stitch in the middle, over one finger, and continue to the front, again over one finger.

Horsehair Feed under the loops sufficient teased horsehair to fill in the groove made by the roll stitching.

Calico Tack the calico with 10 mm (⅜ in) fine tacks.

Inside back

Webbing As the back does not have to withstand nearly as much weight as the seat, secure two webs from the bottom back tacking rail to the top and three webs between the side rails with 13 mm (½ in) fine tacks. Support the back uprights of the chair on a mallet or other block when tacking to avoid strain on the frame.

Hessian This is tacked to cover the area between the bottom and top rails and between the side rails with 13 mm (½ in) fine tacks in the same way as previously described.

Stuffing loops for fibre The upholstery of the back of this chair needs to be fatter at the bottom below the arms to support and fit the small of the back. This is called a lumbar swell and is shown in Figure 38. Make four stuffing loops up both sides of the back from a stitch 10 cm (4 in) into the hessian to the tacking rabbet varying their depth as follows: between the bottom of the back and the arm, make the loop over the whole depth of the hand held

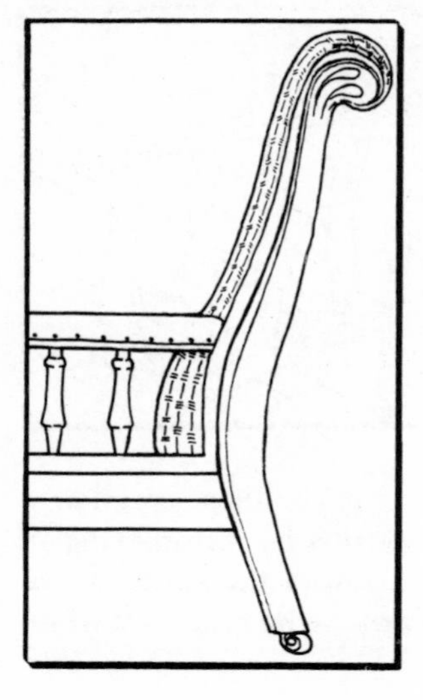

Figure 38 Profile of inside back, showing lumbar swell

vertically on the side rail; the other three loops should be three fingers deep. Place two loops from a line level with the arms to the bottom back tacking rail over the whole depth of the hand. Three further loops should also be made over the depth of the whole hand from the top of the hessian to the wood at the back of the scroll.

Scrim Measure for the scrim allowing for the anticipated depth of the fibre. Fold under the bottom of the scrim and tack it to the bottom back tacking rail only with 10 mm ($\frac{3}{8}$ in) fine tacks and then lay it back over the seat area.

Fibre Tease and feed Algerian grass under the loops and fill in the centre, remembering all the points mentioned in the previous chapter about how this should be done. The outline shape of the back required is shown in Figure 38.

Tacking down the scrim The scrim can now be set loosely, to allow for the contours, at the back of the scroll and more tautly at the sides. Easing the scrim upwards from the bottom back tacking rail, sew 6 bridle ties in an oblong to hold the centre stuffing. Tack the scrim to the wood at the back of the scroll, adding more fibre under the edge and allowing sufficient depth to sew a blind stitch and roll stitch at the back of the scroll and on the side rails around the scroll. Before tacking the sides to the rabbet, add a little extra fibre under the edge and make a cut at the arm rails by laying the scrim back and cutting straight to the wood as shown in Figure 39a. The scrim is fixed in small folds around the scroll (Figure 39b).

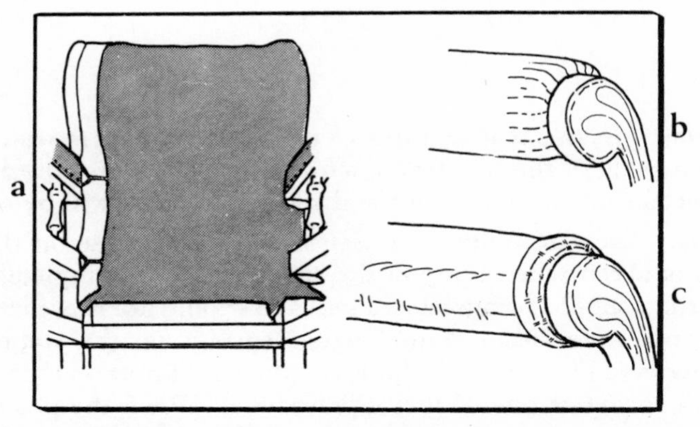

Figure 39 a cuts made at arm and back uprights; **b** pleating around the scroll; **c** stitching along the scroll back

Blind stitch and roll stitch Sew a row of blind stitching in the lumbar swell area below the arms only, 15 mm (½ in) above the tacks. This will give firmness to the deeper upholstery of this part. To prevent damaging the show-wood, use a curved twine needle instead of the mattress needle. Sew a second row of blind stitching along the side rails and around the scroll starting 15 mm (½ in) above the blind stitch in the lumbar swell area tapering to 15 mm (½ in) above the tacks for the rest of the back. Then sew a roll both sides, continuing around the scroll. Watch the profile of the back as you do the stitching and make sure that a shape similar to that in Figure 38 is being achieved.

Now blind stitching and a roll are sewn along the back of the scroll as shown in Figure 39c. For the blind stitching, insert the needle just above the tacks and sew the roll, which should be 25 mm (1 in) deep and not pulled too tightly, 25 mm (1 in) above the blind stitching.

Stuffing loops for horsehair Make three rows of stuffing loops from the bottom of the back to the back of the scroll, making two stitches on the way with the loops two fingers deep.

Horsehair Feed teased horsehair under the loops.

Calico Tack the calico over the horsehair with 10 mm (⅜ in) fine tacks. At the bottom of the back, the calico is taken around the bottom rail and tacked to the outside of the rail. Cut at the arms in the same way as for the scrim and pleat the calico around the scrolls.

Seat

Webbing As this seat requires springs, the webbing is attached to the underside of the seat frame with 16 mm (⅝ in) improved tacks. Five webs from back to front and six webs across will be needed.

Springs The durability of a seat largely depends upon the care which is taken when tying-in the springs. When completely tied, the springs should compress as a unit and should not move laterally.

Arrange nine 20 cm (8 in) 9-gauge springs on the webbing in three rows of three with the knuckle (the wire knot) on the top coil of each spring at one o'clock (Figure 40a). When the position of the springs is satisfactory, ie they are evenly spaced from each other and the bottom coil of each spring is well supported by webbing,

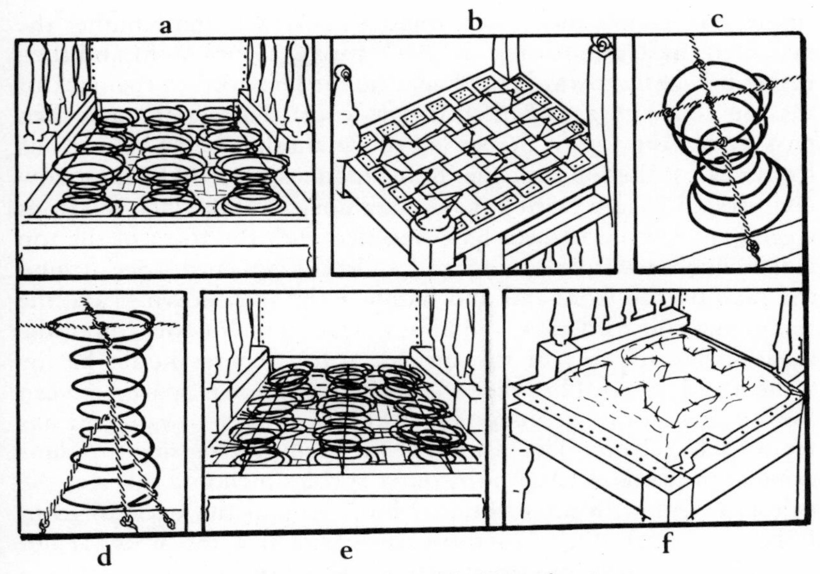

Figure 40 Tying in and lashing of springs

mark around the base of each spring on the webbing with a felt-tipped pen.

The springs can now be tied to the webbing so, with the exception of the back left one, move them all out of the way for ease of working. Then with a spring needle threaded with no. 1 or 2 twine and commencing from the underside of the webbing with an upholsterer's knot, tie each spring down in three places evenly spaced around the bottom coil. Each loop, which is made as closely to and as tightly as possible around the wire, is secured with a single knot on the underside of the webbing before passing to the next stitch. One length of twine should tie in all the springs. Remember to reposition each spring with the top knuckle at one o'clock to ensure that the knuckle will not be in the way when the springs are lashed. Figure 40b shows the underside of the seat when all the springs have been sewn to the webbing.

The top coil of each spring now needs lashing. Place half-sunk 16 mm ($\frac{5}{8}$ in) improved tacks in the middle of the rail at the back, front and sides opposite each row of springs. Measure from the back tack over the springs to the front tack and add half that measurement again to allow for knotting. This gives the length of laid cord which will be required for that row of springs. Tie a single knot in the laid cord around a back tack and hammer the tack right in. Compressing the back spring 25 mm (1 in) and then tilting it slightly towards the back, tie the laid cord to the back of the top coil with a half-hitch (single knot) (Figure 40c) and then pass across the top of the spring to tie another half-hitch on the front edge of the top coil. Tie-in the middle spring in the same row compressed 25 mm (1 in) but standing upright and, when the front spring, again compressed, has been tied with the front of the top coil inclined towards the front rail, twist the laid cord twice around the tack on the front rail and hammer the tack down. Take the remaining laid cord back and knot it around the middle coil of the front spring to support the spring's waist. There should be the same length of cord between the springs as there is space between the springs on the webbing. Tie in the two other rows of springs from back to front. The lashing of the springs from side to side is done in the same way with the outer springs inclining towards the side rails but with an additional loop around the back to front lashings (Figure 40c). On those springs where the waist is not supported, and on the corner springs which must be supported in two directions, use a short length of laid cord to loop the spring at the waist and tie off each end around a tack (Figure 40d). When fully lashed-in (Figure 40e), the springs will have been compressed by 25 mm (1 in).

Hessian The tacking of the hessian with 13 mm (½ in) improved tacks is done in the same way as previously described, the only difference being that it is taken over the top of the springs instead of over the webbing. Although the tension on the hessian should be taut, it should not be so tight that it compresses the springs.

To prevent the springs rubbing against the hessian, the springs must now be tied to the hessian. The same method is followed as for tying them to the webbing except that this time you knot the twine on the top surface using a curved twine needle (Figure 40f).

Stuffing loops for fibre On this seat, three stuffing loops are required along the front rail and one loop on both sides in front of the arm uprights. Commence each loop from the centre of a spring and, allowing sufficient twine to form a right angle above the rail, tie off around a 10 mm (⅜ in) improved tack on the chamfered edge.

Scrim Before stuffing the seat, the scrim should be tacked to the back tacking rail chamfer with 10 mm (⅜ in) improved tacks. With the scrim laid against the inside back upholstery, it will be much easier to stuff fully down the back edge. When measuring for the scrim, you will have to allow for the depth of the stuffing to be placed on the seat.

Fibre Begin at the back, stuffing teased Algerian grass well down between the hessian and the scrim. You can now see why the back of the chair is upholstered before the seat, as this stuffing at the back of the seat ensures that the back and the seat will fit closely. Then feed stuffing under the loops, along the sides and, finally, fill in the centre area of the seat.

Set the scrim on the other three rails, pulling firmly to the front because, with the back of the scrim already tacked down, you will not be able to make any tightening adjustment at the back later. Sew in 9 bridle ties to hold the scrim, fibre and hessian only. Adding extra fibre along the edges, tack the scrim down allowing for stitching in front of the arm uprights and along the front only. Hence the side scrim underneath the arms can be tacked down more tautly. The scrim will need to be cut at the arm uprights in the same way as was done at the arms on the inside back (refer to Figure 39a).

Blind stitch and roll stitch On this seat, the sewing will be done only in front of the arm uprights and along the front. However, as the stuffing is deep, sew three rows of blind stitching with a 15 mm (½ in) space between each row before doing the roll stitch.

Stuffing loops for horsehair Three rows of loops are required from the back of the seat to the top of the front roll with two stitches down the centre. Each loop should be two fingers deep.

Horsehair Feed horsehair under the loops on the top of the seat only, adding a little extra in the centre for doming, if required.

Calico Tack the calico on in the usual way, cutting at the arm uprights and using 10 mm (⅜ in) fine tacks. With this deep seat, it will be best to have a pleat on either side of the front corners.

COVERING

Although the measurements for the covering material were taken before ripping off the old upholstery, they were not completely accurate. So take all measurements again allowing sufficient to tack under the seat rails all round. It is as well to draw a cutting plan to scale before marking out the different covering pieces with tailor's chalk and metre stick on the right side of the material. This plan will ensure the economic use of the fabric and will confirm that there is sufficient material. It will usually be found that the inside back and outside back can be cut from one width.

Seat

Contrary to the order of upholstery, the seat is covered first.

Wadding Lay one layer of lintafelt to cover the top of the seat and to extend halfway down the side upholstery.

Covering material Set the material. Before starting to tack, the material must be cut for the back uprights. Remove the 'setting' tack on the back rail and fold the material back over the seat, making sure that the centre mark on the material is in the middle of the seat. As it is necessary to have sufficient material at the sides to make neat corners, this cut is rather different to the previous cuts you have used and is illustrated in Figure 41. When both cuts have been made, tack along the side of the back rail and under the front rail with 10 mm ($\frac{3}{8}$ in) fine tacks, trimming back the wadding where necessary so that it is above the bottom of the seat rail.

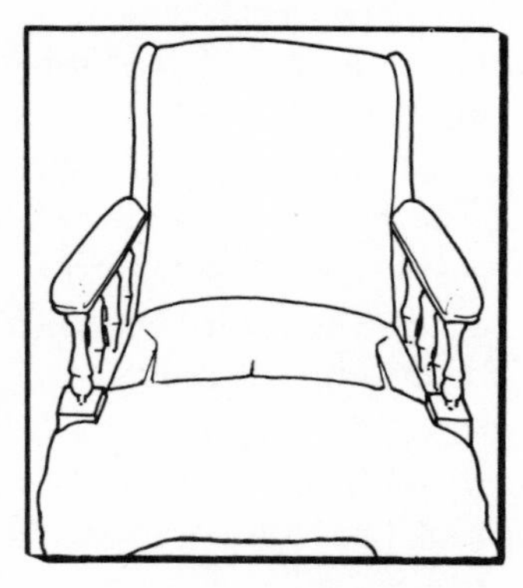

Figure 41 Seat covering material cuts for back leg uprights

Before tacking under the side rails, the arm upright cuts must be made in exactly the same way as was done for the scrim and calico. Due to these cuts, there will be a small area at the bottom of the arm upright on the outside of the chair which the material will not cover. Thus, before tacking both sides, cut a piece of covering material which is wider than the base of the arm upright and long enough to tack from the bottom of the arm upright to under the seat plus 25 mm (1 in) fold-under at the top. Match up any pile or

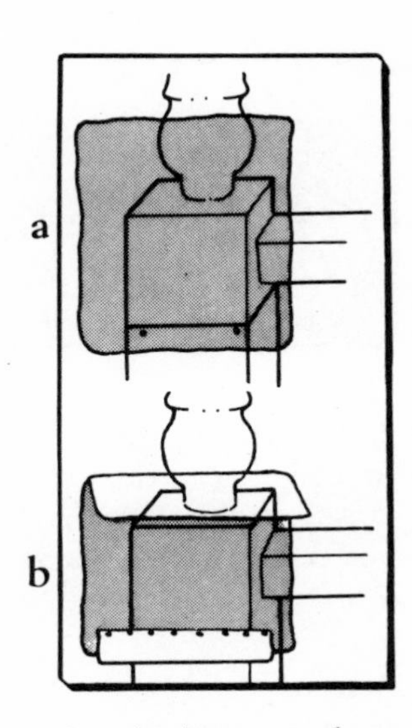

Figure 42 Back tacking

pattern. This piece now has to be 'back tacked', which means that, when completed, the tacks will not be visible. Position the top edge of the material 25 mm (1 in) beneath the show-wood at the base of the arm upright with the wrong side of the material towards you, ie the right side of the material will be lying on the show-wood of the arm upright (Figure 42a). Secure only two 10 mm ($\frac{3}{8}$ in) fine tacks just beneath the show-wood and then fold the material down to ensure that it is correctly positioned. Turning the material up again, lay and then tack a small strip of card, buckram or half a width of webbing along the top edge of the fold (Figure 42b). This will reinforce the tacking line so that when the material is tacked under the seat rail over a layer of skin wadding, the line of the material is smooth and straight.

The covering material can then be tacked under the side rails and the pleats made at the front corners.

Inside back

Wadding Lay two separate layers of skin wadding on the back.

Covering material At the bottom of the inside back, the material is tacked down on top of the tacks holding the seat material. This will prevent a gap at the back of the chair, which is why the seat had to be covered first. The top of the inside back material should be tensioned tightly on the outside edges of the scroll back (Figure 43) so that there is less material to pleat on the scroll sides. If it is

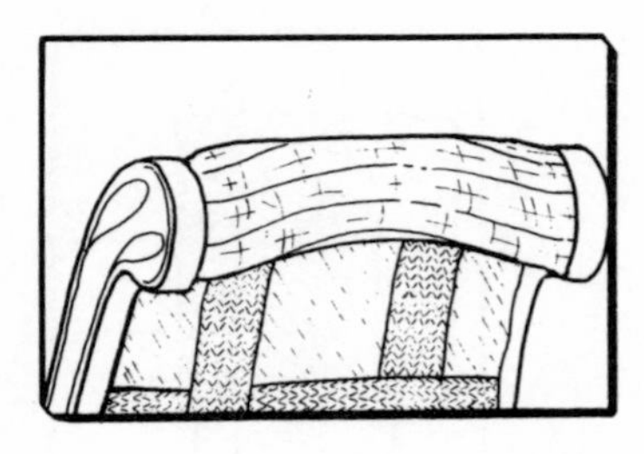

Figure 43 Tensioning of covering material around scroll to ease pleating

difficult to position the pleats around the scroll due to the small space between the upholstery and the show-wood, with twine run one row of gathering stitches on the line where the tacks will be positioned on each side. Draw up the gathers, tying off the twine around a tack, and position the tacks around the scroll.

Arm pads

Wadding Place two layers of skin wadding on each arm.

Covering material It is best to make a single pleat on the front of the arms. A single pleat is also made at the back of the arms but on the sides.

Outside back

Hessian and covering material Measure from under the scroll to the underneath of the chair and between the side rails and add 5 cm (2 in) to each measurement. Cut 305 g (10 oz) hessian and covering material to this size.

The covering material is back tacked under the scroll with the hessian. Lay the covering material wrong side up over the scroll and position three tacks (10 mm ($\frac{3}{8}$ in) fine) to hold the outside edges and centre of the material 25 mm (1 in) from the top edge right up under the scroll. Fold the material down to check that its position is covering all the tacks used when attaching the inside back. When correctly sited, hammer in these three tacks. Now fold under 25 mm (1 in) at the top of the hessian and lay this fold along the line of the three tacks holding the covering material. With 10 mm ($\frac{3}{8}$ in) improved tacks, 25 mm (1 in) apart, tack down the top edge of the hessian, ie at the fold. This method of back tacking is identical to that done at the bottom of the arm uprights except that 'folded under' hessian replaces the card, buckram or webbing. As the outside back on this chair is slightly concave, tack the hessian,

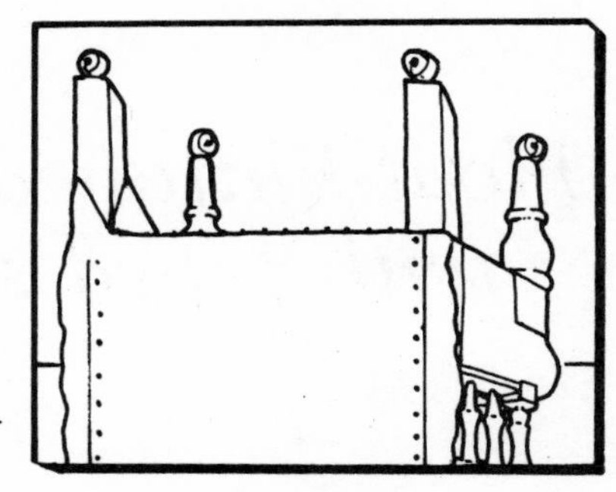

Figure 44 Cuts at the back legs on outside back cover

folded under, down the sides with 10 mm ($\frac{3}{8}$ in) fine tacks before tacking it to the seat rail. Lay one layer of skin wadding over the hessian before folding down the covering material. Tack the covering material singly down each side rail with 10 mm ($\frac{3}{8}$ in) fine tacks before stretching and tacking it to the underside of the seat. The cut required at the back legs is shown in Figure 44.

Braid

Stick braid on the front and sides of the seat and arms and on both sides of the inside and outside back.

Black lining

Tack black lining on the underside of the seat to cover all raw edges and tacks.

Sprung seat

Any sprung seat is always webbed from the underside of the frame. If you have a loose seat or dining chair to be sprung, use four springs and tie them in as described in this chapter. However, as the springs will be shorter, there will be no necessity to support the waists.

Edge springing

The front row of springs on some armchairs and most settees is placed on the front rail. This technique is known as 'edge springing'. The springs are tied in separately and, to learn how to do this, refer to a book on advanced upholstery.

Float-buttoned nursing chair with piped scroll facings

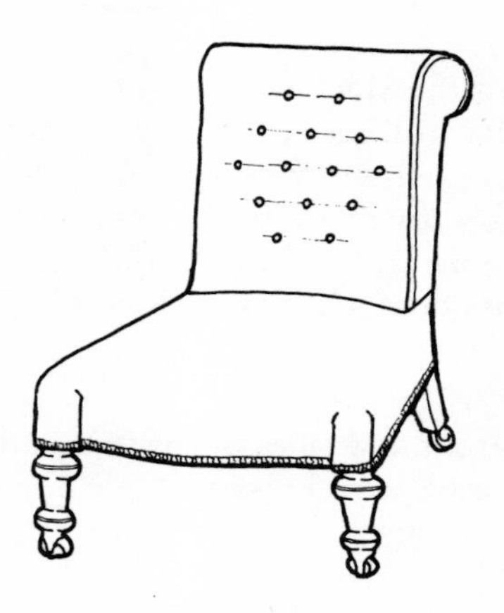

Figure 45

Buttons are used in two ways in upholstery: deep buttoning, which is described in the next chapter, and float or hold buttoning, which is used to add interest on an unpatterned covering material, as in the nursing chair in Figure 45, or where the inside back of a chair is concave and it is difficult to eliminate fullness on the inside back covering material.

Inside back

The inside back of the nursing chair is built up in the same way as the inside back of the chair described in the previous chapter. However, as it is designed to have a straight back, the nursing chair does not require the lumbar swell. After the horsehair has been fed under the stuffing loops, the calico is tacked around the bottom rail and at the back of the scroll as before, but down the sides it is sewn with back stitch under the lip of the roll (Figure 46). Thus the

Figure 46 Back stitch under the lip of the roll

width measurement for the calico needs only to cover the horsehair and extend over the roll on both sides. It is positioned with skewers until stitched.

Seat

The seat has nine springs and is upholstered as detailed for the framed armchair, except that the blind stitch and roll stitch are sewn down both sides as well as along the front.

Covering material Set the seat covering material. The material is cut at the back uprights as described for the armchair but, instead of tacking the corners to the seat side rails, the material is taken to the outside of the back. However, at this stage, hold these back corners with temporary tacks only, as the piped scroll facings are inserted underneath the back corner material.

Inside back and scroll facings

The inside back covering material, piping and scroll facings for this chair are first sewn together and then tacked to the chair. This is how it is done:

Covering material for the inside back Measure from the seat back tacking rail to the back of the scroll plus 5 cm (2 in) for the length and across the width of the inside back from the outer edge of the roll on both sides plus 25 mm (1 in) for the width. Cut the material to this size.

Covering material for the scroll facings Measure the width of the scroll at the widest part, allowing extra if the back of the chair leans backwards, plus 10 cm (4 in) and measure from the top of the scroll to the bottom of the seat rail plus 25 mm (1 in) for the length. Cut two pieces of material this size.

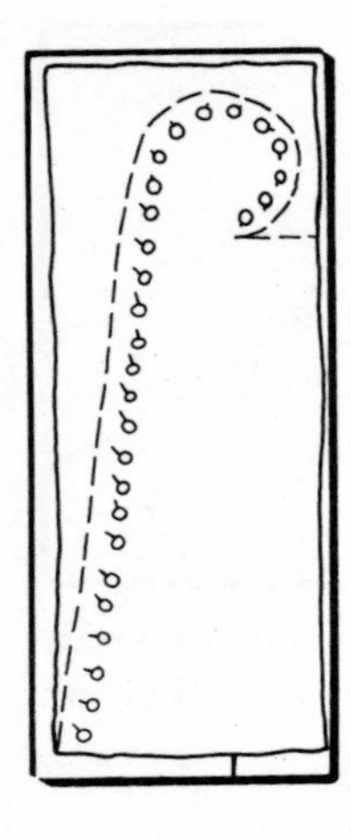

Figure 47 Shaping the scroll facing material on the chair

Inserting plenty of skewers, position one of the pieces of facing material to the top of the roll around the scroll and down the inside back edge. Make sure that the weave of the material is straight. With tailor's chalk, mark a line 15 mm (½ in) to the outside of the skewers (Figure 47). Remove the material from the chair and cut along the chalk line. Lay the shaped facing on top of the other piece of facing material, wrong side to wrong side, so that the second facing will be a mirror image of the first, and cut it to the same shape.

Piping Cut 35 mm (1½ in) wide strips of covering material on the bias (diagonal). The strips, allowing for joining, should be long enough to extend completely around both scroll facings. Keep the strips in the order in which they are cut and the same way up, so that when joined the pile, pattern and weave of the material will run in the same direction.

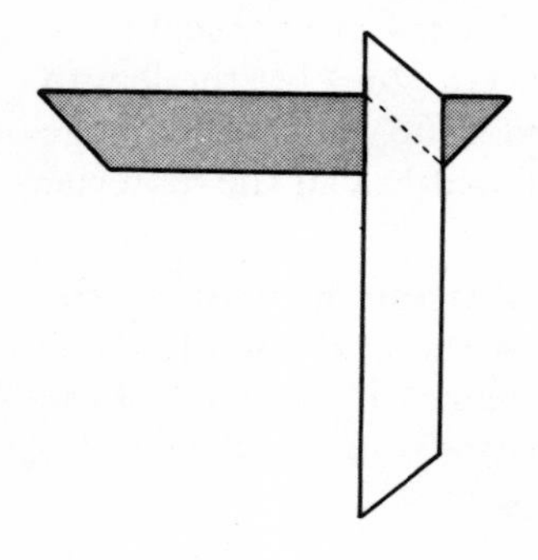

Figure 48 Joining the piping strips

The strips now have to be joined into one length. Follow the method shown in Figure 48, machining them together with button thread for extra strength. Then trim the seams to 10 mm ($\frac{3}{8}$in) and open them out flat. Fold the strip evenly around the piping cord and, with a piping/zipper foot on the machine, sew down the length of the strip.

Next, machine together the inside back covering material, piping and scroll facings with 15 mm ($\frac{1}{2}$ in) seams. As shown in Figure 49, however, leave a length of the piping at the back of each scroll facing long enough to extend down the outside back to the top of the back leg. Do the machining in two stages: first machine the inside back covering material to the piping and then join the facing. Cut into the inside back covering material and piping seam allowances at 25 mm (1 in) intervals in order to machine the inside back to the facing more easily around the scroll.

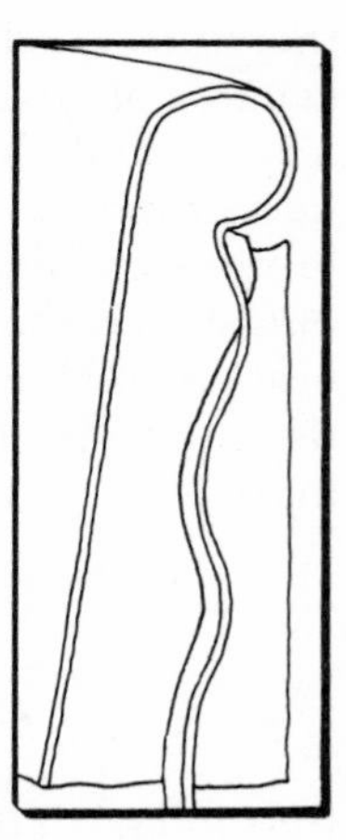

Figure 49 The inside back cover ready to fit on the chair

Wadding for the inside back Cut two layers of skin wadding which are the length of the back to the back of the scroll and wide enough to just cover the roll on both sides.

Tacking down covering material Remove the temporary tacks at the seat back corners and ease the inside back covering material with attached scroll facings over the wadding, tacking the bottom edge to the seat back tacking rail and the top to the back of the scroll. Cut the inside back covering material at the back uprights in the same way as the seat covering material was shaped. Pad the curl of the scroll with enough small pieces of lintafelt so that the bulk of the seam turnings is evened out and the facing is smoothly filled. Then place a layer down the straight part of the facing before tacking the back edge of the facing to the outside of the back rail. Tack the seat covering material at the seat back corners to the outside of the back rail and then tack the loose pieces of piping, slightly proud of the edge, down the length of the back rail, cutting back the piping cord only and turning the piping under at the top of the back legs.

Buttons It is best to have the buttons covered by your local upholsterer or upholstery supply shop, as upholstery covering material is fairly thick, often has a pile, and a satisfactory result cannot be obtained using the do-it-yourself dressmaking button covering kits.

Two machines are used in the process of covering buttons. The first cuts 30 mm (1¼ in) circles of the covering material and you will therefore need to provide the upholsterer with 35 mm (1½ in) squares of covering material for the number of buttons required. The second then wraps the material around the 15 mm ($\frac{9}{16}$ in) button mould and wedges it into the button base. Two types of buttons are available (Figure 50): one has a metal loop like a shoe button and the other a linen back. The one with the linen back is best, as the button sits flat on the base of the upholstery, whereas the one with the metal loop stands proud of it by the depth of the loop.

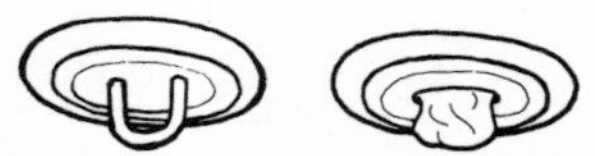

Figure 50 Metal loop and linen back buttons

Buttoning The buttons are positioned so that the spaces between them form diamonds whose length is greater than their width. In addition, the buttons nearest to the outside edges are placed not less than half and not more than the whole width or length of the diamond away from the edge, and the bottom row of buttons should not be set too low.

Bearing these points in mind, mark out the button positions with skewers on the inside back covering material to a design of your choice, following the weave of the material to ensure that the rows are straight. The advantage of using skewers is that they can be repositioned without marking the material. Then, with a tape measure, check the measurements between all the skewers. I cannot

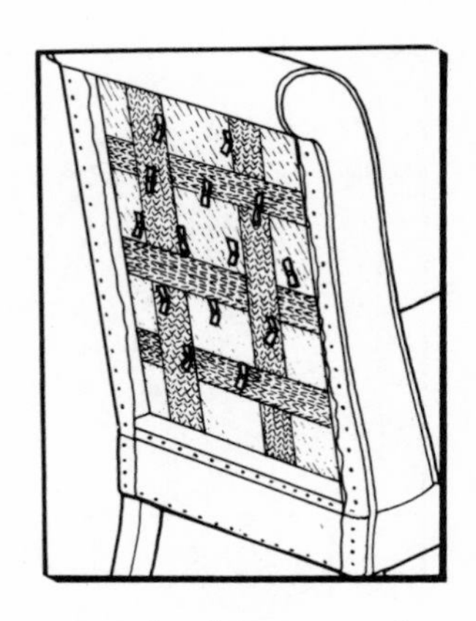

Figure 51 Toggles

stress sufficiently that, to obtain a satisfactory result, this measuring must be done very accurately. Only when you are satisfied that the skewers are evenly spaced should you mark the covering material and the hessian or webbing at the back with small biro dots as you remove each skewer. The size of the diamonds on this nursing chair are 15 cm (6 in) by 8.5 cm (3¾ in).

Always commence buttoning in the centre and work outwards to the other buttons. Thread a mattress needle with twine and put a knot in the end. Insert the needle to one side of the biro dot on the hessian or webbing at the back and bring it out at the biro dot on the covering material. Do not pull the twine right through. Thread the button onto the twine. The needle is now returned through the biro dot to emerge at the back 5 mm (¼ in) away from where it entered. Make an upholsterer's knot but, before tightening it, cut a 25 mm (1 in) piece of webbing, fold it in half widthwise and insert this toggle between the knot and the hessian or webbing to prevent the knot from cutting through the upholstery. Cut off the twine about 15 cm (6 in) from the knot. When all the buttons are tied in, pull the twine on each button to an even tension so that the buttons are just below the level of the upholstery and make two separate half-hitch knots against each upholsterer's knot to prevent it from slipping. Cut off the twine 25 mm (1 in) from the knot (Figure 51).

Outside back

Back tack the hessian and covering material at the back of the scroll as for the armchair. Down the sides, turn the material under the layer of wadding and hold the fold with skewers against the piping.

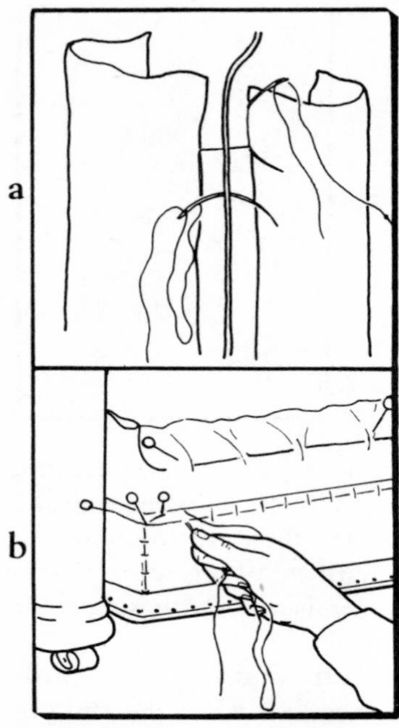

Figure 52 a slip stitch; b over and over stitch

With a small, fine, curved needle and carpet thread, sew the outside back cover to the piping and scroll facing with slip stitch, as follows: take a 5 mm (¼ in) stitch through the fold of the outside back covering material, then pass the needle through the piping on the machine stitching and take another 5 mm (¼ in) stitch through the scroll facing material. Bring the needle back through the piping again and repeat these stitches (Figure 52a). This technique makes a continuous running stitch joining the back cover, piping and scroll facing together and when the thread is pulled tight, no stitches show.

Piped border

On a chair which has a piped border on the front of the seat, the calico and seat covering material are sewn with back stitch under the lip of the roll. The piping is machined to the border and the piped border is then positioned, with skewers, to the front roll ensuring that it is at an even height above the front tacking rail. Pushing the skewers into the upholstery as far as possible, lift up the border and insert further skewers through the piping and border seam allowances. Then, with curved needle and twine, sew the piping and border seam allowances to the seat covering material, calico and scrim with an over and over stitch (Figure 52b). Turn the border down again and, using the small curved sewing needle and carpet thread, sew the piping to the seat covering material with slip stitch by taking a stitch at the back of the piping and the next stitch through the seat covering material and repeat.

You will realize that the border has been sewn twice. The over and over stitching through the seam allowances is the strong stitching which keeps the border in position: it does not sew the piping itself to the seat covering material. The slip stitch does this, but on its own this stitching is not sufficiently strong.

With the stitching complete, fold up the border and sew stuffing loops for a little horsehair from top to bottom of the edge upholstery. Cover the horsehair with a layer of lintafelt and tack the border under the front rail.

Deep-buttoned Victorian piano stool

Figure 53

I appreciate that to some, upholstery is synonymous with deep buttoning and that, for this reason, people want to try their hand at it, even though they have relatively little experience. As an introduction, therefore, I have chosen the small stool in Figure 53. However, I do emphasize that deep buttoning is an advanced technique, which demands very neat work and, above all, the greatest care when marking out the positions for the buttons both on the stool itself and on the covering material.

Ripping off The seat on this stool untwists from the tripod legs and the metal shaft then unscrews from the seat portion. You can therefore work on it more easily as it lies flat on the bench and the centre buttoning hole is also uncovered. Check that the top edge of the base has a bevel and, if not, rub down the sharp edge with a wood rasp.

Hessian Webbing is not required on this type of stool, but tack on a piece of mangled hessian to cover the holes and, if the circular

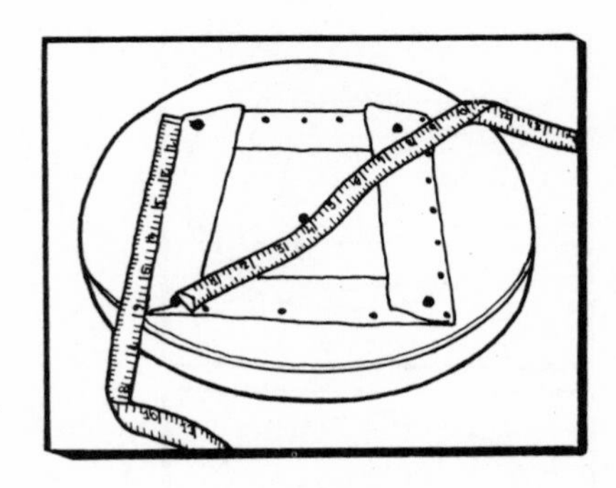

Figure 54 Checking the button positions on the base

piano stool base is of a different type, any open areas, with 10 mm ($\frac{3}{8}$ in) improved tacks.

Marking button positions on the base Although on most buttonwork the button positions form diamonds, on this particular stool they have to be where the holes are in the wood. With biro, mark the top of the hessian above the holes. The centre mark is 10 cm (4 in) from each outer mark and each outer mark is 14 cm ($5\frac{3}{4}$ in) from the one on either side of it, as shown in Figure 54. On circular piano stools without a solid wood base, the place for the centre button is determined by the hole through the frame. Insert a skewer straight through the hessian at this point to mark the spot. The other four buttons have to be positioned on the hessian over the open part of the seat, so that the five buttons will form four equal-sided half diamonds with each outer button being at an equal distance from the centre button and the same distance from the two outer buttons next to it. Use skewers to mark the other four button places. Then check the position of each skewer measuring with a tape from the centre to the outer skewers and between outer skewers. Take great care to ensure that these measurements are exact before marking the top and the underside of the hessian with small biro dots.

Stuffing loops On all deep buttonwork it is necessary to build up an edge to the upholstery which will be firm and give shape. With a felt-tipped pen or biro draw a circle 7.5 cm (3 in) in from the outside edge using a tape measure or 7.5 cm (3 in) stick, as a guide (Figure 55a). It is preferable if the marked button positions are in the central area away from the edge upholstery, but this is not possible on this stool.

Five or six stuffing loops are needed around the base. Make a stitch through the hessian on the drawn line and take the loop over

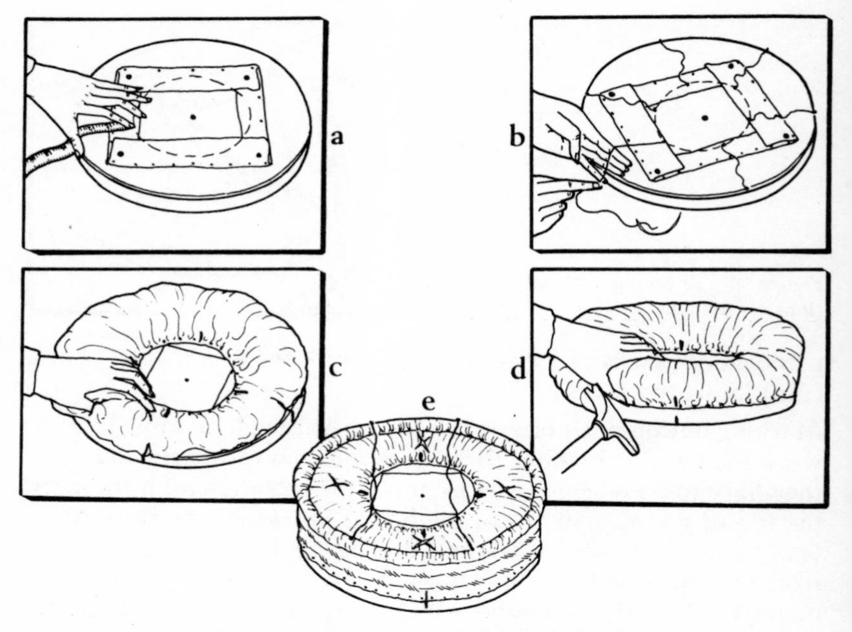

Figure 55 Building up the edge upholstery

three fingers held vertically on the edge to a tack on the bevel (Figure 55b).

Scrim Cut a piece of scrim 18 cm (7 in) wide and as long as the circumference of the base plus 7.5 cm (3 in) overlap. Make a 15 mm (½ in) fold along one side of the length. The folded edge now has to be tacked, where possible, or sewn to the line, pleating to absorb the fullness. It is easier to allocate the amount of fullness on this circular top if the quarter circle points are marked on the tacking edge and if the scrim is folded and marked at the quarter points on both edges, remembering to exclude the 7.5 cm (3 in) overlap from the measurements. If these marked points are matched up as the pleated fold is tacked or sewn on the line, you can check that the fold is pleated to the right amount to allow sufficient scrim to go around the circumference (Figure 55c). At the end, fold 25 mm (1 in) of the overlap under to make a neat join.

Horsehair As horsehair is used to stuff the area to be buttoned, it is also best to use it for the edge upholstery.

Fold the scrim into the centre of the stool out of the way and stuff horsehair under the loops. These need to be well packed.

Adding more hair under the edge, tuck the scrim under the hair and tack it to the chamfered edge with 10 mm (⅜ in) improved tacks. Match up the marks on the scrim with those on the wood as you tack on the edge (Figure 55d).

Blind stitch and roll stitch Regulating the hair to the edge of the frame, sew a row of blind stitching 15 mm (½ in) above the tacks. Then make a second row of blind stitching 15 mm (½ in) above the first row. Finally, sew the roll with roll stitch 15 mm (½ in) above the second row of blind stitching. Do regulate the hair between each stitch to ensure that the edge will be firm and at right angles to the base (Figure 55e).

As the outer button positions have been covered by the edge upholstery, it is now necessary to push a skewer up from the base of the stool, either through the holes or straight up at the biro marks, and to make X-shaped nicks in the scrim where the skewers emerge at each button position. To ensure that the buttons will subsequently sink down to the base when pulled tight, push a finger down through the cuts to the base.

Stuffing loops for horsehair Sew two loops from the top of the roll on one side of the base to the top of the roll on the other side (Figure 55e).

Horsehair Tease and well fill the central area with horsehair to a slightly greater depth than the edge upholstery.

Wadding Over the horsehair, place a layer of lintafelt which is large enough to cover the top and extend half way down to the tacking edge.

Covering material When measuring covering material for deep buttoning a flat surface, an extra 4 cm (1½ in) has to be allowed across the width and down the length of each diamond over and above the measurements marked on the base.

Measure from the tacking edge across the top of the seat to the tacking edge on the other side and add 10 cm (4 in) plus 8 cm (3 in) for the buttoning. Cut a square piece of material to this size. Measuring with a yardstick diagonally across from the corners, insert a skewer into the centre point.

It will be easier to mark out the other button positions for this stool if we imagine that there are going to be buttons north, south, east and west of the centre button, as there would be if a larger area were being buttoned. The distance between the outer buttons

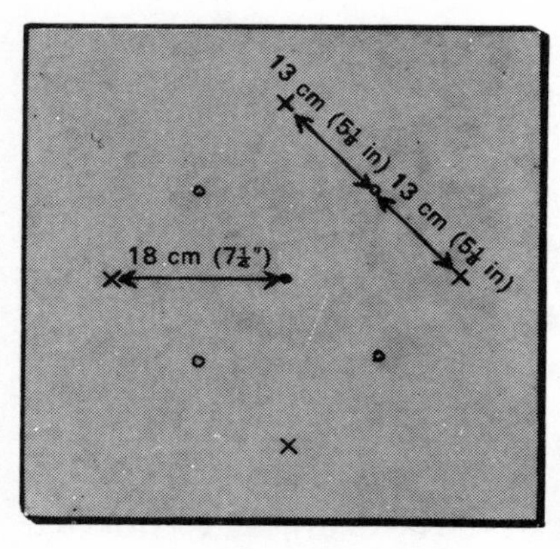

Figure 56 Button positions on the covering material

on the base was 14 cm (5¾ in) to which 4 cm (1½ in) must be added on the covering material. Therefore, following the weave of the material to keep a straight line, insert skewers 18 cm (7¼ in) to the north, south, east and west of the centre skewer. Check that the measurements between the outer skewers are all the same. If adjustment is necessary, then make sure that the distance from the centre skewer to each outer skewer has remained equal. In Figure 56, these skewers are indicated with an 'x'.

Half the distance between these outer skewers locates the required outer button positions. These positions are indicated by an 'o' in Figure 56.

Very thorough checking of all the measurements is now required, particularly between all the 'o' skewers and the centre skewer. If the measurements are not exact, a satisfactory result is impossible and you will find the buttoning very difficult to do.

Remove only the 'x' skewers as these markers are no longer required. You will be left with five skewers indicating the positions of the five buttons. As you take out each skewer, mark the material on the right side with a small biro dot.

Lay the material on top of the wadding and tie in the centre button as detailed for the nursing chair. As it is difficult to return the needle through the small hole in the wooden base from the top, unthread the needle and, from the underside of the base, take the needle, eye first, through the hole to emerge at the biro dot on the covering material. Leaving the needle in the upholstery, rethread it and pull it back down through the hole again. Make an upholsterer's knot and pull so that the button is drawn in half the depth of the upholstery. Cut off the twine about 15 cm (6 in) from the base.

Tie in all the buttons in the same way. If they are being tied into an open area of the base, then, before pulling the upholsterer's knot, insert a toggle between the knot and the hessian as described in the previous chapter.

With all the buttons pulled in half way, the pleats between them can now be formed. When the buttoning is on a vertical surface, the pleats are folded downwards so that dust cannot collect in them. On this stool, the folds lie as shown in Figure 57. With a pile material, the pleats must lie in the direction of the pile. Using the flat end of the regulator, the material can be manipulated to form the pleats. Put the regulator underneath the centre button and arrange the material so that the beginning of the pleat emerges from under the button along the same line as the main part of the pleat. Adjust the end of the pleat under the outer button in the same way. When the four pleats have been set, lift the covering material and wadding and, with the flat end of the regulator, push more horsehair if necessary into the button areas so that the material is fully padded out. You will then probably need to add a little more horsehair on the outer edge.

Four further pleats will leave each outer button, on the same line and lying in the same direction as the pleats from the centre button, and be taken down to the tacking edge. Again a little extra horsehair may have to be added in the button areas before the pleats are tacked down temporarily.

The buttons can now be pulled down tightly. On a wooden base, temporary tack two 13 mm (½ in) fine tacks adjacent to each hole on the underside. Starting in the centre, push down on the button from the top side to make sure that it sinks in as far as possible.

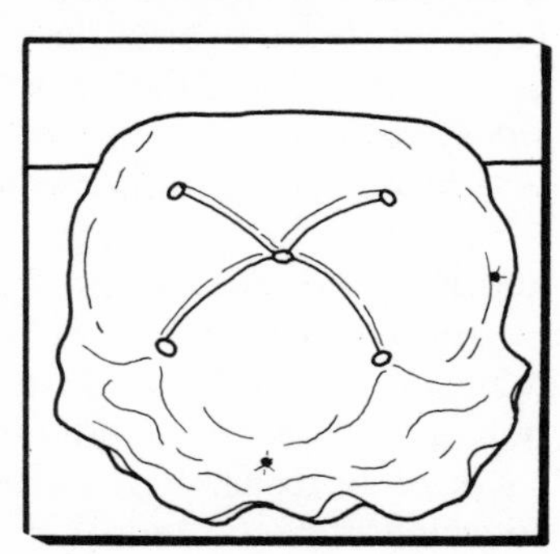

Figure 57 Direction of pleats between the buttons

Pulling the twine tight, wrap it in a 'figure of eight' around the tacks and hammer the tacks in. Do the same with the other four buttons. Where the button is in an open part of the frame, press down on the button and pull the upholsterer's knot tight against the toggle. Then make two separate half-hitch knots against the upholsterer's knot to prevent the upholsterer's knot from slipping. Cut off the twine 25 mm (1 in) from the knot or tack.

Now make final adjustments to the pleats. If you took care in measuring out the base and the material, you will find that the pleats have fallen neatly into place.

With 10 mm ($\frac{3}{8}$ in) fine tacks, tack the material to the wooden edge. Follow a line of the weave in an area between two outer buttons to ensure that you begin tacking on the straight of the material. You will then find that the fullness can be incorporated into the four pleats.

Braid Cut off the spare material with a knife and stick braid over the tacks.

Deep buttoning curved surfaces

The method described in this chapter applies to all deep buttoning. However, whereas for this stool and other flat surfaces an additional 4 cm ($1\frac{1}{2}$ in) is allowed on the covering material, over and above the length and width of each diamond measurement on the base, some chairs require different allowances to accommodate the buttoning to their shape.

For example, the inside back of a chair may sometimes be slightly concave side to side to fit the shape of the body. Mark out the base in the same way and in this case, on the covering material add 4 cm ($1\frac{1}{2}$ in) as before to the length of the diamonds and to their width on the flat part of the back. Where the back begins to curve at the sides, however, reduce the extra covering material required on the width only of each diamond to 25 mm (1 in).

On the other hand, the back of a chesterfield settee is convex and here the adjustment is made over the length of the diamonds on the covering material, with the extra width needed for each diamond remaining at 4 cm ($1\frac{1}{2}$ in). On the length there are usually one and a half diamonds, ie three rows of half diamonds or four rows of buttons. It is easier in this case to work out the extra covering material required if you calculate per half diamond. On

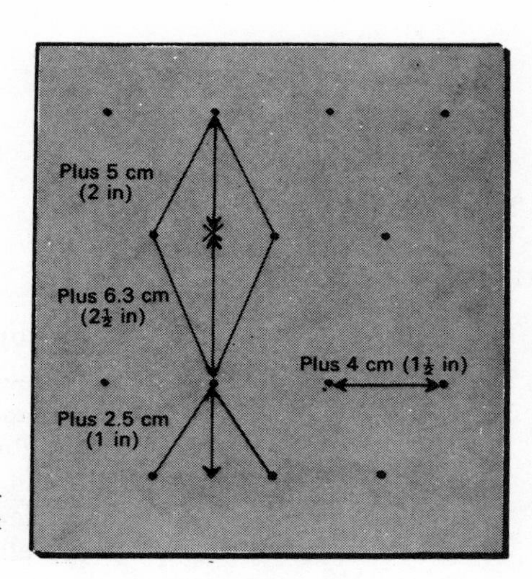

Figure 58 Marking out the covering material on a portion of the back of a chesterfield settee

the first half diamond above the seat allow 25 mm (1 in). A total of 12 cm (4½ in) then has to be allowed on the length of the whole diamond above the half diamond. This is broken down into 7 cm (2½ in) on the bottom half and 5 cm (2 in) on the top half, making 12 cm (4½ in) in total (Figure 58).

Upholstery suppliers

The publishers have a list of upholstery suppliers in the United Kingdom which they will send to readers on request. Please write to 'Upholstery', Frederick Warne (Publishers) Ltd, Warne House, Vincent Lane, Dorking, Surrey RH4 3FW, enclosing a large (A4), stamped, self-addressed envelope clearly marked 'Upholstery Suppliers'. Alternatively, look in your Yellow Pages under *Upholsterer's Supplies*. Although some of the suppliers listed are wholesalers, they will often be able to give you the name of a retailer.

Index

N
W
E
S
1
10
15
6
9
14
7
2
3
11
12
8
4
13
5

LONGSTONE

A DCI RYAN MYSTERY

LONGSTONE

A DCI RYAN MYSTERY

LJ ROSS

ISBN: 978-1-912310-10-4

First published in 2018 by LJ Ross

This edition published in September 2020 by Dark Skies Publishing

Author photo by Gareth Iwan Jones

Cover layout by Stuart Bache

Cover artwork and map by Andrew Davidson

Typeset by Riverside Publishing Solutions Limited

Printed and bound by CPI Goup (UK) Limited

“Beware the wolf in sheep’s clothing”

—Aesop

PROLOGUE

Autumn, 1995

Seahouses, Northumberland

The man they called 'Hutch' watched a woman wind her way through the punters in the main bar. His heart quickened at the sight of Gemma, just like the very first time he'd seen her, when they were only kids in the school playground. She was a woman now, no doubt about that. Tall and slim, with long blonde hair that fell in shining waves down her back, and the kind of self-assurance beautiful women often had; the kind that came from knowing they had only to look a certain way to have men like him falling at their feet.

The Cockle Inn was surprisingly busy for a Thursday night off-season and he watched as she fought her way past a rowdy crowd of locals, like an exotic flower trying to pick its way through thorny undergrowth, her eyes searching the sea of familiar faces as she made her way towards the bar.

Towards him.

He continued to pull pints, keeping his eyes firmly on his task.

“Hiya, Hutch,” she said. “Y’ seen Kris anywhere?”

His lips twisted.

“I thought you two were taking the boat out, today?” he said, buying himself more time.

“He was supposed to meet me at the harbour twenty minutes ago,” she muttered, casting a quick glance up at the old wooden clock on the wall.

“Only twenty minutes?” He smiled. “I’ve waited longer than that for Kris to turn up.”

When she smiled back, it was like a knife in his gut.

“I know,” she said. “He’s never on time. Maybe I should just head back down to the harbour and see if he’s there now—”

“Might as well stay inside, where it’s warm,” he said quickly. “How about a drink?”

He moved towards the shelf where he kept the white wine he knew she preferred, but Gemma shook her head.

“No, not today,” she said. “I’ll just have a coke, thanks.”

He shrugged.

“So, how’ve you been?”

Gemma slid onto a stool and folded her arms on the bar, only half listening.

“What? Oh, fine, thanks. Just trying to get *Shell Seekers* up and running but it’s the wrong time of year. Hardly anybody wants to go diving when the weather’s like this.”

He made a rumbling sound of agreement. Autumn in Northumberland was not the best time to start a new diving school; only the keenest amateur and professional divers would want to go down into the freezing depths of the North Sea and they already had their own diving gear—and probably their own boats, too.

But he didn't have the heart to tell her any of that.

"They found another wreck near Beadnell," he said instead. "That's bound to attract a bit of new interest."

The North-Eastern coastline boasted a high number of shipwrecks; unfortunate galleons and cargo ships, paddle steamers and military vessels having been lost to its rocky shoreline and tempestuous weather over the centuries. Whenever a new wreck was found, it attracted salvage divers and marine archaeologists from around the world.

"Hopefully," she murmured. "I—"

Whatever she'd been about to say was cut off as a pair of sinewy arms wrapped around her waist.

"Here you are!"

Kristopher Reid—'The Kraken', to his friends—smiled broadly and then lowered his dark head to nuzzle at Gemma's neck with an elaborate growl, which made her laugh. Hutch turned away to busy himself with the next order, trying to block out the image of her enraptured face, trying to forget the way it had come alive when she'd caught sight of his younger brother.

"I've been looking for you," Kris lied, as he lifted his head. "D' you still fancy a run out?"

Gemma's forehead crinkled in a frown.

"I was down at the harbour. I thought we agreed to meet there—?"

"No, babe, we decided to meet *here*, don't you remember?" He gave her a patient look, then brushed his lips against hers. "Oh well, it doesn't matter now, does it?"

Looking into his deep brown eyes, she might have believed anything.

"Sure, it doesn't matter," she agreed, all smiles again. "We can go now, if you like?"

With a wink for his brother, Kris helped her down from the stool and, a moment later, they were gone. Very carefully, Hutch set the glass of coke down on a bar mat, untouched. He watched his brother leave with the woman he loved, watched his hand trail down her back and further still, watched her pause and reach up to kiss him, lost in the moment.

Then he turned away, unable to watch any longer.

Three days later

He found Gemma on the beach at Bamburgh, a mile or so north of Seahouses. It was practically deserted at that hour of the morning and she was sitting amongst the sand dunes staring out to sea, lost in her own thoughts. It was a beautiful spot; a golden, sandy beach swept out for miles beneath a mighty castle fortress perched on a craggy hilltop where, once, early kings of England had reigned.

"Gemma?"

She turned distractedly.

"Hutch?"

His feet sank into the fine sand as he made his way over the dunes to join her, turning up his collar against the sharp wind rolling in with the tide.

"Mind if I join you?"

Close up, he could see the ravages of tears that had dried in salty tracks against her pale skin.

"He hasn't come back," she said brokenly. "Kris left, and he hasn't come back."

"It's only been a couple of days," he replied. "You know what Kris is like—"

She closed her eyes and another tear escaped.

"This is different," she said, raggedly. "He—I—"

Unable to stop himself, he reached across to grasp her hand, finding it limp and cold.

"I-I told him about the baby," she whispered. "I told him he was going to be a father and, the next morning, he was gone."

Hutch felt something inside him shatter, some hitherto untouched area of his heart breaking into tiny pieces. His eyes strayed down to her belly, hidden beneath the folds of her jacket. It was still flat but, somewhere within, life had blossomed.

"What did Kris say when you told him?" he asked quietly, working hard to keep his anger in check.

She raised shaking fingers to wipe away fresh tears.

"He was…surprised, at first. Then, he seemed happy. I thought he was happy," she repeated, her voice breaking on the last word. "But I know he's been worrying about money, about the business."

Hutch knew it too. Kris had already come to him twice for hand-outs, although she knew nothing about that.

"We went to bed and, when I woke up in the morning, he was gone."

"And you've heard nothing since?"

She sniffed and shook her head.

"I know—I know he's not ready to be a father," she said. "But that doesn't mean he would be a bad one. I tried to tell him it would be okay, that we'd be *fine*."

Hutch said nothing.

"He hasn't gone to your mum's house," she continued. "I already rang her. I don't have his dad's number, though—"

The two brothers shared a mother but had different fathers.

"I'll find it," he said.

"But, if—if he isn't there, I don't know what to do. I don't know what *we'll* do."

His hand tightened on hers and he opened his mouth to say all that he longed to say, all the words of love he carried like a weight against his chest, but she was not ready to hear them.

"If Kris isn't there, we'll call the police," he told her. "If they can't help, maybe he doesn't *want* to be found."

His jaw tightened, thinking of the man who was his brother, of the years of disappointment and frustration.

Kris had been blessed with a strong body and mind—and the kind of good looks that meant he would never be lonely. But he took them for granted, never thinking of the hurt and destruction he could wield.

He hated him.

Hutch sighed deeply, trying to expel the feeling, to cast it out, but it returned stronger, waves upon waves of hatred coursing through his body as he looked upon the devastation of the woman he loved.

"You'll never be alone," he promised her. "I'll look after you."

But Gemma wasn't listening; she was far away, watching the sea roll back and forth against the shore in a timeless dance. On the far horizon, a boat bobbed across the water, only a speck against the sky that was awash with colour as the day came alive.

After a moment, she turned and looked at the man sitting beside her. There was a slight family resemblance, she thought. But where Kris's eyes were dark brown, Paul Hutchison's were a bright, bold blue and swirling with emotion.

She looked away, brushing away tears with the heels of her hands.

"I-I should get back," she whispered.

He helped her to her feet.

"Thank you," she said softly. "I—"

But she merely shook her head and turned away, walking across the dunes; away from him, and the life he had offered.

CHAPTER 1

Thursday, 1st November 2018

Twenty-three years later

The sun was setting on the horizon, casting wide arcs of blazing amber light over the serene waters of the North Sea as it prepared to slip off the edge of the world. The little dive boat chugged through the waves, rocking precariously and tipping up at the bow as water swelled against its sides then fizzled away, before the cycle began all over again. It was a slow journey as Iain Tucker navigated his way through treacherous currents, renowned for centuries as a graveyard for much bigger vessels than the modest little boat he was proud to call his own.

The Farne Islands consisted of between fifteen and twenty-eight small islands depending on the tide, including a nature reserve that was home to thousands of protected birds and a pair of lighthouses that had been warding ships from the rocks for nearly two hundred years. All the same, they hadn't been able to prevent the destruction of countless vessels whose skeletons lay beneath the darkening waters far below. It took an experienced sailor to command a boat on these waters, and an even more experienced diver to explore the underwater cemetery below.

Iain narrowed his eyes against the sun, calculating the amount of time he had left before the light would be lost completely.

Fifteen minutes, tops.

It would take thirty to get back to the harbour at Seahouses and he'd be foolish to traverse the narrow, rocky channels of the Farnes after dark without good reason.

All the same…

He thought of the charts he had painstakingly compiled over the past few years, of the countless diving trips and hours spent researching the past. He felt sure there was an undiscovered wreck somewhere beneath the choppy waters, one that would make headlines around the world.

If only he could find it.

Coming to a sudden decision, he changed course and swung the boat around, back towards the islands. If he was quick, there would be time for one last dive before nightfall.

As the boat turned aft, a white light began to blink through the dusk, flashing its warning at regular intervals. A foghorn followed, sounding two loud blasts into the surrounding air. Iain's hands tightened on the wheel and his eyes skittered across to where a lighthouse was silhouetted against the purple-blue sky.

Go home, it said. *Turn back.*

He shook his head, gripping the wheel more tightly. There was always time for one last dive.

"*Daisy*!"

Gemma Dawson watched as the young barmaid flitted about the dining area of *The Cockle Inn*, chatting and laughing with the locals who'd come in for their usual Friday night fish 'n' chips. It was all very well being friendly, she thought irritably, but dirty plates were stacking up and empty glasses needed refilling.

Deciding to have a firm word later, she tucked a tea towel into the back pocket of her jeans and moved quickly around the room, gathering the plates herself and taking new orders for drinks.

Daisy hurried over.

"Sorry, Gemma—"

"Never mind," the other woman snapped, with a little more force than she'd intended. "Just take these through to the kitchen."

She thrust a stack of plates into Daisy's arms.

"Number nine needs two pints of Guinness and number fourteen wants a large glass of chardonnay and a diet coke."

Daisy nodded vigorously and bustled away.

Watching her, Gemma raised a hand to her aching temple and sighed deeply.

"Rough night?"

Hutch appeared beside her and gave her back a rub. If his hand lingered a fraction too long, neither of them mentioned it.

"No more than usual," she replied, trying to ignore the loud clatter of plates coming from the general direction of the kitchen. "Business is good."

They looked around the busy dining area where tourists and locals mingled, chattering about everything from *Love Island* to American politics. The atmosphere was warm, with a large fire crackling in the new log-burner. They'd renovated the old shipping inn over the past few years to create an upmarket place for people to come and stay, without becoming so fancy that their local punters would feel out of place. It seemed they'd found the right balance.

"Aye, it's doing well," Hutch agreed, looking across at her with a smile. "That's down to you. I don't have your eye for what goes where, or what needs painting in Pigeon's Breath or Elephant's Dung—"

Gemma laughed.

"It wasn't all down to the paint. You've done a wonderful job with the place, Hutch. I'm only grateful—"

"Now, don't start that again."

She twisted the tea towel in her hands.

"I mean it," she said softly. "I'm grateful you put a roof over our heads, all those years ago. I wasn't sure I'd take to managing this place, but I've grown to love it."

But not him, his heart whispered.

Never him.

"It's your home," he told her, and cleared his throat. "I, ah, haven't seen much of Josh the past few days."

Gemma closed her eyes, suddenly weary.

"Neither have I," she confessed. Her son was becoming more like his father with every passing year: headstrong, handsome and with little regard for anyone or anything except his precious boat.

"He seems to be making a go of it, taking care of *Shell Seekers,*" Hutch pointed out.

When Josh Dawson had taken an interest in running his mother's old diving school, it was fair to say that nobody had really expected it to last. There had been other projects, other ventures, none of which he'd stuck to, until now.

"He loves the sea," Gemma replied. "Josh has always had an affinity with it, just like—"

Just like Kris, she'd been about to say.

Hutch rubbed her back again, in a silent gesture of support. It had been around the same time of year that Kris had gone, over twenty years ago, and the pain could still slice through the barriers they'd both built to guard against it.

"Speak of the Devil," Hutch said quietly, and broke into an easy smile for the young man who sauntered into the main bar, the spitting image of his brother. So much so, his heart gave a funny little lurch and his smile slipped, just a bit.

"Hi," Josh greeted them, leaning down to bestow a quick peck on Gemma's cheek before casting his eyes around the room. "Any chance of a bite to eat?"

"Might have known you'd be thinking of your stomach," Hutch chuckled. "What'll it be?"

"Ah—" Josh looked around the room again. "Is Daisy working tonight?"

Gemma's mouth flattened.

"*Yes*, and don't go distracting her, either," she warned him. "That girl needs no encouragement."

"Wouldn't dream of it," he said, and then flashed a roguish smile as he caught sight of the petite brunette crossing the room laden with steaming plates of food. "In fact, I'll lend a hand."

"We don't need—"

But Gemma's words were lost on the air as her son moved to take the plates from Daisy, gallantly dishing them out to waiting customers as the girl looked on with stars in her eyes. A fierce, unexpected pain stabbed at her chest as she recognised that look; it was one she had worn herself, many years ago.

"They're only young," Hutch murmured, steering her away.

"So was I," she said huskily. "I just—"

She broke off as the door to the main bar was flung open and Iain Tucker burst into the room bringing a rush of cool, salty air with him. He still wore his diving suit with a pair of worn trainers and an overcoat slung on top of it all.

"Evening, Iain," Hutch said, affably. "You lookin' for a spot of dinner?"

The other man grinned like a fool and shook his balding head, which glistened beneath the overhead lights as drops of sea spray fell onto his shoulders.

"I couldn't eat," he said, excitedly. "But I'll have a glass of champagne. *No!* Make that a bottle—and I'll buy a drink for everybody else, as well!"

Gemma and Hutch exchanged an amused glance, while his loud declaration earned several curious stares.

"You won the lottery or something?" Josh called out.

"Better than that," Iain said, still grinning. "Much better than that. I've found it! I've found the wreck!"

Across the room, Daisy slopped a bowl of pea and ham soup into a customer's lap.

"For goodness' sake," Gemma muttered, and hurried over to minimise the damage.

"You want to be careful shouting about things like that," Hutch turned back to Iain, speaking in an undertone. "Most of the people in here are divers themselves, and one or two have been known to loot the old wrecks for stuff they can hock to foreign collectors. Be careful somebody doesn't beat you to it."

"They could try, but they'd never find it," Iain said, confidently. "It's taken me thirty years to find the right spot and I'm not even sure I'll be able to find it again."

Hutch shrugged and handed the man his champagne, before starting to hand out the drinks orders around the room. When Iain took himself off to the guest suite he occupied upstairs to shower and change, Josh stepped behind the bar and nudged his uncle.

"What d' you make of that, then?"

Hutch didn't so much as look up.

"Iain's been coming here every year looking for some old Viking longboat he read about sometime or other. Even *if* it existed, it would probably have been lost to the sea centuries ago, but try telling Iain that. He's obsessed." Hutch paused to hand out a couple of glasses of wine, before continuing. "Once or twice, he found some bits and bobs, cannons or old swords from the eighteenth century. Mind you, I've never seen him this excited," he admitted, with a slight frown. "Maybe he's finally found something big, after all."

"Don't know how he can be sure," Josh remarked. "It's darker than Satan's heart, out there."

Hutch made a murmuring sound of agreement, then nodded towards the ceiling and the room that Iain occupied upstairs.

"All the same, he should be careful what he says. There've been plenty of businesses going under these past few years, enough to make people desperate. Back in my day, people would go out on the water at all hours of the night to loot a wreck, if they thought it was worth their while."

Josh shuffled uncomfortably.

"They wouldn't find much, since nobody knows where to go."

"Aye," Hutch said, giving him a long, level look. "Maybe that's just as well."

CHAPTER 2

Friday, 2nd November

Doctor Anna Taylor-Ryan steered her car along the winding country lane towards the historic fishing village of Seahouses, enjoying the dappled light as it filtered through the trees on both sides. It was a road she knew well from childhood, having been born only fifteen miles further north on the tiny, scenic island of Lindisfarne. As she wound through the hedgerows and followed the coastline towards the village, she reflected that it had been a while since she'd visited her childhood home. Perhaps it was time to go back and rediscover the island with fresh eyes, ones that were untainted by death and sadness.

But even as she thought of it, her mind slipped back to a time when she'd almost lost her life and when others had been even less fortunate.

No, she thought. It had not been long enough to overcome the nightmares that had plagued her since the last time she'd made the journey across the causeway.

"Maybe next year," she murmured.

As she reached the outer limits of Seahouses, she shook off the memories and slowed the car to a crawl as she followed the main road towards the seafront. The long promenade overlooked a quaint harbour with multi-coloured boats and kiosks advertising diving excursions and trips to see the puffins and seals. Amusement arcades and numerous fish restaurants touted the catch of the day and the place bustled with life, despite the fact autumn was swiftly marching towards winter and the tourists would soon return home.

Close to the harbour, she spotted an old stone building which bore a hand-painted sign declaring it to be *The Cockle Inn* and pulled into the small car park alongside. Stepping out of her car, she breathed deeply of the damp air that slapped against her skin and whipped through her hair, raising her face to the wind as if to capture the scent of the sea before heading across to the main entrance.

Inside, Anna found the place almost empty except for a couple of residents polishing off the last of their Full English Breakfasts.

"Would you like a menu?"

She turned to face a tall, broad-shouldered man of around fifty. His face was pleasantly weathered by the sun and rain, telling tales of a life spent outdoors whenever he got the chance.

"Ah, no, thank you," she replied. "I'm here to see Iain Tucker, if he's around?"

Hutch eyed the tall, lovely-looking brunette with frank scepticism.

"Iain? Ah, I don't think he's come down yet. Must be having a lie-in. D' you want me to call up and see?"

Anna checked her watch, which read quarter-past-ten.

"He said to meet him here at ten o'clock, but I don't want to disturb him, if he's still sleeping. Let's give it another fifteen minutes."

Hutch nodded politely.

"Would you like a coffee, while you wait?"

Anna smiled.

"You just said the magic word," she replied. "Black, please, no sugar."

Fifteen minutes later, there was still no sign of Iain.

"How'd you say you knew him?"

Hutch paused in his task of emptying the dishwasher and leaned against the bar, wincing as Daisy cleared the breakfast plates with a noisy clatter.

"I didn't," Anna said, with a small smile. "But he's a colleague of mine from Durham University. He's part of the Archaeology Department, specialising in marine archaeology, whereas my focus is on early religious history in Northumberland. Our paths sometimes cross and he asked me to come along for a chat about something he'd found yesterday."

Hutch nodded.

"Aye, he was in here last night, raving about it," he said. "Said he'd found some old Viking wreck and then offered to buy everyone a drink."

"He must have found something important," she murmured, excitement creeping into her voice. "I wonder what's keeping him?"

Hutch glanced up at the clock.

"It's been more than fifteen minutes now," he said. "I'll go upstairs and knock on his door."

Anna waited while he climbed to the first floor, listening to the creaks and moans of the old building as the beams contracted beneath his weight.

But a couple of minutes later, Hutch returned alone.

"Nobody's answering," he told her. "Are you sure he said ten o'clock?"

Anna nodded.

"I wonder where he's got to."

"Where who's got to?"

They both turned at the sound of a new voice, this time from a blonde woman who entered the room carrying a cardboard box full of small packets of bar snacks.

"This should do us," Gemma said, setting the box on the bar.

"Have you seen Iain, this morning?" Hutch asked her. "This lady was expecting to meet him at ten."

Gemma gave Anna a quick, discreet assessment.

"No, I haven't seen him at all. Haven't heard anybody moving about, either," she added, as an afterthought.

"Come to think of it, that's a bit unusual for Iain. He's usually up at the crack of dawn. Let me check with Daisy, in case he came down earlier."

She headed off to find the barmaid.

"I'll try calling him," Anna said, reaching for her mobile.

But the number rang out.

"Daisy says she hasn't seen him," Gemma said, returning to the bar. "Have you called him?"

Anna nodded, holding up the phone that was still in her hand.

"I've left a message," she said. "It's not like Iain to be late for an appointment. He's usually a stickler for punctuality."

"He might have passed out with a hangover," Gemma joked. "He took a bottle of champagne upstairs with him last night, so he probably missed his alarm."

"I'll try his door again and take the master key, just in case," Hutch decided. "Why don't you ring Josh and ask if he can see Iain's boat in the harbour?"

"Good idea," Gemma said, from her position beside one of the windows. "Iain's car's still outside, so he can't have gone far. Maybe he got his times mixed up and decided to go out on the water, since the weather's fine. He was hopping around with excitement, last night."

Anna waited while the other woman put a call through to her son, at the *Shell Seekers* diving school.

"There you go," Gemma said, after the call ended. "Josh says the boat isn't in the harbour, so Iain must have got up early this morning and taken it out for a spin."

"Not in his room," Hutch said, returning to the dining area. "I let myself in, just to check. Bit weird, though—it doesn't look as though he slept at all last night."

Having started to relax, Anna's system went back on full alert.

"What do you mean?"

Hutch shrugged.

"The bed was still made, and he's hardly touched his champagne," he said, looking between the pair of them. "It was still sitting there, on the coffee table, with a full glass beside it."

Anna felt something curl in her stomach, something like dread.

"What's the name of his boat?"

"The *Viking Princess*," Gemma replied. "Why?"

"Because I need to know what to tell the Coastguard."

CHAPTER 3

Fifty miles further south, Detective Chief Inspector Maxwell Finley-Ryan stepped into the open-plan office area of the Northumbria Criminal Investigation Department. He had barely crossed the threshold before coming to a skidding halt at the unexpected sight of an enormous, mechanical snowman. It stood in the central aisle separating the rows of workstations on either side and was at least six feet tall, with a carrot-shaped nose that looked sharp enough to cause grievous bodily harm. While there were very few certainties in life, Ryan knew he could be sure of one thing: the expression in its glassy black eyes would haunt him for years to come.

"Frank!"

His sergeant's balding, salt-and-pepper head popped around the side of a nearby computer screen.

"Mornin'!"

Ryan kept an eye on the snowman, half expecting it to morph into life and come charging at his jugular.

"What the hell is that... *thing* doing in CID?"

Detective Sergeant Frank Phillips swung around in his desk chair to face the six-foot effigy.

"D' you like it? They had them on offer down at the garden centre," he said, cheerfully. "Thought it might brighten the place up a bit."

Giving the snowman a wide berth, Ryan shrugged out of his jacket and slung it over the back of his own chair.

"It's...certainly bright."

"Aye, and it plays Christmas carols, too. Here, I'll show y—"

"Don't even think about it," Ryan growled. "For one thing, it's barely November, and, for another, it's just plain... creepy."

"Aw, howay, man, it's not that bad."

"Its eyes are staring into my soul," Detective Inspector Denise MacKenzie chimed in, from across the room. "Small wonder they were selling them off for peanuts!"

Phillips swung around to grin at his senior officer and—as it happened—his new wife.

"It's not that bad," he argued. "Once we get a few fairy-lights up, it'll be grand. Besides, it was only a few quid and they threw in some fake snow, too."

"You were robbed," Ryan muttered. "For God's sake, Frank, shove it in a cupboard before it gives us all nightmares."

With a sigh, Phillips heaved himself out of his chair and slung a companionable arm around the snowman's plastic shoulders.

"C'mon, big lad. Some people just don't know how to get into the festive spirit."

While he dragged it off, Ryan turned to MacKenzie.

"Good luck keeping that thing out of the house," he said.

"Over my dead body," she vowed. "Speaking of which, Control have just sent through a new one. Unidentified male, washed up on the rocks at Longstone lighthouse."

"Longstone?" Ryan frowned. "Where have I heard that name before?"

"You probably recognise it from the story of Grace Darling," MacKenzie replied. "She was the young lighthouse keeper's daughter who helped to rescue survivors from the *Forfarshire* in the 1800s. Longstone was the lighthouse where she lived with her family, on Outer Farne—it's northernmost island in the Farne Islands."

Ryan remembered the tale, and the afternoon he'd spent with Anna at the Grace Darling Museum in Bamburgh. He considered himself lucky she wasn't there to witness the fact he'd retained very little of their excursion, particularly given her enthusiasm for local history.

"Looks like the rocks around there have claimed another life," he said. "Did his boat capsize?"

MacKenzie lifted a shoulder.

"Too early to say. There's no sign of a boat but Control have dispatched a team of first responders and notified the coastguard, who'll send a lifeboat out to help to transfer the body across to the mainland."

"Anybody reported missing lately?"

"Plenty," she replied. "But none from the local area. The body was reported by the lighthouse keeper, who was running a boat tour when he spotted it."

"Not what you need, just after breakfast," Ryan said.

MacKenzie nodded.

"You can get a boat across from Beadnell or—"

"Seahouses," Ryan put in, as his phone began to rumble, and his wife's number flashed on the screen. It was the same place Anna had been headed, that very morning.

He exchanged a look with MacKenzie, all business now.

"Tell Phillips to put his wellies on," he said. "We're going to the seaside."

It was an hour's drive from Northumbria Police Headquarters, in the old shipping heart of Newcastle, to the coastal village of Seahouses. Thanks to a combination of bad luck and lunchtime traffic, Ryan and Phillips found themselves caught behind a slow-moving tractor and several lorries making their routine journey to Scotland along a stretch of the A1 that was not a fully operational dual carriageway.

"You'd think they'd widen the road a bit, after all these years," Phillips complained. "Even I could drive a bit faster than this."

Ryan's lips twitched. It was a truth universally acknowledged that his sergeant was a cautious driver.

"Careful, Frank. Next thing, you'll be telling me you're buying a motorbike and touring South America."

The very thought was enough to bring Phillips out in a cold sweat, but he wasn't about to admit that. Instead, he folded his arms across his burly chest and fixed his younger companion with a dignified stare.

"The trouble with your generation is, you think anybody over a certain age has lost their sense of adventure. I could ride a motorcycle, y' nah, if I wanted to."

"Of course you could."

"And I could tour South America and see the pyramids," Phillips continued.

"They're in Egypt," Ryan said, dryly.

"Eh? Maybe I'm thinking of the other pyramids."

"Promise me, whenever the grand tour does happen, you'll take a map," Ryan muttered, putting the car back in gear as the traffic began to move again. "Only another few miles to go, now. Has anything else come through?"

Phillips checked the e-mails on his work phone, then shook his head.

"Nothing we don't already know. Some feller was found on the rocks at Longstone lighthouse, just after eleven this morning. No identity yet, and that could take a while depending on the state of the body," Phillips added, with a note of sympathy. "Did you say Anna reckons she knows who it could be?"

"It's a possibility," Ryan said, slowing the car to indicate right. "She heard from a colleague of hers—Iain Tucker—late last night. He's some kind of marine archaeologist who reckoned he'd found a Viking shipwreck. He wanted to speak to Anna about it, to verify dates or something."

"She thinks the body could be him?"

Ryan nodded.

"She drove up to Seahouses this morning, for a meeting they'd arranged for ten o'clock. He never turned up, and nobody has seen him since last night. Apparently, Tucker's car is still parked beside the inn where he was staying but his boat is missing from the harbour."

"Aye," Phillips mused. "He must've taken it out and run into some trouble. The waters around the Farnes are dangerous. It wouldn't take much more than a few heavy waves or a jagged rock to take a boat under—and him with it. Wouldn't be the first time that's happened, although you'd think he'd have put a call through to the Coastguard."

Ryan nodded.

"You'd think."

"Still, it might be nothing suspicious." Phillips was ever the optimist. "It's bad luck if the bloke took a tumble, but we have no reason to think anybody wanted him dead, do we? It might not be a case for CID, at all."

"I'm not so sure about that," Ryan surprised him by saying. "If the body turns out to be Iain Tucker, he might have made a big discovery. What if somebody got wind of it and decided they wanted it for themselves?"

Phillips snorted.

"Sounds a bit far-flung, if y' ask me. It's not as if he'll have found a chest of gold doubloons." He barked out a laugh.

"More likely, some old duffer had one too many pints last night and lost control of his boat."

As they approached the village, they spotted a couple of squad cars parked by the harbour wall and a growing crowd of locals who had come to witness what the sea had tossed up. Ryan parked the car as close as he could and, after a brief discussion with the first police responders, they began to make their way down the slipway to where the lifeboat had just returned from its grisly task.

"Come on," Ryan said. "Let's see whether Iain Tucker has turned up, safe and sound."

CHAPTER 4

The man who had been Iain Tucker might now be safe, but he was no longer sound.

He was little more than a bloated shell, a beached carcass that had once been a man, and the two murder detectives looked upon the wasted life with eyes that were twin reflections of compassion.

"Poor bastard," Phillips said, gruffly.

Ryan simply nodded.

The body had been strapped to a lifeboat stretcher and was afforded some protection from the elements—and the prying eyes—by a thick body bag, which was unzipped to allow the two men to view the damage.

Phillips felt his stomach perform an uncomfortable somersault and the gentle sway of the lifeboat did little to help matters.

"I'll, ah, I'll just—"

"Take a breather, Frank."

Ryan didn't begrudge his sergeant a moment's respite; it was all he could do to keep his own system in check.

A crowd had gathered by the harbour wall, wrapped up warm in overcoats and woollen hats as if it were a variety show, and a couple of local police had been dispatched to keep them as far back as possible. All the same, Ryan could feel their eyes boring into his back as he disembarked the lifeboat a minute or two later and stepped aside to allow a pair of technicians to transport the man to the mortuary, where a full post-mortem would be carried out.

"What d' you reckon, then?" Phillips asked, once they were back on firm ground. "At least we know for certain that it's Iain."

They had recovered a sodden wallet from the inner zipped pocket of the dead man's coat and, while much of its contents had been reduced to pulp, the plastic cards had survived to help identify their owner.

"We know that he had Iain's wallet," Ryan said. "But we need to track down a next of kin, if there is one. Somebody needs to make a formal identification."

It was a grim task, one he regretted having to ask of anyone, but necessary all the same.

"I'll ask Yates to get on to it," Phillips said, referring to Trainee Detective Melanie Yates, who was manning a desk back at CID. "It looked to me as though he'd been bashed about a fair bit, so it's hard to tell how long he'd been underwater. Then there's the birds and the fish."

On that last meaningful observation, Ryan stuck his hands in his pockets and looked out across the sea, thinking of what gallons of salty water and sharp rocks did to a man. The image of Iain Tucker's swollen flesh, of the skin that had been flayed from his body, imprinted itself upon his memory like the shutter of an old camera.

"The pathologist will be able to help with post-mortem interval," was all he said. "I'm more concerned about the fact he wasn't found in his diving gear."

Phillips rubbed his chilly hands together.

"Why?"

"Because Iain Tucker was here to dive. It was the only reason for him to be out on the water, of his own accord. Why else would he head out, at night or in the early morning?"

Phillips nodded slowly.

"You're thinking someone forced him out there, or maybe he was meeting someone?"

Ryan squinted as the sun broke through the clouds and burnished the water in gleaming light, so that it lapped against the harbour walls like molten silver.

"I don't know what to think. We need to have a word with the coastguard, the lighthouse keeper, and then find Anna and speak to the people who were the last to see him alive."

"Did somebody call for a coastguard?"

When Ryan and Phillips spun around, they were greeted by a man who might have stepped straight off a Californian beach and not a windswept Northumbrian shoreline. The coastguard was a little under six feet and unseasonably bronzed, dressed in all-weather uniform. A pair of expensive-looking sunglasses were propped in his gravity-defying blond hair and, when he flashed a smile, they were treated to a line of blinding white teeth.

"Well, look what the tide dragged in," Ryan said, before he was enveloped in a bear hug. "It's been a while."

"Aye, good to see you," Phillips said, and accepted a dose of the same medicine.

Coastal Area Commander Alex Walker stepped back and looked between the pair of them.

"Haven't seen you both since the wedding, last year," he said, referring to Ryan and Anna's quiet, romantic nuptials the previous summer. "Shame that you're here on business—not that it isn't great to see you two reprobates," he added.

"Thankfully, the circumstances are different from the last time we were in the area on business," Ryan said. "We don't know whether there's anything to investigate, yet."

Walker reached inside one of the pockets of his waterproof coat and pulled out a packet of mints, which he offered around. The past was painful, not least because it had been his own father who had perpetrated a series of vicious murders on Lindisfarne three years before. The awful truth of it had nearly destroyed his family, not to mention his friendship with Anna and Ryan, and any reminder of that time in his life was a topic best avoided.

"Well, that's something," he said, grasping around for a change of subject. "I hear congratulations are in order, Frank? Denise finally made an honest man of you, eh?"

Phillips beamed.

"Aye, I'm a lucky man," he said, thinking of how lovely Denise had looked standing beside him at the altar in Florence. Lord knew what she saw in him, but he was wise enough not to question it.

"Give the new Mrs Phillips a kiss from me," Alex winked.

"Aye, you'd be lucky," Phillips growled, good-naturedly. "Besides, that's still *MacKenzie*, to you."

"Modern woman, eh?"

"She's a brave one, that's for sure," Ryan chipped in, and steered the conversation gently back to the matters at hand. "Talk us through what happened in the last hour, Alex."

The coastguard blew out a windy breath.

"Let's see, now. The call came through from HQ in Humberside to the Coastguard here in Seahouses around an hour ago," he began. "Turns out, Anna had already been around to the office asking after Iain Tucker."

"And had they heard anything?" Ryan asked.

Walker shook his head.

"No, they hadn't heard a thing, so they rang Lindisfarne to ask whether we'd received any distress signals or pan-pans—"

"Panna-whatty?" Phillips asked.

"Pan-pan is an urgency signal," Alex explained. "It's the signal people use if they're in an urgent situation but not one that poses an immediate danger to life or to the vessel. If there was imminent danger, they'd send a mayday signal."

"And you hadn't received either?"

"Not a peep," Walker confirmed. "Same for Howick and Berwick-upon-Tweed. None of the nearby coastguard stations received anything from Tucker, and there's no sign of his vessel on the radar, either. My best guess would be that it went under sometime during the night or it's out of range."

He nodded towards the sea which seemed so placid, then pointed towards the dark clouds that rumbled in the distance.

"Storm came in through the night," he told them. "It's moving out, now, but if he was out on the water after dark, Tucker might've found himself caught up in it."

"You'd have to be a bloody fruitcake to go out on the water in the dead of night," Phillips declared.

"A fruitcake, or just a fool in love," Ryan muttered, with a trace of embarrassment. A few years before, it had been Alex Walker he had to thank for guiding him through the rocks and safely into Lindisfarne Harbour so that he could reach Anna in the nick of time. He'd never known anything like the fear he'd experienced manning a tin-pot boat against all the might of the North Sea. Give him murderers and psychopaths; he'd take them over a fight against Nature, any day.

"I was lucky that night," he said, with his usual flair for understatement. "But Iain Tucker wasn't. How come there was no alert, if his boat got into trouble?"

Walker slipped his sunglasses onto the end of his nose as another bright shaft of light broke through the clouds.

"Good question. If he didn't send a manual 'mayday' or urgency signal over the radio, Tucker could have pressed the distress button on his radio, if it was equipped with DSC—"

"I need a glossary here, man," Phillips complained.

"It's Digital Selective Calling over the VHF…that's Very High Frequency channel sixteen, on the marine radio," Ryan explained.

"Might've known you'd be clued up about it all," Phillips grumbled. "If that Tuscan villa's anything to go by, you probably have a super-yacht stashed away in your back garden."

"Har har," Ryan replied

"Villa?" Walker's eyes lit up. "What villa?"

"I'll tell you later," Ryan muttered. "You were saying there should have been other ways for Tucker to send a distress signal?"

Walker nodded.

"I'd need to know more about his boat but, theoretically, yes. It should have had an Automatic Identification System and an Emergency Position-Indicating Radio Beacon with an in-built GPS receiver. Hell, he could have sent up a flare and done it the old-fashioned way."

"The boat *should* have had GPS?" Ryan queried.

"Yeah, *should've*. Except, it's looking like the boat's EPIRB wasn't registered on our system," he said, and pulled an expressive face. "That would've made life a lot easier, if it had been. As it is, we're pissing in the dark."

The other two men nodded sagely.

"Best thing would be to speak to the Harbour Master," Walker advised. "They should have a record of when Tucker's boat left the harbour, as well as its vital statistics."

He turned and pointed towards a squat, boxy building on the far side of the pier.

"Harbour Office is right over there."

CHAPTER 5

Far from being the gnarly old sea captain they might have expected, the Harbour Master turned out to be a glamorous woman in her late forties, who managed the turnover of boats in and out of Seahouses Harbour with a pair of capable and impressively manicured hands.

"Amanda Jones?"

She held up a single, blue-painted fingernail as she spoke rapidly into her radio and then swung around in her desk chair to face the newcomers. While her eye passed over Phillips with what he considered to be indecent haste, it lingered for a noticeably longer time on the tall, cool, raven-haired drink of water standing beside him.

"Yes?" she said.

"My name is Detective Chief Inspector Ryan, and this is Detective Sergeant Frank Phillips."

He held up his warrant card for her inspection.

"Call me Mandy," she said, barely glancing at his warrant card. "I guess you're here about Iain."

"Yes," Ryan nodded. "We're hoping you can help us by answering a few questions."

"Anything for you," she said.

"Thank you," Ryan said, trying not to feel disconcerted by what appeared to be a thorough inspection of his jean-clad legs. "To begin with, can you give us a brief description of Iain Tucker's boat?"

"The *Viking Princess*?"

"That's the one."

"Let me see," she turned back to one of the computer screens on her desk, nestled alongside the remnants of a half-eaten pain au chocolat and a stack of glossy magazines.

"Here we are," she said. "The *Viking Princess* is listed as being a passenger vessel equipped with diving lift, eight by four metres, blue and red painted stripes with a max speed of thirty knots. Do you want the MMSI?"

Phillips rolled his eyes.

"Maritime Mobile Service Identity," Ryan murmured, for his benefit. "No, that's alright, we'll follow up with a formal statement later. Can you tell us who was on shift here, last night?"

"Sure, that would be me, same as every night. I started at midday, finished around nine."

"Who fills in the rest of the time?"

"I've got a deputy," she said. "The Commissioners spring for extra staff in High Season but, since it's autumn, it's just the two of us at the moment. Carl did the six a.m. to midday shift, yesterday."

"So who logs the boats after dark, when neither of you are around?"

Mandy leaned back and crossed her legs.

"In the first place, hardly anybody would take a boat out in the dead of night around these parts. It'd be tantamount to suicide, especially with a storm raging off-shore," she said. "But aside from that, we use a VTS system. That's the Vessel Traffic Service," she explained. "It's a monitoring system, a bit like air traffic control. We use a vessel's Automatic Identification System, radar and VHF radio to keep track of all the vessels coming in and out. Whenever a new boat comes within range, it gets flagged up, not only to us but to each other. It's a public system, so the boats can avoid a collision."

Ryan thought of what Alex Walker had already told him about the boat's GPS.

"Do you have any automated record of the *Viking Princess*?" he asked.

"Iain's boat?"

Ryan inclined his head and Mandy tapped a few keys on her desktop, then clucked her tongue.

"That's weird," she muttered.

"What is?"

She leaned back and ran agitated fingers through her stylish blonde bob.

"It looks like Iain's AIS wasn't activated," she said. "I guess because I always saw him coming in or out, I never stopped to check if he was transmitting."

"Isn't it a legal requirement?" Phillips asked, without rancour.

"It is, of all passenger vessels regardless of size, and international voyagers above a certain weight," she told him. "There's no legal requirement for other boats to have one."

"Besides which, an AIS can be deactivated," Ryan added. "Marine authorities sometimes do it if they want to take pirates by surprise, or sail beneath the radar. The reverse is also true."

"That's right," she agreed. "The whole reason to have AIS is to make your boat visible to other boats in the area but, around here, the boats are mostly smaller until you get further out—and then you're talking about tankers and cruise ships. I can't think why Iain would want to deactivate his."

Her face took on a thoughtful, troubled expression, and Ryan thought privately that a man in search of an important archaeological find might have had plenty of reasons to keep his precise location a secret.

"Does that mean you can't tell us what time the *Viking Princess* left the harbour, last night?"

She had the grace to look abashed.

"Without an automatic log on the system? No, I can't. I can only tell you the boat was still here when I finished my shift, at nine."

"What about a Personal Locator Beacon?" he asked, and worked hard to rein in his mounting frustration. "Had Tucker registered one of those?"

Mandy brought up another database and performed a quick search. PLBs had a unique identification number and were designed to be carried on a person's clothing during situations with a high risk of 'man overboard' or in other similarly dangerous scenarios. There was a chance—just a *chance*—that Iain Tucker had carried one.

"Yes," she said, excited to have redeemed herself. "There's one registered here, with details of the *Viking Princess*. I can tell the Coastguard—"

Ryan thought quickly. There had been no PLB recovered with Tucker's body, but it might still be with the missing boat. When they found the boat, they may find further clues as to how a mild-mannered university archaeologist wound up dead on the rocks.

He looked at Phillips, who read the silent message in his eyes.

"I'll get in touch with them now," he said. "They can get a search underway."

As Phillips stepped outside to make the call, Ryan turned back to the Harbour Master.

"What about CCTV? There must be something covering the harbour."

"Yes, we've got two small cameras," she told him. "Would you like to see?"

Without waiting for a response, she turned and clicked another button to bring up the visuals.

"Camera One looks out over the east pier, so you can see the boats leaving the harbour."

He looked over her shoulder.

"And the other camera?" Ryan asked.

Mandy pointed at a plain black screen.

"Camera Two is broken," she said. "It looks out over the north pier and slipway, usually, but it's due to be replaced."

"Vandals?" Ryan said. *Or somebody else.* "How long has it been down?"

"Oh, at least a week. It was probably the birds," Mandy said, with a chuckle. "The gulls are a bloody nightmare, sometimes. I've had a couple fly straight into the window, and they'll nest anywhere there's a cosy nook. The camera was covered in bird mess."

Phillips stepped back inside the office and caught Ryan's eye.

"All taken care of," he said.

"With your permission, I'll ask one of our team to check that camera," Ryan turned back to Mandy, who nodded her assent. "In the meantime, can you tell us whether you noticed anything unusual about the *Viking Princess*, before you left last night? Anybody sniffing around?"

She held up a finger again as the radio crackled into life and she had a brief exchange with a seafarer's disembodied voice before turning back.

"Just a boat tour, wondering if they were okay to leave," she explained, with a vague wave of her hand. "Ah, well, I can't say I noticed anything especially unusual—sorry. All I know is that he came back into the harbour just before five, docked his boat over on the north pier next to the rest of them. Like I said, I clocked off around nine and it was still sitting there, as far as I know."

Ryan paused, looking out of the expansive windows and across the picturesque harbour, thinking of a dead man's last movements.

"Alright, thank you, Ms Jones. We'll be in touch. In the meantime, if you remember anything else, please call us."

He set his business card on her desk and the action drew attention to the third finger of his left hand, which bore a platinum band.

"All the best ones are taken," she said, with a slow smile.

In silent accord, both men beat a hasty retreat.

Outside, Ryan turned to his sergeant.

"Frank, what the hell just happened in there?"

"I think she was puttin' the moves on you, son."

Ryan looked at him in blank confusion.

"Aye, I nah, it's been a long time since anybody except Anna looked twice, hasn't it?" Phillips said, patting his tall, good-looking friend's shoulder. "Me, on the other hand? I'm practically fighting them off."

"Naturally," Ryan said, recovering himself. "Denise must be a very understanding woman, constantly having to fight off the hordes of adoring women clamouring at your door."

"Aye, it's a full-time occupation," Phillips chuckled, as he thought of the quiet, happy life he shared with his new wife.

"It's an odd time for Iain to go out on the water, after dark, without a good reason," Ryan said, returning to their current problem.

Phillips turned to him.

"Sounds like you think it's a bit suspicious," he said, with a knowing glint.

Ryan weighed up everything they knew so far against everything they had yet to learn, and came to a decision.

"Given the state of the body, it was impossible to tell at a glance whether any of the injuries were sustained before Tucker went into the water. All we know is that he acted out of character and that his vessel is missing in unexplained circumstances. That sounds suspicious enough to me."

Phillips rubbed his hands together.

"Goody. I like a bit of murder on the high seas."

Ryan huffed out a laugh.

"You're an odd man, Frank. God knows why I like that about you."

"Great minds, and all that," came the pithy response.

CHAPTER 6

Seahouses Police Station shared its premises with the local fire station and was set back from the harbour, towards the historic heart of the village. However, they had hardly made it halfway along Main Street when Phillips was waylaid by a small bakery shop called *Trotters*.

He came to an emergency stop and raised his nose to the air, like a bloodhound.

"I smell stottie," he declared, and peered through the shop window. "*There*, I knew it!"

He turned to Ryan with a look that would have put Oliver Twist to shame.

"Howay, lad, have pity. I didn't have time for breakfast…"

Ryan raised a single, disbelieving eyebrow.

"That'll be the day," he said.

"Alreet," Phillips relented, and put his cards on the table. "I might have managed a couple of Weetabix. But a bit of dried grass isn't enough to keep a man with muscles like mine going all day, is it?"

The last statement was said with such breath-taking sincerity that Ryan was moved.

"Fine. You've got two minutes to grab something and another two minutes to eat it before we get to the station," he warned.

Phillips needed no further bidding, and soon returned brandishing two fresh bacon stotties, one of which he offered to his friend.

"Thanks," Ryan said, and took a grateful bite.

"Y'nesdf pbbty bcon," Phillips mumbled.

"What?"

Phillips swallowed and tried again.

"I was sayin', you need plenty of bacon in weather like this. It's all very well being *athletic*," he said, with a sideways glance at Ryan. "But it'll be a long, cold winter. You've got to give the lasses something to snuggle up to, y'nah."

"I'll keep it in mind," Ryan assured him.

A minute later, Phillips was licking his chops like a satisfied lion.

"Better hurry up and finish—" He watched, open-mouthed, as Ryan threw away the remainder of his sandwich. "What the heck did you go and do *that* for?"

"I was full," Ryan explained, as if to a child.

"But—why..." Phillips said, weakly. "It's the southerner in you, that's what it is."

Ryan put a hand on his shoulder.

"We've just seen the corpse of a man who was dragged from the water, but you didn't look half as horrified then as you did just now."

Phillips let out a quivering breath.

"I've seen some things in my time, but nobody's ever thrown away half a stottie. Not in my lifetime."

Ryan burst out laughing.

"Let's take your mind off it by talking to the man who found Iain Tucker."

They pushed open a toughened Perspex door leading to the foyer of the Police and Fire Station and were met by a local sergeant by the name of Carole Kirby. She was dressed in uniform and had been looking forward to a quiet day occupied by petty crime and domestic disturbance until the unfortunate events of the morning had unfolded.

"DCI Ryan, DS Phillips? Thanks for getting down here so quickly," she said, shaking hands. "Sad business, isn't it?"

It was a hackneyed remark, but one that was true nonetheless.

"You said on the phone that it was the lighthouse keeper who found the body? Is he here?"

"Yes," she nodded, tucking curly brown hair behind one ear in an unmistakably feminine gesture. She might have been pushing fifty, but she still had eyes in her head and there was no crime in looking. The police grapevine was a very active network and she'd heard plenty about the man who was now standing in front of her; remarks ranging from 'film-star handsome' to 'cool and aloof', depending on the messenger.

It turned out they hadn't been wrong on either score.

"I've put him in one of the meeting rooms for the time being. He was a bit shaken up," she said, in her most professional voice.

"Can't blame him," Ryan said. "This way?"

She nodded, leading them towards one of the smaller rooms before knocking and opening the door.

"If you need anything, let me know."

Ryan nodded his thanks, and Phillips gave him a subtle nudge as she walked away.

"Full house for you, today," he joked. "Looked like she was having a hot flush—"

"Shut it," Ryan muttered, and stepped inside the meeting room.

"Mr Tawny?"

A fit-looking man of around forty came to attention, sloshing the milky tea he cradled in his hands.

"I'm DCI Ryan and this is DS Phillips, we're from Northumbria CID."

Ryan produced his warrant card and then nodded towards the cooling mug the man held in his hands.

"Would you like a fresh one?"

Pete Tawny looked down at the chipped 'Fire and Rescue' mug and shook his head.

"No—no, thanks."

Phillips shut the door behind them and both men took a seat at a cheap coffee table that had been placed too close to the chairs surrounding it, so they were forced to re-shuffle the seating arrangement before they could be comfortable.

Finally, Ryan leaned forward and rested his forearms on his knees.

"So, it seems you got more than you bargained for when you left the house this morning, Mr Tawny," he began, aiming for a touch of levity.

"You can say that again," Tawny agreed. "You'd think, in all the years I've been a keeper, I'd have seen a body before. But that was the first."

"Hopefully, the only," Ryan said, with a trace of sympathy. "I know it's unpleasant, but it would be very helpful if you could tell us how you came to find the body. It might help to get it off your chest, too."

The other man nodded and set the untouched tea back down on the table, clasping his hands together instead.

"I'm—ah, I'm not sure where to start."

"Why don't you begin by telling us about your work," Phillips suggested, to put him at ease. "I hear you're the lighthouse keeper? Must be an interesting job."

On safe ground for the moment, Tawny started to speak.

"Well, Longstone is operated remotely, nowadays, by a central office which oversees various lighthouses around the country. It's a lot safer than the old days, when Grace Darling's family lived there all year round and had to keep the light burning," he said. "Still, I look after the place and run tours around the Farnes and into the lighthouse, itself. There's a museum in there, if you ever fancy it."

Ryan nodded, and didn't have the heart to say he'd been blessed with a live-in historian at home, one who had already satisfied his appetite for local history for at least three lifetimes.

“Were you running a tour this morning?”

“Yes,” Tawny nodded. “We left Seahouses at around nine and reached the Farnes at about half-past, give or take. By the time we reached Outer Farne, it must have been well past ten o’clock.”

“Can you describe how you came to find the body?”

Tawny nodded slowly, remembering.

“I brought the boat around. There were six passengers on board, this morning. Not bad, considering the time of year,” he added, mostly to himself. “Anyhow, I skirted around the headland towards the landing point but, as we got closer, I spotted him. He was washed up on the rocks directly at the foot of the lighthouse, all tangled up. His arms and legs were…they were…”

He swallowed bile.

“What did you do, next?” Ryan interjected, firmly. It helped to focus on the facts, and not on the memory of how Iain Tucker had looked.

“Next? I radioed the coastguard,” he said. “Told them to get a rescue boat across as soon as they could, and I turned my boat around because I didn’t want anybody else to see. There were kids on board,” he explained.

They both nodded their understanding.

“Did you recognise the person on the rocks?” Phillips asked.

Pete shook his head.

"No, I wasn't close enough and, even if I had been, I'm not sure I would have been able to recognise him," he said, honestly. "I thought it was a man, judging by the general build."

There was a short pause.

"Who was it?"

"I'm afraid we can't discuss the identity until their next of kin has been informed," Ryan replied.

"Of course," Pete nodded. "When you're able, can you let me know? A few of us would like to club together and send some flowers to his family."

"That's good of you," Ryan replied, and looked towards Phillips, who shook his head. "I think that's all we wanted to discuss, at this stage. We'll most likely be in touch again but, if you remember anything you feel might be important, please contact us."

The lighthouse keeper nodded, and it seemed he was about to say more.

"Was there something else?" Ryan asked.

"I'm not sure...well, I wondered if it might have been Iain."

"Iain?"

"My mate, Iain Tucker. He's a marine archaeologist. I've seen him out that way quite a bit, recently, and I haven't been able to get hold of him this morning."

Ryan and Phillips exchanged another look, and decided to make an exception to the usual procedure.

"In the strictest of confidence, I can tell you we strongly suspect the body is that of Iain Tucker."

Pete Tawny's face crumpled like paper in front of them.

"I'm sorry," Ryan murmured.

Pete scrubbed his face, embarrassed to find tears in his eyes.

"Daft old bugger," he said, tremulously. "I *told* him he should've taken a diving partner."

"I need to ask whether you knew of any reason why Mr Tucker would have been out on the water alone, or whether he had arranged to meet anyone?"

"There was only one reason Iain ever went out," Tawny replied, sadly. "He was searching for a Viking longship. Didn't matter how often we told him he was wasting his time, it fell on deaf ears. Knew it'd kill him, one day."

His voice thickened with grief.

"I bloody knew it."

They spent another thirty minutes with Pete Tawny and agreed to take a trip across the water the following day to see the lighthouse for themselves, weather permitting.

"It'll be good to get the lay of the land," Phillips said, as they made their way back towards the harbour. "Can't say I'm over-keen about getting on a boat, mind."

Ryan held off a smile.

"Is there any form of transport that isn't the Devil's Work?" he enquired.

Phillips gave it some thought. He'd tried a pedal bike when he'd been at the Academy, years ago, before he could afford a car. But that had been a non-starter, considering the number of near-misses he'd had with other road users and he strongly suspected he'd been the common denominator in all of them.

He'd tried buses, instead, but didn't feel entirely confident at the mercy of some of the kamikaze drivers, who clearly had a sweepstake going on how many passengers they could unbalance during a single journey.

As soon as he'd been able, he'd bought a natty little MG Midget in jazzy red, which he'd enjoyed cruising to the end of his street and back. On the open road, he'd been at the mercy of much larger vehicles and he'd found the whole experience mildly traumatic.

And that only covered *land* transportation; air and water travel were other matters, entirely.

"Look, son," he said. "If God had intended us to gad about like birds, he'd have given us wings. As it is, I've got two stubby legs and they get me where I need to go. My Volvo does the rest."

"That it does, Frank. Eventually."

"Oh, haddaway, y' cheeky git. It'll not be like that, when your fancy Merc breaks down on the A1 because it's too chilly. You'll be glad of the trusty Volvo, then."

"I'll be eating humble pie," Ryan agreed, and spotted *Trotters* as they passed by. "Don't even think about it, by the way," he said, by way of a pre-emptive strike.

"The thought never even crossed my mind," Phillips said, gravely, and put his plans for an early lunch on hold.

CHAPTER 7

The Cockle Inn commanded a relatively isolated position on the far side of the harbour, overlooking the sea and the dunes which spread northward towards Bamburgh. When Ryan and Phillips stepped inside, they found it teeming with locals who were enjoying more than just a pub lunch. Heads were bent and voices hushed as they chewed the fat, drumming up all manner of wild theories about how Iain Tucker, Professor of Marine Archaeology, had come to die. Gossip was ripe on the air and Ryan spotted at least one person skipping from table to table, presumably comparing notes.

"It's like Chinese Whispers in 'ere!" Phillips exclaimed. "Anyone'd think this was the most exciting thing that's ever happened since Robson Green's *Tales From Northumberland*."

As several heads swivelled in their direction, Ryan took hold of his sergeant's arm.

"Perhaps it is," he muttered. "Quick, let's find Anna, before we're cornered."

They rounded the bar and spotted Ryan's wife perched on one of the stools. He allowed himself a moment to admire the elegance of her profile, the sweep of long leg as she crossed one over the other. Sensing him, she turned and he watched her face light up in a broad smile, the kind she reserved only for him. Just the sight of her was enough to banish the recent memory of Tucker's broken body, if only for a while.

"Hello stranger," he said, and leaned down to brush his lips against hers.

When Phillips cleared his throat, he became acutely aware that he was still very much *on duty*.

"This must be your husband," the woman behind the bar said.

"Yes. Gemma Dawson, this is Detective Chief Inspector Ryan and Detective Sergeant Phillips."

They nodded politely.

"Are you the landlady?" Ryan asked, switching easily back to business.

"You could say that," she replied. "Hutch is the one who owns the place, but I help him run it. I s'pose you need to have a word with us about poor Iain?"

Grief flitted across her face and she shook her head.

"Awful, what's happened. I can hardly believe he was here one minute and then just… gone."

Ryan nodded again. There wasn't much he could offer in the way of platitudes.

"Perhaps you could arrange a private room, where we could sit down and take a preliminary statement from both of you—and anybody who was working here last night?"

Gemma nodded.

"I'll see to it."

They left Gemma to her work and stepped out into the beer garden at the back of the inn, which was blessedly empty. Sea winds had swept away the cloudy morning and left blue skies overhead, but the air was unmistakably cold and nipped at their skin.

It was still preferable to the metaphorical hot-house they'd left behind.

"How're you doing, lass?" Phillips asked of Anna, as they seated themselves around a wooden picnic table. One would be forgiven for thinking that Anna Taylor-Ryan carried bad luck around with her, judging by the number of police investigations she found herself embroiled in.

"Ah, I'm fine. Really," she said, rooting around her bag for a pair of gloves. "I'm just so sorry this has happened to Iain."

"I wish it had been anyone but you he'd called," Ryan confessed. "Morrison won't like it when I tell her you're mixed up in another one."

Their Chief Constable was a fair woman, but the desk she occupied demanded that things were not only done by the book, but that they were *seen* to be done by the book. When the wife of her most high-profile murder detective found herself a party to one too many of her husband's investigations, it didn't look good.

"I can hardly help who Iain chose to call, last night," Anna said, a bit testily. "Besides, right at this moment, I couldn't give a flying…*fig* what Morrison thinks. I'm more concerned with finding out what happened to a good colleague of mine. Iain has family who will miss him."

Ryan reached across to give her hand a squeeze.

"We'll do all we can."

"I know you will," she said, returning the pressure. There was nobody in the world she trusted more to seek justice for the dead and those they left behind.

"Yates came back with the details about Tucker's next of kin," Phillips put in. "He was divorced, but he has a son who's twenty-one."

"Sounds about right," Anna said.

"MacKenzie's contacted him, anyhow. The lad's away at university but he's heading back today. He and his mother are going over to the hospital together to make the identification."

"Decent of her," Ryan said quietly. In his experience, death was a great leveller.

He was momentarily distracted from his chain of thought by a flock of ducks which had wandered into the garden and found their way beneath the picnic table.

"I didn't know they had eider ducks here," he said, idly.

"That's southern talk," Anna said, with the ghost of a smile. "Around these parts, we call them 'cuddy' ducks."

As always, Ryan found there was more to learn about his adoptive home.

"What's the difference?"

"Nothing, except legend has it Saint Cuthbert made lifelong friends with the ducks while he was a hermit on one of the Farne Islands, back in the Seventh Century. Apparently, they were so tame you could stroke them. 'Cuddy' is local slang for 'Cuthbert.'"

The local area had a long Christian tradition and the saintly, duck-loving Cuthbert had lived most of his life at the priory on Lindisfarne, except for a short stint living on one of the smaller, uninhabited islands where, presumably, he could commune with his God.

"Aye, I bet they taste nice with a bit of hoisin sauce, n'all," Phillips joked, earning himself a playful nudge.

"I wouldn't risk it," Anna laughed. "The birds are protected around these parts. The Farnes themselves are a nature reserve, under the custodianship of National Heritage."

As if to reinforce the point, one of the ducks gave a loud *quack*.

"There, there," Phillips patted its head. "Keep your feathers on, I was only joking."

Bemused, Ryan shook his head.

"I know you got the call from Iain at about five o'clock, yesterday," he picked up the thread of their conversation. "Can you remember exactly what was said?"

Anna cast her mind back.

"I was a bit surprised to hear from him," she began. "Iain Tucker was a colleague, but I wouldn't have said we were close enough to be called friends, so it was unusual for him to ring me at home on my personal mobile. There's a list of our contact details on the internal database at the university but it's usually for emergencies only."

"Perhaps he thought it *was* an emergency," Phillips murmured, while he stroked the downy head of one of the ducks that had flapped up onto the bench beside him.

"Did he sound nervous? Worried?" Ryan asked.

"No, he sounded excited," Anna replied, after a moment's thought. "He was talking so quickly, I had to tell him to slow down. He said I needed to hurry up to Seahouses first thing in the morning because he'd made a major find and he wanted to ask me a couple of questions."

She smiled at the memory.

"He told me he'd found the Viking shipwreck he'd been searching for all his professional life. He'd seen artefacts, treasure, and, according to him, the ship was mostly intact."

"Did you believe him?"

Anna lifted a hand and then let it fall away again.

"Iain was a reasonable man. If anything, he could be a bit of a nit-picker on procedure and university bureaucracy. But when it came to his pet project, he was like another person. Diving for wreckage was his passion," she said, thinking of the man she had known. "And he was so certain there would be wreckage found somewhere off Lindisfarne. To be honest, I wasn't sure what to think. I didn't *disbelieve* him, but I wondered if his enthusiasm might have got the better of him. Does that make sense?"

"Perfectly," Ryan assured her. "Did he tell you anything else about it?"

Anna turned up her collar against a sudden rush of wind, while she considered the question.

"Well, it was no secret around the university that Iain was searching for something specific, but he rarely went into details. It was a private project, something he kept out-of-hours. All we knew was it concerned the Viking era, specifically around Lindisfarne—but that's been so heavily researched and documented I don't know what he hoped to add, particularly as a marine archaeologist. There's never been a Viking shipwreck, or, at least, we've never discovered one around here. There have been other Viking boats discovered in Scandinavia..."

She trailed off as her mind wandered, struggling to remember the snatches of conversation they'd shared.

"I remember he was very interested in a discovery we made on land a couple of years ago, but I don't understand how that would relate to this project. It wasn't Viking, for one thing."

"What was it?" Ryan asked, curious despite himself.

"It was an excavation of an old Pagan burial site beside the Drake Stone, up near Morpeth," she replied, with a slight shrug. "The practice was for people to be buried with their most prized possessions, so it was a fairly interesting discovery but not particularly unusual from a historical perspective. We found nothing associated with the Viking tradition, as I recall. The bodies were dated to at least fifty years prior to the first Viking raid on Lindisfarne, in 793 A.D."

"Sounds unconnected," Ryan agreed, and shelved it for now. "Did he tell you anything about what he'd actually discovered—and where?"

Anna shook her head.

"He was very tight-lipped about its location," she said. "Iain told me half the village would love to find it for themselves, so he couldn't afford to take any chances."

"Is that true?" Phillips asked. "Do you think he would have been in any real danger?"

"I thought it was paranoia talking," Anna admitted. "But then, this has happened—"

"We don't know what's happened, yet."

She nodded, drawing strength from Ryan's steady gaze.

"I told Iain to report his discovery to the proper authorities, but I don't know whether he took my advice."

"Who are the proper authorities in a case like this?" Ryan asked. Shipwrecks were hardly his usual milieu.

"If treasure is found, it must be reported to the Receiver of Wreck within a certain timeframe," Anna said. "There are strict rules about it all. They supervise the salvage of the wreck and produce a report which manages all the competing demands from interested parties."

"I thought it was a case of 'Finders Keepers'?" Phillips put in.

"It would be simpler," she smiled. "Unfortunately, there are all kinds of rules and regulations around marine archaeology, surveying and salvage. It differs, too, depending on the kind of wreck. Either way, Iain could never have claimed any booty as his own."

"How come?" Ryan asked, in surprise. "I presumed that was why he was so excited about it."

"Archaeologists are prevented from asserting any form of ownership over treasure like that," she said. "It's presumed that their job is to further the body of evidence for the benefit of an ongoing historical record, for future generations."

"You're telling me he wouldn't even get a penny piece?" Phillips was outraged, and the duck let out an indignant *quack*. "What if he uncovered rubies, pearls…*diamonds*?"

"Sounds like you're getting gold rush fever," Anna said, with a grin. "He might have been allowed to keep a couple of mementos, as a salvage reward, but Iain was a respected marine archaeologist. He wanted to uncover the wreck not for the fortune, but for the fame. If he made an important find, it had the potential to turn him into a household name and he'd be touring the lecture circuit for years to come."

"Him and a bunch of former prime ministers," Ryan said, which earned a bark of laughter from Phillips. "Here's the thing I still don't understand: what could possibly be rich enough, or important enough, to kill for?"

"*If* he was killed," Phillips was obliged to say, and Ryan nodded.

"*If* Tucker was killed, what could be important enough? There've been wrecks before, plenty of them over the years, and nobody's bothered to kill for them."

Anna realised she had simply assumed they knew enough about regional history to understand the potential significance.

"Perhaps I wasn't clear," she said, looking between them with dark, serious eyes. "The Viking raid on Lindisfarne in 793 A.D. is the first known Viking raid in history. It marks the beginning of the Viking era, between the eighth and twelfth centuries. Aside from a sketchy record of three Viking longboats beaching at Weymouth four years before that, there are no other records to suggest any Viking landings before that time. No longboats have been discovered on the coastline, until now."

Anna paused, choosing her next words with care.

"The discovery of a Viking longboat in these waters isn't just remarkable from an archaeological perspective," she said. "Depending on the date of Iain's find, it has the potential to rewrite the whole timeframe of the Viking era, as we know it."

Ryan was a quick study.

"That's the kind of fame somebody could kill for," he said, and turned to Phillips with renewed energy. "C'mon Doctor Dolittle. Let's find out whether any of the locals wanted a taste of immortality."

CHAPTER 8

"What d' you think happened to him?"

Daisy spoke in a stage whisper, fearful that, by saying the words aloud, she would be struck down by the same fate as the man who now lay on a cold metal slab.

"How should I know?" Josh replied. "The police are looking into it, aren't they?"

He let out a short grunt as he lifted a fresh barrel of beer and began connecting the pipes to supply the tap somewhere above their heads. Nobody wanted to go diving today, so he might as well make himself useful.

"What if there's a killer on the loose?" she tried again, enjoying the play of muscle as he hauled the keg upright.

"Don't be daft," he muttered.

"I'm not," she insisted, her mouth pouting in a way that both infuriated and aroused him. "It's bad, what happened to Iain. Nobody knows why he was on the water so late and Hutch says he'd hardly touched his champagne, which means he must've left pretty soon after nightfall. I can ask my mum about it."

"She probably isn't allowed to tell you," Josh said, straightening up again. "The Harbour Master is supposed to keep an official log—"

"Exactly," Daisy interrupted him, and hitched herself up onto one of the scarred wooden benches in the basement of the inn. "She has a log, so she'll know for sure."

Josh sighed. Some things weren't worth fighting over.

"Anyway," she said, her tone changing. "Would you protect me, if there *was* a psycho killer on the loose?"

Deciding to play along, Josh smiled and walked across to her.

"What if *I'm* the psycho killer?" he said, and wriggled his eyebrows to make her laugh. "What if I lured you down here, just to have my wicked way with you?"

Quick as a flash, one hand whipped up to circle her neck. Her eyes widened in alarm, then relaxed again as his hand fell away, just as quickly as it had come.

As her arms came up to wind around his neck, they heard the basement door creak open and, a moment later, his mother's voice called down to them.

"Josh! Have you finished hooking up the line, yet?"

He hissed out a short, frustrated breath while Daisy stifled a laugh.

"Yep! All done!"

"Good, because the police are here and they need to speak to all of us. Come on up to the sitting room," she said, referring to the cosy front room they shared in a small apartment Hutch had set aside for them on the first floor.

The Manager's Apartment, he called it.

Charity, she called it.

"I'll be up in a minute—"

"Tell Daisy to come up with you," Gemma added, taking the wind out of his sails completely. "They need to speak to her, too."

When the door slammed shut, Josh pulled Daisy in for a hard kiss.

"We'll go up in a minute," he whispered.

While a small team of Crime Scene Investigators combed the room Iain had occupied at the *Cockle,* Ryan and Phillips settled themselves a few doors along, in an upstairs sitting room. It formed part of a small but perfectly proportioned apartment which, Gemma had told them, she still shared with her son.

"In my day, you left home at eighteen—sixteen, sometimes—and made your own way in the world," Phillips remarked, after Gemma left to seek out their first interviewee. "It's all different now, though. The kids go off to university, or stay and do an apprenticeship or whatever, and they don't leave until they're starting to go grey themselves."

"Maybe some parents like having their kids stay at home for longer," Ryan remarked.

"Howay, man. They'd never be able to get their leg owa."

Ryan was confused.

"Owa?"

"Y'nah, leg *over*, a bit o' nookie, a bit of a snuggle, that sort of thing."

"Ah," Ryan said.

Phillips folded his arms as he warmed to his topic.

"Take this place," he gestured to the comfortable sitting room with its framed pictures of Josh and chintzy curtains that were back in fashion. "I'll bet you can hear every creak and moan…pardon the pun."

He let out a laugh that Sid James would have been proud of, while Ryan hoped for the ground to swallow him up.

"I, ah, see your point," he managed.

"Anyhow, all I'm saying is, it's no good having your grown-up kids wandering about if you're into Naked Tuesdays."

"Words to live by," Ryan said, and made a mental note never to visit Phillips' home on any given Tuesday.

"What about the lad's father? Doesn't seem to be on the scene."

"Josh took his mother's surname," Ryan said quietly, as they heard footsteps approaching. "Who died and made you Jeremy Kyle, anyway?"

Phillips let out another bark of laughter, then the door to the sitting room opened and Gemma stepped inside, balancing a large tray of tea and biscuits from the kitchen downstairs.

"Thought you might need a bit of sustenance," she said. "I don't suppose you've had time for any lunch."

Phillips' stomach rumbled, right on cue.

"Thanks, Ms Dawson," Ryan said, and waited for her to sit down on the sofa opposite.

"Daisy and my son, Josh, will be along in a minute. Hutch is just dealing with customers, but he'll pop up when he can. Who would you like to speak to, first?"

"Well, since you're here, why don't we start with you?" Ryan said, with an easy smile.

She settled herself on a chair and began to pour the tea.

"Of course," she said, handing him a cup. "Anything I can do to help."

"Let's start at the beginning, then," Ryan said, taking a polite sip. "How long had you known Professor Tucker?"

She blew out a gusty breath.

"It must be getting on for ten years, now. He'd been coming to Seahouses for years before then, but I'd say he started staying at the inn regularly around ten years ago. That's when we started renovating the place, too."

"And you've been working here all that time?"

She nodded.

"Oh yes," she let out a short, mirthless laugh. "I've been working and living here for twenty-three years and counting, back when Hutch's dad still owned the place."

"You don't sound very happy about it," Phillips was bound to say.

Gemma looked down at the tea she held in her hand, then set it back on the table.

"It's a long story," she murmured.

Ryan tried another tack.

"How would you have described Iain Tucker?"

Her eyebrows raised briefly, then fell into a soft frown as she thought of the man she had known.

"I suppose I just saw him as another punter," she confessed, with an apologetic smile. "Better than most. He was always polite, never broke anything or upset any of the other customers. A bit miserly with the tips but, hey, that's almost everyone. He kept himself mostly to himself, except for the odd bit of chit-chat at the bar or when he was ordering dinner."

"I see." Ryan nodded, while Phillips made brief notes in an ancient, dog-eared notepad. "I understand he was a keen diver."

"One of the best," she told him. "It was his profession and he knew the sea like the back of his hand. Everyone knew Iain and he's worked with most of the other serious divers around here, on one project or another."

Ryan nodded.

"Would you be able to give us a list of their names?"

"Happy to," she said. "But I warn you, my knowledge is a bit out of date. I hardly ever go down, now, so I couldn't really tell you who Iain spent most of his underwater time with. Josh would know all about the diving scene, nowadays," she added.

"We understand; just tell us what you can," Ryan reassured her. "To your knowledge, had Iain ever run into any trouble over the years?"

Gemma took a thoughtful gulp of tea.

"Not in all the time I'd known him, and I would probably have heard. It's a small place."

"How about issues on land?" Phillips asked. "Did he ever mention any trouble he was having with anyone?"

Her face registered mild shock.

"No, not at all. As far as I'm aware, everyone liked Iain. He was well-known in diving circles and well-respected. Amateur shipwreck divers would sometimes bend his ear to go over their charts or join them on an expedition."

"What about on the personal front?" Ryan prodded, although he had a feeling he already knew the answer. "Did Iain mention any personal troubles or worries he was having? Financial concerns?"

Gemma cradled her cup in her hands, warming her fingers as a cold draught seeped through the cracks in the old building.

"I get a lot of people telling me their woes," she said. "The younger ones look up to me as a surrogate mum and the older ones look for a bit of fun, or a way to forget their normal lives. I've never been interested in any of that," she said, firmly. "But it doesn't stop them trying. I'll be honest and tell you that Iain tried it on, just once, after he and his wife divorced. He took it on the chin when I knocked him back, but he was going through a hard time. That's all I can really think of."

"I see," Ryan murmured, and supposed she would be a beacon for all kinds of male attention. It was hard to see it, when he was so much in love with another woman, but if he looked with detachment, he imagined Gemma Dawson had enjoyed her fair share of admirers over the years.

"People get lonely," she continued, softly. "That night, Iain had had one too many drinks and I suppose he thought he knew me well enough to give it a try. He was a lovely guy and would've been a great catch for a lot of women, and I told him as much. It softened the blow a bit."

Phillips remembered his own pain after his first wife had died following a long battle with cancer. It was a different kind of struggle he'd gone through, but he felt a kinship with Iain Tucker and the kind of loneliness that came with loss of any kind.

He cleared his throat.

"How about yesterday?" he asked. "Can you tell us Iain's movements, to the best of your knowledge?"

Gemma shuffled in her chair, as if changing gears in her mind.

"Yes, I'll try. He was a creature of habit, so I can say that he was up with the larks at around six-fifteen to have an early breakfast and get a start on the day. That was his way," she explained. "When Iain was on a diving trip, he liked to make the most of the daylight."

"What did he do after breakfast?"

"I assume he went out on the water," she replied. "I didn't ask him, but I'd assume that was where he went. He headed out at around seven."

That tallied with the logs they had from the Harbour Master, Ryan thought.

"And when did you next see him?"

"Oh, gosh. It would have been around five, maybe ten-past five? It was already dark, and the early dinner crowd was starting to get busy so perhaps it could have been half-past. Anyway, Iain burst into the dining area dripping with rain and dragging half the sea in with him," she said, blinking away unexpected tears. Iain had been eccentric, she thought, but she'd miss him. "He told us he'd found a Viking wreck. Practically shouted it from the rooftops."

"Told who?"

She looked between them.

"The whole dining area," she said. "Probably the bar area too, since his voice carried. In fact, Hutch warned him he should keep it down a bit. Not because he was rowdy, but because…well, people have been known to poach a wreck, if they think it's worth their while."

"Anyone in particular?" Ryan asked.

But a shutter seemed to come down across her eyes and she was, once more, the polite hostess.

"Nobody that springs to mind."

"Alright," Ryan said, deciding to play along, for now. "Could you write us a list of all the people you remember being in the dining area when Iain made his announcement?"

She frowned.

"Yes, but you don't think—you can't *possibly* think one of the locals would hurt him?" she said. "Poaching a wreck is one thing, but nobody in their right mind would kill for that. Especially not Iain; he was like one of us."

"Whoever said we were looking for somebody in their right mind?" Ryan murmured, after Gemma left the room to hurry along their next interviewee. "I wonder if they know Iain Tucker contacted the Receiver of Wreck before he died?"

They'd put a call through to the Receiver's office less than twenty minutes ago, only to be informed the man was already en route to Seahouses and would be there within the hour. Professor Iain Tucker's reputation for marine archaeology preceded him, it seemed, and the Receiver had caught the first available flight from Southampton to come and see the discovery. Unfortunately, Tucker hadn't told them the coordinates of the wreckage, since he'd planned to unveil it himself. Nobody had imagined his life would be cut short in the space of a few short hours.

"Question is whether anybody'll find the wreck before the authorities get here," Phillips said.

Ryan stood up abruptly, moving to the window to stare out at the water and the boats bobbing across it, and wondered which of their masters had been at the inn to hear Tucker's declaration, the night before.

"If only we knew the coordinates," he said. "We could watch the area and see who goes down."

But they didn't. So far, all they had was supposition and hearsay.

"You think it's definitely murder, then?"

Ryan glanced back over his shoulder with serious grey eyes.

"Well, I definitely don't think the guy left here and decided to throw himself overboard, that's for sure."

CHAPTER 9

While Ryan and Phillips talked of murder, Anna made her way to the Coastguard's Office where she had been summoned to attend a meeting. It was located a short distance from the harbour, inside an unremarkable one-storey pre-fab that might have been found in any seaside town across the land. Two large, all-terrain vehicles were parked on the forecourt next to an even larger high-spec SUV, which looked distinctly out of place alongside such an inauspicious building.

Stepping inside, Anna passed through a small foyer papered with leaflets and posters advertising local charity ventures, before entering the main workspace.

"Doctor Taylor, I'm glad you could join us."

The greeting came from a tall, smartly-dressed man in his late forties who might easily have been ten years younger. She recognised Jasper Vaughn immediately as a colleague of the late Iain Tucker, hailing from the Department of Marine Archaeology at Durham. Now that the latter was dead, she found herself wondering whether the younger man would be a strong contender to become Acting Head of Department.

"It's Taylor-*Ryan*," she corrected automatically, and shook his outstretched hand. "Good to see you again, Jasper."

She might belong to a different university faculty, but they still worked together from time to time and it was Anna's policy to treat everyone as a potential ally, unless circumstances proved otherwise. Unfortunately, most of the interactions she'd had with Jasper Vaughn had thus far ranged from the bizarre to the ridiculous, owing to the man's enormous ego.

"Likewise," he said, then turned to introduce the other people hovering a short distance away. "I believe you already know the Coastal Area Commander, Alex Walker? He tells me you're old friends."

There was a question in his eyes, Anna thought, and an impertinent one she had no intention of answering. Luckily, Vaughn didn't wait for any reply before moving on to his next introduction.

"This is Hector Sayer, Her Majesty's Receiver of Wreck, who's flown all the way up from the south coast. Finally, Ursula Tan, from the Marine Archaeology Sea Trust," he added, clearly as an afterthought.

Interesting.

After the obligatory round of hand-shaking, they were shown into the tiny break room where a Formica table had been set up to accommodate their meeting.

"I want to thank you all for coming at short notice," Sayer began, taking his rightful place as chairman. Anna judged him to be somewhere in his fifties with the ruddy complexion of one who either spent much of his time outdoors, drank to excess, or both.

"I received a phone call from Professor Iain Tucker at about five o'clock last night, informing me of a major discovery of treasure in the form of artefacts and an intact Viking longboat located off the coast of the Farne Islands."

He paused to let that sink in.

"Since Professor Tucker refused to disclose any further particulars over the telephone, I agreed to travel and accompany him to the site in person," he continued, fiddling with a half-chewed biro lying on the table. "Unfortunately, while in transit, I received a call from the police informing me that Tucker passed away overnight and they are treating his death as suspicious."

He spread his hands.

"This is an unusual scenario, as I'm sure you will appreciate. During my tenure as Receiver of Wreck, I've never been called upon to report a wreck in circumstances where the registrant has died prior to my arrival. Additionally, I'm facing the problem of not being able to confirm the status of the wreck, since I haven't been provided with any coordinates for its location. That being the case, I felt it prudent to ask you to join me, today, so we can pool our collective resources and determine whether to proceed with a salvage investigation."

"I'm not really sure how I can help you," Anna felt obliged to say. "Marine archaeology isn't my field, nor am I an experienced diver—"

"Yes, but I understand you were a colleague of the late Professor Tucker, one he obviously trusted enough to call. Perhaps you might be able to help us locate the find, given your knowledge of the local area?"

It was possible, she thought.

Still…

"How does it work, in terms of registering the finder of a wreck?" Vaughn asked suddenly, from his position at the other end of the table. "Does Tucker's name still go on the paperwork, even though he hasn't technically provided you with the location of the wreck? Anybody could *claim* to have found treasure, but surely only the person who fully registers the details ought to be listed as its rightful discoverer."

"I hardly think it's the time to quibble over the paperwork, do you, Jasper?"

Anna's softly-spoken voice held a thread of steel. It was remarkable, she thought, how quickly the vultures began to circle.

"I agree," Sayer nodded. "My immediate concern is in confirming the existence of a find of the magnitude Tucker described, not merely in the interests of my office but to assist the police in their ongoing investigations, alongside the Coastguard. We can argue semantics later."

Walker took his cue and leaned forward, folding a pair of muscular forearms on the table.

"We still haven't located Tucker's diving boat, the *Viking Princess*, although we've managed to trace the dinghy which had become detached from the main boat. It carried a Personal Locator Beacon on board, which allowed us to find it quickly. We'll be turning over the dinghy to the police and their CSIs but, from our perspective, it doesn't reveal anything further about the location of Tucker's find."

"Why not?" Anna said. "Can't you look at the surrounding area where the dinghy was recovered?"

"Not really," Walker replied. "It had probably been floating throughout the night, carried on the tide. It could have started out anywhere in a ten or even fifteen-mile radius of the harbour."

"What about notes, records?" asked Ursula. "Surely, the professor kept detailed charts?"

"I can look in his office, when I return to the university," Vaughn offered, with a studied nonchalance Anna found vaguely insulting to their collective intelligence.

"The *police* will conduct a search of his office and possessions," she told him. "If there's anything that proves helpful, I'm sure they'll pass it on."

"I suppose it's too much to hope that he told *you* the coordinates?"

Anna shook her head.

"No such luck," she said. "Iain contacted me primarily, I think, because of my knowledge of early Christian history in the region, including the Viking era as it applies to the

North-East. I believe he wanted to verify his own suspicions about what he'd found and to talk it over."

"We've been conducting a longitudinal study of the waters around the Farnes," Ursula interjected, a bit defensively. "We would know if there was any wreckage of the kind Tucker described. It would have been found long before now."

Vaughn gave a haughty laugh.

"Ah, *yes*, I forgot. Marine archaeologists from MAST are the only ones who are capable of finding or excavating early shipwrecks," he sneered. "Of course, my department would argue otherwise, considering the large number of new wrecks we've discovered in the past ten years—"

"You've always had a chip on your shoulder, Jasper. The fact is, National Heritage commissioned MAST to conduct a study of the area, rather than your team at the university. We *asked* if you wanted to be a consultant but playing second fiddle wasn't good enough for you—"

Anna rubbed a tired hand across her eyes.

"This isn't the time to decide who's got the bigger dick," she muttered, and watched jaws drop around the table with the notable exception of Alex Walker, who let out a hoot of laughter instead.

"I hardly think it's helpful to start name-calling," Jasper began, self-righteously.

"It's hardly helpful to start picking over the bloke's legacy, either," Alex shot back. "Iain Tucker isn't even in his grave yet."

Anna sucked in a deep breath.

"All I mean is, we need to pull together if we're going to find Iain's wreck. It doesn't help to argue over whose team is the most qualified to do that."

"Hear, hear," Sayer said, in a booming tone reminiscent of Father Christmas. "Let's concentrate on whether we believe there's anything to find. There doesn't appear to be any evidence to support a Viking wreck, nothing that's survived."

Anna opened her mouth to speak, but Vaughn cut across her.

"Logically, for there to have been a wreck of the kind of age Tucker was talking about, and for it to have been intact as he described, we should be searching deep water where the water is largely deoxygenated," he offered, lazily. "There's no way that the timber would have survived, otherwise."

"That's a good starting point," Sayer said, and turned to the coastguard. "Do you have a chart showing water depths in the area?"

In answer, Walker pushed away from his chair and walked across to a large map that hung on the wall.

"The deepest diving waters around the Farnes are generally up to thirty-five metres," he explained, tapping a finger against several well-known diving spots. "Anything deeper and Tucker would have needed more specialist equipment than just a set of tanks and his flippers."

"What if it isn't depth we're looking for, but mud, or silt? Anaerobic conditions found in something like an underwater bog?" Anna thought aloud.

Not so long ago, Ryan had investigated the case of a mummified body that had lain beneath the bed of a reservoir for years. Why not a ship?

"Hardly likely," Vaughn scoffed, but she could almost see the wheels turning in his mind. "Besides, as Ursula has already pointed out, that sort of thing would have been discovered before now."

"Not necessarily," Sayer put in. "There are frequent shifts in tide and current that alter the state of the seabed, sometimes only for short periods. Perhaps something has been uncovered that we're not aware of."

"You mean like the Bamburgh Wreck?" Ursula said. "That was a major discovery a few years ago, an old ship lying on its side on the beach but only visible at certain times of the day. The rest of the time, you'd never know it was there."

"It's possible," Vaughn acknowledged, grudgingly. "But we still have no idea where to look."

"I'll ask around," Walker suggested. "See if any of the fishermen saw Iain out and about while he was staying here. Maybe one of them will know where to look. I'll have a word with the volunteers here—maybe somebody saw Iain in the same area, more than once."

"And maybe it'll be a complete waste of time," Ursula replied, with an air of impatience. "I'm not here to help with some kind of wild goose chase, I have *real* work to be getting on with."

"Feel free to leave anytime you like," Vaughn said, with an oily smile. "We can handle things here without you."

"And leave you to take all the credit? Not likely—"

Anna listened to their bickering with a heavy heart and thought that power, when left in the wrong hands, could corrupt just as easily as a silver Viking sword could corrode. She turned to the window and saw that, outside, the weather had changed again. Gone were the blue skies of earlier, replaced by the deepening clouds of grey that foretold of more stormy weather before the day was out. As the debate raged on, so too did the rain, which began to patter at first, then pummelled away at the window panes as though it were demanding to be heard.

She shivered at the sound and found herself wondering whether they were trespassing, treading across the graveyard of souls who had been lost, long before any of them were born.

Perhaps whatever Iain had found was best left to the sea.

CHAPTER 10

A few streets away, Josh Dawson faced the two murder detectives with the same confident demeanour he adopted in most situations, especially those where he felt out of his depth.

"You seem nervous," Ryan remarked, in what he hoped was an unthreatening tone. "Try to relax. We only want to know what you can tell us about Iain Tucker."

Josh let out an irritable sigh.

"Look, I don't know how I can help," he said. "My mum probably told you all about it and I'm supposed to be at work."

"We'd like to hear your version, if it isn't too much trouble."

Another sigh.

"Fine," he rolled his shoulders. "Iain was a regular around here. He'd been coming for years."

"Since you were a nipper?" Phillips said.

"Yeah, since I was twelve or thirteen, I guess. He was..." Josh scrubbed a hand over his face then let it fall away again. "He was a decent bloke, alright? He let me tag along with some of the other divers when I was a kid. He showed me how to check tanks, that sort of thing."

"Didn't your mum own a diving school?" Ryan asked.

"Yeah, but she was too busy to teach me. Besides, she kind of closed it down after—after my dad left," he said. "*Shell Seekers* was mostly his, anyway."

Or so he'd been told.

Ryan and Phillips exchanged a brief glance. To the untrained eye, there would have been nothing untoward in what Josh had just told them. No malice, no upset—just a statement of fact. But the delivery was too clipped and too rehearsed, as if Josh Dawson had spent his whole life trying to convince himself that the absence of his father meant nothing to him.

But it did.

"I, ah, understand you've started the diving school up again?" Phillips said, after an awkward pause. "Must be a good diver, yourself?"

Josh shrugged, and his face adopted its confident expression once more.

"Yeah, I suppose you could say I get by."

Ryan wondered idly whether he, too, had been as cocky at the same age and was forced to admit that the answer was likely to be in the affirmative.

"Right. So you knew Iain Tucker pretty well."

"As well as anyone here," Josh said. "Iain mostly hung out with Diarmuid O'Brien, but he went back to Ireland a couple of years back. Runs a diving school off the west coast."

Phillips made a note of the name.

"Anyone else he spent a lot of time with?"

Josh fiddled with the edge of a plaid shirt, which he wore open over a plain white vest. Leather bracelets circled his wrists and a small tattoo graced the underside of his left wrist.

"Well, I s'pose he would have a pint with Hutch, if he was in the mood," Josh replied. "But Iain wasn't really a social butterfly, you know? He was friendly enough but he wouldn't hang around to chat about the weather, if you know what I mean."

They nodded.

"Did he have a regular diving partner or a group he'd go down with?"

Josh sighed.

"You're supposed to," he replied. "Iain knew that, but I'd see him going out alone all the time. He just didn't want to share his secrets."

There was a note in his voice that Ryan couldn't quite place. It sounded like resentment.

"Did you ask to go down with him? To get in on the action?"

Josh's eyes flitted away, to a spot somewhere just to the left of Phillips' head.

"Are you kidding? I have a business to run," he said, affecting a bored tone. "Nobody really believed all that stuff about a Viking wreck, anyway. People searched all the time—"

He broke off, suddenly.

"They searched—?"

"I mean, there are loads of diving and shipwreck tours. *Shell Seekers* runs a couple of tours a day in summer, and that's just us. People would have seen something like a Viking longboat before now, wouldn't they?"

Ryan merely smiled.

"Let's talk about what happened yesterday. When did you last see Iain?"

There was an infinitesimal pause.

"Ah, about five-thirty," he replied. "He came into the dining room downstairs and announced that he'd found a wreck. He ordered some champagne and then offered to buy everyone a drink. It was big of him, since the room was packed out."

"Can you give us a list of everyone who was there?" Ryan asked. It would be useful to compare Josh's recollection with his mother's.

"Sure, but why does it matter?"

They didn't immediately respond, so the question hung on the air for the few seconds it took Josh to put two and two together.

"You think somebody went after him? After the treasure?"

Josh ran both hands through shaggy, overlong hair.

"You must be kidding. He probably fell, that's all."

"Let's hope so," Ryan agreed.

A few hundred feet away, inside the Harbour Office, Mandy Jones slipped her mobile phone back inside the pocket of her jeans and walked across to the window. She needed time to think, to process what was happening and make sense of it all.

She could hardly believe it.

Last night, she'd watched Iain's boat heading back out onto the water, in the darkness. But she hadn't been able to sit around and worry about it all night; she had a life to lead, didn't she? She worked hard, she was a good mother to Daisy—or, at least, she tried to be—and she deserved some time to herself.

Or, as it happened, some alone time with the latest man in her life.

She knew it wouldn't last; it never did, and she'd stopped believing in the fairy-tale of True Love when she was a girl. All the same, it had been nice to have somebody to spend time with, to be close with.

Was that too much to ask?

She heaved a sigh as she watched the people of the town walking past the office, chattering about Iain, no doubt.

She struggled to make sense of it all; to believe what her mind was telling her.

After a pleasant, if short-lived, rendezvous the previous evening, she had popped back into the office to collect the emergency radio she'd forgotten in her earlier rush to get away. She'd clattered into the room on four-inch heels, a bit woozy after a few glasses of wine, and rummaged about to find it. It would have looked bad, if anything had come through and she wasn't there to receive the message, but thankfully nobody would be any the wiser.

She remembered grasping the radio in her hand and flicking off the lights, starting to turn away from the window, when she'd spotted something in the distance. A tiny flicker, nothing more than a torchlight entering the darkened harbour. She'd thought her eyes had been playing tricks, that she'd had one too many glasses of Merlot.

But then the shape had come into view.

A dinghy.

It had steered carefully away from the east pier, away from the working camera, but she only realised it had been deliberate afterwards. She'd watched from her darkened office, waited with idle curiosity to see who had managed to come into the harbour as a storm began to rage.

And she'd seen who it was.

Still, it had been no more than a passing curiosity, an idle observation, until she'd heard that the coastguard had found a dinghy and that it belonged to Iain's missing boat. The possibilities had spiralled throughout the day and she'd warred with herself. She knew she should speak to the police, to the tall detective and his sergeant.

That would be the right thing to do.

But then, she'd never been much of a one for always doing the right thing. Not when there was something to be gained.

Smiling now, she reached for her coat and decided to make a short, very personal, house call.

Time to collect.

CHAPTER 11

As the light faded and rain clattered against the roof of the old shipping inn, Ryan and Phillips made their way to the bedroom Iain Tucker had routinely used on his trips to Seahouses.

"Same room every time," Phillips said. "Had his breakfast at the same time every day, ate his dinner around the same time too."

"Dangerous," Ryan said softly. "It's dangerous to be so predictable."

Phillips found himself wondering whether he was growing too predictable in his old age, and made a mental note to ask MacKenzie about it. There was a woman who was unafraid to give him the full, unvarnished truth—usually several times a day.

"Aye, if the wrong kind of person is watching, you're a sitting duck."

"You and your ducks," Ryan said, coming to stand outside one of the bedrooms. It bore a carved wooden nameplate marked 'ST. AIDAN', after another local saint.

He reached inside his pocket for a fresh set of shoe coveralls and snapped the elastic over his boots before drawing on a pair of nitrile gloves. Phillips did the same and they tapped on the door, which opened to reveal a figure which, at first glance, was not dissimilar to the snowman they'd seen earlier in the day.

"Afternoon, lads." Tom Faulkner, the Senior CSI attached to Northumbria CID, was dressed head to toe in a white polypropylene boiler suit, complete with hairnet and hood so that only his mild brown eyes remained visible behind his goggles.

"Tom." Ryan nodded a greeting. "Found anything interesting inside?"

"Come and have a look for yourself."

Faulkner's suit rustled as he led them into the bedroom, where Ryan's cool gaze swept over the details of the furniture, cataloguing the scene and committing it to memory. A small double bed dominated the room, still fully made-up with the kind of attention to detail employed by an experienced chambermaid. A tartan headboard was fitted to the wall above it and, further above that, there was a decorative stag's skull Ryan found mildly disconcerting. On the far side of the room, a large mullioned window overlooked the sea and, beneath it, a small bureau and chair had been set up. A suitcase lay open on the floor containing a few personal effects and clothes, and a brief glance through the open doorway to the en suite revealed Tucker's missing diving gear, which hung from a clothes hanger over the shower rail to dry out.

"Why would a man intending to go back out on the water not take his diving gear?" Ryan asked, of nobody in particular. "He orders champagne, he gets changed and hangs his suit up to dry. Why would he do all that, if he was planning to head out again? Those are the actions of a man who was settling in for the night."

"He can't have drunk more than a single glass of champagne," Faulkner chipped in. "The bottle and glass are still here on the bedside table. Just one set of full prints, another partial, but we'll probably find that the partial belongs to whoever gave him the glass at the bar downstairs."

"We can ask for voluntary prints from the residents here," Phillips said. "Start ruling people out."

Ryan continued his survey of the room.

"No papers, folders, notebooks?"

"Not so far," Faulkner said. "Were you expecting any?"

"How about a laptop or iPad? A tablet of any kind?"

"No, nothing like that, although we found a mobile phone. I've bagged it up—it was on the bathroom shelf, just there."

He turned and pointed towards a small marker which had been left in its place.

"Probably checked his messages while he was sitting on the throne," Phillips said.

Ryan pulled a face.

"Bit unhygienic," he observed, and Phillips reddened a bit.

"Aye, well, I'm just saying that's what *he* might have done."

"Right. The important thing is whether he had anything interesting to say while he was contemplating state business."

"I had a quick look before the battery died," Faulkner said. "Password was a simple '1234', so it wasn't like cracking the enigma code. There were a couple of messages from his son, a couple that look work-related, and one from a woman called 'Sandy' who was asking if he still wanted to have dinner next week. None of them mentioned the wreck, but there were a couple of outgoing calls on his list—one to Anna and a couple to some area codes I didn't recognise. Few missed calls from this morning, too."

"We'll check it all out," Ryan said. "One of them was probably the Receiver of Wreck, another would have been Anna."

Faulkner nodded.

"There was one funny thing," he said. "I looked for Iain's phone charger but couldn't find it anywhere."

"Could have forgotten to bring it with him," Phillips offered.

"Seems unlikely," Ryan said. "Iain had been here for over a week. No way he managed to survive on a single battery charge that whole time."

"Could have left it on the boat?" Phillips tried again, but that seemed unlikely too, since there wasn't much in the way of electricity supply on a dive boat.

"No electronics, no papers," Ryan murmured.

He could almost imagine it, could almost see a shadow moving through the nondescript bedroom, hurriedly snatching up Iain's belongings, taking anything that might contain details of the location of his discovery.

"Somebody's been in here," he said aloud. "They've removed anything incriminating but, in their rush, they took the phone charger without remembering to take the phone."

Phillips felt a tingle, the kind an experienced hunter gets when they first scent their quarry.

"Nobody ever thinks to check the netty," he said, sagely.

"In terms of finding anything else remotely useful in here, I'm sorry to tell you there isn't much," Faulkner said. "The place is covered in prints, most of them probably quite old, and the recent ones will belong to Iain and whoever has been coming in to clean his room. We'll swab as much as we can, but it'll be the same story for bodily fluids. No blood spatter anywhere, either."

Ryan stuck his hands in the pockets of his jeans in a gesture they'd come to recognise as frustration.

"Who's in the room next door?" he asked, suddenly. "A man doesn't just disappear in a place this small. Somebody must have heard him coming in or out."

"I didn't see any cameras inside," Phillips said. "But there might be one outside. Hutch would know."

Ryan took one last look around the room, then nodded.

"Let's ask him."

CHAPTER 12

"You alright?"

Anna turned and smiled at the man she'd known since nursery school. He was grown, now, and life had changed them both since the days when they'd chased each other around the playground. By rights, there shouldn't be much of a friendship left between them, not after all that had happened on the island, but she supposed that was a testament to the human spirit and its power of forgiveness—of each other, of those who had hurt them, and of themselves.

"Just coming up for air," she replied, and leaned back against the wall of the Coastguard's Office. The rain had eased off, temporarily, as if the gods had known she needed to escape the cloying, competitive atmosphere within and feel the misty air cleanse her skin and her mind.

"This reminds me of school," Alex said, with a smile. "Back then, we'd have been pretending to smoke cigarettes around the back of the bike shed, not talking about murder and shipwrecks."

Anna laughed.

"*You'd* have been smoking. I'd have been in the library," she reminded him.

"You always were a nerd."

She gave him a half-hearted shove.

"How's life treating you, Alex? Have you—" She stopped herself, wondering whether it would be insensitive to ask about relationships. Three years before, the man Alex loved had been murdered—brutally, and by Alex's own father. That was enough for any heart to withstand in the space of a lifetime but, by the same token, the capacity for love was unlimited, or so she had always believed. If a person had loved once, they could do so again.

"Have I met anyone, you mean?" Alex came to lean against the wall beside her. "If you'd asked me a year ago, I'd have said I'd never be interested in meeting anyone ever again. Then, I realised something important. Loneliness isn't what Rob would have wanted for me, or what I would have expected of him, if the situation were reversed. I grieved…I still do," he amended quietly. "And I miss him all the time. But I've started to say 'yes' when people suggest a drink or a bit of dinner. It's a start."

Anna reached over to clasp his hand.

"You deserve a bit of happiness."

"Thanks. I didn't think I deserved anything after—well, after what my father did. It took everything I had in me, just to go back to work and hold my head up high. I thought people would want nothing to do with me, that they would think I was just like *him*."

"People are idiots," she acknowledged, and made him laugh. It was only the truth, after all. "But you didn't kill anyone, Alex, and you couldn't be more different from your father."

It was the biggest compliment she could have paid.

"Thanks," he said, and pulled her in for a hug.

"Well, well," a voice drawled, and they pulled apart in surprise. "Oh, don't let me interrupt your little…reunion."

Alex's face fell into hard lines of anger.

"I think we'd both appreciate it if you'd keep your sly little innuendos to yourself. Doctor Taylor-Ryan is a very good, very *married* friend of mine. I'm proud to call her husband a friend, too."

"Alex—"

She laid a hand on his arm and tried to tell him he was wasting his breath on a man like Jasper, but he was already in full flow.

"You need to grow up, mate, before you really offend someone. In other circumstances, I'd be flattered that you think she'd even look twice, but there's one thing you're forgetting."

Vaughn's face was flushed with embarrassment, but he chose to brazen it out.

"Oh? And what's that?"

Walker came to stand directly in front of him, almost toe to toe. He smiled slowly, put his hand on the man's chest and affected a suggestive whisper.

"I'm *gay*, sweetheart."

Their laughter rang in Jasper Vaughn's ears as he stormed back inside the office, fuelled by homophobic outrage and humiliation. Nobody laughed at his expense and got away with it.

Nobody.

They'd see who had the last laugh.

Back at the *Cockle,* Paul Hutchinson was seated inside a small, windowless cubby-hole which passed for an office, hidden behind a door marked 'PRIVATE'. It contained only a small desk and chair, floor-to-ceiling shelving, and the remaining wall space was plastered with photographs and memorabilia. He paused in the act of going through a stack of invoices and studied them, transporting himself back in time for a few precious moments.

Where had all the years gone? he wondered.

His eyes skimmed over faded colour photographs of Gemma and Josh, splashing about on the beach twenty years ago. He remembered capturing the moment of mother and son together before he'd whisked the little boy up and onto his shoulders and pretended to be a horse, clacking his teeth as his nephew giggled and begged for more. He remembered her laughter, the light that had shone briefly in her eyes, before it had faded again like waves retreating from the shore.

There were very few of the three of them captured together but his favourite rested in an expensive silver frame on his desk, so he could look at it often. It showed him and Gemma at the hospital just after Josh was born; she, cradling the tiny baby in her arms, while he kneeled beside her beaming like a new father.

Except, of course, he was *not* the boy's father.

How many times he had wanted to adopt Josh as his own and to make Gemma his wife. He would have shouted his love from the rooftops of the village, cherished her for the rest of their days, if only she would let him.

But then, he had never really asked. He'd never found the courage to say the words, to speak them aloud and let his fate be decided.

Just in case she said '*no*'.

Coward, his mind whispered.

They lived in a strange purgatory, he and Gemma, moving around one another as if in a tango. Their fingers brushed, their hands touched, but never for long. She was warm and welcoming with everyone and that was one of the many reasons he loved her.

And yet, also one of the reasons he was frustrated by her.

She must *know* how he felt. Gemma was a woman, not a girl. She knew when a man looked at her the way he did, knew the depth of emotion written in his eyes.

Softly, his mind cautioned. *Gently.*

Hutch took a deep, shaky breath and wondered again how twenty-three years had slipped by. It was written on his face when he looked in the mirror every morning, the unmistakable evidence that life continued to march onward, unstoppable. He wished he could make it stand still, or even turn back so that he could start all over again. He thought of all the things he would say, all the things he would do.

And of all the things he wouldn't do.

With a trembling hand, Hutch reached for a small wooden box on one of the higher shelves. It was dusty from lack of use but, when he flipped open the lid, the photographs inside were as fresh as the last time he'd plucked up the courage to look. He sat there for long minutes staring down at the laughing face of his younger brother, whose features so resembled his son that it was becoming an effort to look Josh in the eye.

A moment later, he slammed the box shut and shoved it back on the shelf.

Thief, his mind whispered.

When Ryan and Phillips tracked him down, Hutch was happily engrossed in the task of balancing his books. A low-hanging pendant light in a fashionable, vintage style—another one of Gemma's acquisitions—shone a moody light over his greying head and an ancient golden retriever was curled in a basket by his feet, snoring softly.

"Mind if we disturb you for a minute?"

He looked up at the sound of Ryan's voice and removed a pair of cheap magnifiers he'd bought at the local pharmacy.

"Sure, do you want a coffee in the main bar? Or I think you can both just about squeeze in here if you'd rather."

"Here's fine," Ryan assured him, and then immediately regretted it. Standing a couple of inches over six feet put him at a disadvantage in the confined space with its sloping ceilings and exposed beams.

"Nice photos," Phillips said, taking a good look around. "It's like a treasure trove in here."

Hutch smiled, never more conscious that the majority of his gallery was devoted to Gemma and Josh, as if they were his own.

"I suppose you need to ask me about Iain?"

"Yes, if it's a convenient moment?"

He linked his fingers.

"Now's as good a time as any."

"Thanks. Can you start by telling us how long you'd known Iain Tucker?"

Hutch's chair squeaked as he leaned back against the wood.

"Oh, God. Must be over twenty years," he said. "Iain used to rent a holiday cottage down by the fire station when he was younger, but he'd still come in here for a drink or a bar meal. That was before we gave the place a bit of a facelift."

"We understand he started staying here regularly around ten years ago?"

Hutch nodded.

"Sounds about right."

"Would you say you two were pally, then?" Phillips asked, and dragged his eyes away from a large photograph of Gemma as a younger woman, dressed only in swimwear.

"Yeah, I suppose I would," Hutch agreed, shifting uncomfortably as he followed Phillips' line of sight. "Iain was a decent bloke, always had a smile on his face, you know? I wouldn't say he was chatty but, whenever Iain *was* feeling talkative, he only ever had something interesting to say."

"Did he ever get chatty about the Viking wreck?" Ryan asked.

Hutch shook his head.

"He told me there was one in particular he wanted to find, one he was sure was down there. He said he'd been piecing things together for years but, to be honest, I never really asked him about it. History was never my strong point," he said, apologetically. "I'm more interested in the wildlife."

"Oh? You a bird man, then?" Phillips said.

Hutch let out a short laugh.

"That's one way of putting it," he said. "I volunteer sometimes with waste collection to keep the beaches clean and I've helped Gemma and Josh run seal trips once or twice, but this place takes up most of my time. If you want a bird fanatic, you should see Janine."

"Janine?"

Hutch nodded, scratching the side of his jaw.

"Janine Richardson. Works for National Heritage and lives on Inner Farne, like Saint Cuthbert," he said, with a note of admiration. "She makes sure nobody trespasses or lands a boat without permission. Takes a certain personality to spend most of their life surrounded by thousands of birds, day and night."

Phillips immediately thought of the famous Hitchcock film and gave an involuntary shiver.

"Aye," he said. "Wouldn't fancy it, myself."

"Takes all sorts," Hutch said easily. "There's nothing she couldn't tell you about the Farnes."

That caught Ryan's attention.

"She lives there all year round?"

"Apart from the odd trip to the mainland for supplies and whatnot, yes."

Ryan made a mental note to take a detour to Inner Farne on their boat trip the next day.

"Thanks for the tip. Coming back to what happened yesterday, do you remember anything about Iain's behaviour that concerned you? Did he seem worried, at all?"

"Exactly the opposite," Hutch said, confirming what everyone else had told them. "I'd never seen him happier."

"That's a hat-trick," Phillips murmured.

"Tell me, who occupied the room next to Iain's?"

"ST. OSWALD, you mean? Nobody had that room, last night. We only had Iain and another couple and their kids staying with us."

"How many guest bedrooms do you have here, in total?"

"Ten," Hutch replied. "Three were in use last night, including Iain's. The Shaeffer family had two connecting doubles on the top floor."

"We already know that Gemma and Josh share an apartment on the first floor. Do you live here too?"

Hutch gave a tight smile. He understood how it looked to the outside world, their unusual living arrangements. He knew what they must be thinking, wondering…

He thought he saw pity reflected in their eyes, and hated them for it.

"Mr Hutchinson?"

He gave himself a mental shake and sat up in his chair.

"Yes, I have a couple of rooms on the top floor, too. Directly above Gemma and Josh, as it happens."

"Finally, could you tell us where the CCTV cameras are, in the inn?"

"Well, we only have a couple. There're two on either side of the bar overlooking both cash registers—one on the dining room side and one in the main bar. There's another overlooking the car park and one at the main entrance."

Ryan thought of at least two other side doors; a back door leading out to the beer garden and another side door leading down to the main road, on the opposite side to the car park, neither of which were covered by CCTV.

"Mind if we take a look at the footage?"

"Be my guest."

Fifteen minutes later, Ryan's suspicions were confirmed. While the camera overlooking the main entrance had picked up Iain Tucker's return to the inn at five-twenty-seven the previous evening, there was no record of him leaving again sometime later, never to return.

"If he was in the habit of using the main entrance, why the hell would he have used the side entrance, all of a sudden?" Ryan muttered. "Unless somebody else suggested it."

Phillips let out a grunt as they made their way along the harbour road towards the Coastguard's Office.

"Seems everyone was struck deaf or blind, n'all," he added. "Everybody heard Tucker say he'd found a wreck, but nobody remembers a thing, after that."

"The Shaeffer family thought they heard a tapping sound on the floor below, sometime around nine," Ryan said. "Could have been someone knocking on Tucker's door."

"Aye, but it could just as easily have been old plumbing or floorboards."

Ryan knew it.

"Even if they did hear something, it only confirms what we already know, which is that Iain left the inn— but with who? There was a roomful of people sitting in the dining room when he spilled his guts about the wreck, most of whom he would have known, and no camera to capture which one of them slipped away to knock on his door later on."

He blew against his chilly hands. The temperature had dropped significantly as night drew in, and the wind had begun to howl, rushing past their ears as another storm swept up fallen leaves and other debris from the pavement.

"Looks like we're in for another miserable night," Phillips said, reading his thoughts. "We know one thing, guv. Whoever led him astray must have been someone Iain trusted."

"And that could have been anyone," Ryan said. "Iain was well-known around the area, that's something everyone agrees on."

"And it's unlikely to have been one of them at the inn," Phillips said, following Ryan's next train of thought with practised ease. "Hutch, Gemma, Josh and Daisy were all still serving at the bar. Daisy says she didn't knock off work until around eleven-thirty."

Ryan nodded, feeling his eyes begin to water as a gush of icy sea wind hit him like a fist to the face.

"It had to be someone who knew the layout of the pub, but who also knew they wouldn't be missed. Let's run a background check on all of them," he said.

Phillips nodded, and thought of all the ordinary men and women of the village who carried on with their lives, never suspecting that malice lived and walked amongst them.

Ryan paused with his hand on the door to the Coastguard's Office and spoke in an undertone.

"This morning, I told Alex Walker the investigation had nothing in common with what happened on the island three years ago," he said. "But I'm starting to think I was wrong. There are currents, here, Frank. Tensions running beneath the surface and lies woven into the stories they've told us. It's a tight-knit community here and I recognise it."

"We've seen it before," Phillips agreed. Truth be told, he'd felt the same, nagging concern throughout the course of the day. "You don't think there's anything sinister, underneath it?"

"More sinister than murder?" Ryan asked, with a flash of humour. "I have no idea. But I intend to find out."

With that, he yanked open the door.

CHAPTER 13

Without any clue as to the location of what had come to be known as 'Iain's Wreck', the Receiver, Hector Sayer, had reluctantly come to the decision that there was nothing for him to investigate and informed the remaining members of the makeshift salvage team that he would be returning to Southampton the next day. The news came as no surprise to any of them and, by the time Ryan and Phillips stepped inside the little break room at the Coastguard's Office, morale was at a low ebb.

Summing up the mood in the room, Ryan injected a little more energy into his own voice.

"Any progress on locating the wreck?" he asked, and moved across to where Anna was seated on a plastic tub chair. One glance told him all he needed to know, and he touched gentle fingers to her pale face, in silent support.

"We don't have the time or the resources to begin a speculative search," Ursula Tan explained, as she gathered up her notepad and briefcase. "Even a focused excavation costs thousands of pounds in machinery and resources; you can imagine what it would take to search the Farnes in expanding circles. We've spent years already."

Ryan nodded his understanding.

"The body was found on Outer Farne," he said. "We had a conversation with the lighthouse keeper earlier today, who confirmed that Iain spent a lot of his time in that section of water. It could be nothing, of course, but it could be something."

Jasper Vaughn pushed away from the table and snatched his jacket from the back of the chair he'd occupied for the past three hours.

"It's as I always suspected," he snapped. "Iain was nothing but a dreamer. You can see it in the wild theories he espouses in his books. History is like a science; it requires rigour, not flights of fantasy."

"Iain's reputation is beyond reproach," Anna shot back, visibly holding her anger in check. "Without his backing, your last project wouldn't have gone ahead."

Vaughn turned an unattractive shade of puce.

"That's utter rubbish," he blustered. "Iain had nothing to do with my last research project."

"Speak to the Dean," she advised him. "Then ask yourself whether you should be showing Iain, and his memory, a bit more respect."

"It was only out of a sense of obligation that I came here in the first place," Vaughn said, snidely.

"You hot-footed it down here pretty quick, for somebody who isn't all that bothered," Phillips said. "Could've sent somebody else or waited to hear whether there was anything to look at before you drove all the way out here."

Ursula let out a tinkling laugh.

"He heard I was coming," she told them, with a smug expression. "There's nothing Jasper hates more than missing out on an opportunity—isn't that right, Jas?"

"I think I've heard just about enough for one day," Vaughn said, and stalked towards the door. "Call me when you actually find anything real."

Ryan's voice stopped him at the door.

"We have one or two questions to ask you, Mr Vaughn, whenever you have a moment."

"*Doctor* Vaughn."

Ryan smiled.

"We'll be in touch."

As the door slammed shut behind him, Ryan turned to the remaining occupants.

"We believe Iain did find something, or that somebody believed he had found something, and it was enough to kill for. That alone warrants further investigation."

"I agree," Sayer said. "But it's a big ocean out there and I can't step outside my jurisdiction."

"What if we manage to find a lead? Would you re-open the matter?"

"Get us some coordinates to work with and we'll take another look," Ursula told them. "All we need is a starting point, then we have ways and means—but it will take time either way."

"Good enough," Ryan decided, and bade them farewell.

Once the door clicked shut behind the two subsea experts, he cast his eye around the space they had vacated. It wasn't much to write home about, but it had all they needed, including a blank wall for him to graffiti.

"Can we commandeer this room for a couple of days, Alex?"

The coastguard nodded.

"I'll clear it. Why?"

"Because we need an Incident Room in the heart of the village, so I can feel its pulse," Ryan said. "Somebody knows what happened to Iain Tucker, and why. I want them to know we're here and I want them to feel nervous about it. Nervous people make mistakes."

"Haven't heard from the pathologist yet, lad," Phillips cautioned. "There's still a chance it was death by misadventure."

Ryan turned to look at him squarely.

"That'll be for the coroner to decide, once we've done our jobs. Something's off, here. I can feel it."

Phillips opened his mouth to argue, then thought better of it. In the early days, he might have turned up his nose at what some called 'intuitive policing'. But he'd worked with Ryan for years and his instincts had never been wrong.

He simply nodded.

"Call in the troops, Frank. We're setting up camp first thing tomorrow."

Long after Ryan made his impassioned call to arms, Mandy Jones shivered as she made her way quickly through the back roads of the village, head lowered against the wind. She glanced over her shoulder now and then, just to be sure nobody was following, but could barely see a few metres in either direction. The streets were shadowed and empty, the misty outline of periodic street lamps shining their watery light through the thick sea fret that had rolled in and curled itself around the buildings, like tentacles.

She heard only the soft *click* of her shoes against the pavement and the crash of distant waves against the sea wall. Nobody was on the streets at that hour; the people of the village were tucked up in their beds for the night, clinging tightly to their loved ones as the storm gathered force around them.

As she neared the meeting point, Mandy's steps slowed and she wondered again whether she had made the right decision in coming here. She thought of Daisy, asleep back in the cottage where she'd been born half a mile away. She supposed there were few things she could be truly proud of, but her daughter was one of them.

Perhaps the only thing.

Rounding the corner, she found she was the first to arrive. She shuffled her feet to keep warm, and thought of the day Daisy had come into the world. It had been a night not dissimilar to this, she remembered, and her mother had perched beside her on the bed, clutching her hand while the midwife told her to *push*. It was funny, the things you remembered. Like the smooth feel of her mother's hand and the scent of her skin as she'd held on; crying, begging for the pain to be over. She'd stroked that same hand to sleep when the cancer finally claimed her mother eight years later, and her scent had been different; the odd, sickly-sweet scent of the dying had circled around the hospital bed and she'd never forgotten it.

Daisy was so different, she thought, so fearless. Her daughter was unafraid of life, or death, for that matter. Since her very first moments, she'd been eager to grasp everything life had to offer and never shied away from the tough parts, whereas Mandy had spent a lifetime running away. Lord knew, Daisy wasn't the academic type, but she was a beauty and she had a good heart.

A better heart than her mother, Mandy thought, and felt her chest contract.

Just then, she heard a whisper of sound somewhere to her left. She flattened herself against the wall where she stood and watched a figure emerge from the gloom.

"You came, then."

"Isn't that what you wanted?"

"Look, I'm not here for the chit-chat," Mandy said, with more bravado than she felt. "I told you what I think—what I *know*."

"You know nothing."

"Oh, I think we both know that I do. Otherwise, you wouldn't have come here, sneaking about like a thief in the night," Mandy replied, getting into the swing of it.

For Daisy, she thought. *For her future.*

"You know where the wreck is," she whispered. "You killed Iain because you wanted to keep the treasure for yourself."

Silence.

"You can deny it all you want—"

"I haven't denied it."

Mandy swallowed a sharp knot of fear while a small part of her brain told her to *run!*

Run, now!

But she had come this far. In another minute or two, it would be over and they would go their separate ways and never speak of it again. That was their bargain.

"I want half," she said quickly. "Give me half and I won't breathe a word. I'll resign my job and go away, leave you to it."

"How can I be sure?"

"You'll have to trust me," Mandy said.

Soft, harsh laughter.

"Or, I can go straight to the police," Mandy threatened, feeling angry now, fuelled by indignant rage at having been scorned. "Maybe I'll tell them who I saw skulking back into the harbour last night, in Iain's dinghy. I'm sure they'll be very interested to hear all about it."

There came a short pause.

"I don't have anything with me now. Meet me here again at first light and I'll show you where it is."

Mandy searched their face for signs of deception but could find nothing in the semi-darkness.

"Alright," she said, nervously. "But if you mess me around, that'll be it."

Their business concluded for the evening, she turned to leave, already imagining the new life she and her daughter would enjoy. Her heart soared at the prospect of riches, of status, and of the anonymity wealth could bring.

She didn't hear any movement until it was too late.

Something hard connected with the back of her head, cracking the skull with a sickening *crunch*. Her body fell forward in a heap of flesh, the fragile bones in her face shattering against the stone arch of the old lime kiln by the water's edge, and she let out a single, muted cry that was lost on the wind. Her killer waited with cold, impassive eyes until Mandy's limbs stopped twitching, the fight having drained out of her in less than half a minute. It was terrifying to feel the old power return, stronger this time, but the course had been set and there was no going back now.

You could never go back.

Moments later, muffled footsteps melted back into the darkness, as swiftly as they had come.

CHAPTER 14

Saturday, 3rd November

Red sky in the morning, sailor's warning.

That's what they said, Gemma thought, as she strapped the dog's lead onto his collar and set out into the early morning. The sky was blood-red, melting into shades of fiery orange and yellow as the sun rose higher in the sky to herald the dawning of a new day. It was peaceful at that hour, the small businesses only just beginning to open their doors to the Saturday crowd that had not yet awakened.

"Come on, lad," she murmured. "Let's shake off the cobwebs."

She paused outside the inn, deciding whether to turn north towards the dunes and Bamburgh Castle, or south into the centre of the village. When the dog nosed towards the village, she was happy enough to follow.

"Alright then, lazy-bones," she said. "Don't feel like a long walk today, eh?"

She smiled ruefully at the old retriever and remembered when Hutch had first brought him into their lives, as a present for Josh. The boy had been delighted at first, and entertained by the novelty of an adoring, fluffy-haired animal to play with. But, soon enough, his interest had worn off and the dog had learned not to expect much, turning instead to the other two people who showed him affection and, most importantly, saw to his basic needs.

Gemma's hand reached down to rub between the dog's ears, careful not to love it too much, frightened to invest too much of herself in another living thing because she *knew* what would happen. It was inevitable.

The dog would leave her.

Just as Kris had done, and as her parents had done before him. She seldom chose to think about it but, there, in the quiet morning breeze, she fumbled around the recesses of her mind for the hazy, snatched memories she had left of her mother. She recalled a young blonde woman with sad, unfocused eyes she later learned were a product of her love affair with heroin. As a mother herself, Gemma could hardly stomach the thought of it, failing to understand how any parent could put their addiction above their children. But, unpalatable though it was, that was the unhappy story of her early childhood; a product of two parents whose interests rested only with themselves, and with finding the next hit.

"Shh," she soothed the dog as it tugged her along the harbour road. "Not so fast."

As they reached the top of the harbour wall, directly above the old lime kilns built into the stonework below, she paused to look across at the shimmering water. It was like a watercolour, she thought; a perfect, blurred reflection of the blended colours of the sky. It was so different to the light-polluted cityscape she had known until the age of four, when a strange man and woman had come to collect her from the police station, after she'd been picked up once again for wandering the streets after dark. She'd been so frightened, then, so angry that they had taken her away from the world she was used to; the only one she knew.

The four-year-old girl hadn't wanted clean sheets and clean clothes, softly-spoken words or a full belly. She hadn't wanted the pity nor the kindness of strangers; hadn't wanted the toys they'd gifted her, nor the trips to the park. She hadn't wanted to see how much she had been missing, because the contrast was too painful.

She'd wanted her mother. Her stupid, messed-up, drug-addled mother, who'd given her life.

But soon, other feelings crept in. Disloyal, hopeful dreams where her stomach never ate its own lining, and nobody ever shouted or smacked or rolled around on the floor crying and laughing, like a mad person.

That's when she'd run away from the foster home, back to where she belonged. It was wrong to dream like that.

Except, when she got back home, she didn't belong. Not anymore.

With six-year-old eyes, she'd looked afresh and realised she was no longer a part of that old world and, soon enough, a family had come along, one who'd wanted the pretty little girl with sunshine blonde hair and big blue eyes. She'd looked nice in their family photos, not at all like the street urchin she'd once been and that was, she supposed, still buried deep inside.

Gemma let out a long breath, watching a flock of guillemots swoop low across the water. What good did it do to remember? It would only bring more pain. She didn't want to think of her well-meaning adoptive parents who'd tried so hard to change her, to mould her into what they'd wanted. She didn't want to remember her first, heady taste of love when she'd seen Kris Reid smile at her across the classroom of her new school.

Kris.

Her chest rose and fell as she fought to keep her emotions in check. Everybody left, including him, including Josh. She could see it happening a little more each day and she wanted to claw him back, to keep him close. But she couldn't. She could only set the bird free.

Losing patience, the dog tugged again on its leash and she relented, allowing him to lead the way, following his nose around the harbour, down the slipway and towards the tall arches on the harbourside.

"What've you found, boy? Fish?"

Gemma's footsteps slowed as they followed the stone pathway towards the cloistered lime kilns, a remnant from the eighteenth century when lime was quarried nearby and stored at Seahouses before it was shipped elsewhere. Nowadays, they were a visitor attraction, a pretty architectural talking point where kids sometimes gathered to smoke their first joint.

As they neared the second arch, the dog began to bark, straining against his leash with all the strength left in his ageing body.

"For goodness' sake," Gemma told him. "Calm *down*!"

At first, she saw nothing inside the archway but, as the clouds shifted, so too did the shadows. She grasped the lead tighter, her knuckles turning white against the frayed leather strap as she fought to drag the dog away, bearing down against the sickening waves of nausea.

"Help," she mumbled, and then tried again, louder this time. "*Help*!"

But, for once, Hutch wasn't there.

Forty miles further south, Ryan watched the changing shape of the sky.

He stood beside a set of tall glass doors leading off the living room onto a wide veranda, which held unspoilt views of the valley beyond. He cupped a mug of steaming coffee in one hand while he rested his long body against the edge of the frame, sipping from time to time as the morning came to life. They'd built a good life together, he and Anna. Despite all they had lost and all they had suffered, theirs was a charmed existence. Unlike so many people who grew up imagining they'd find a soulmate, marry and have children, Ryan had never thought it would be possible. It was a Hallmark card, a rom-com, a story people told their children—not real life. He hadn't thought there was a person alive who could not only tolerate but *understand* the vocation he followed and his need to avenge the dead. How could they, when he was only beginning to understand it himself?

Then, he'd met Anna.

A historian who was anything but stuffy; a woman who liked eighties music and slapstick humour, with soft brown eyes and a sharp tongue to match an even sharper mind. A woman who seldom required an explanation, who had only to look at him or hear the tone of his voice to understand his innermost thoughts. He remembered how it had felt when they'd first met, because it was something he'd been unconsciously searching for his whole life: it had felt like *home*.

He stayed there for a while longer, quietly contemplating the world, and Anna watched him from the doorway, unwilling to interrupt the serenity of the moment, wishing she could capture it instead. It was rare that Ryan allowed raw emotion so near the surface, but it was written there now, for all to see. His blue-grey eyes shone with child-like wonder as he traced the path of the clouds across the sky, lost in the beauty of the infinite cosmos and not in the tawdry, visceral world of murder that took up so much of his waking life. His face—so strong, so beautiful to her—was relaxed in profile and a smile played around his lips as he watched a pair of squirrels chase one another around the garden they were cultivating outside.

"Penny for them," she murmured.

When he turned, her heart gave a funny little lurch. *Funny*, she thought, even after all their time together he could move her with nothing more than a look.

"I was thinking we should plant some more trees," he said. "Give those squirrels something to fight over."

She smiled, pleased to talk about the mundane, simple things in life for a change.

"I thought we could plant some wildflowers, too, and create a meadow at the bottom of the garden."

Ryan nodded, silently curving an arm around her waist as she joined him beside the window.

"You were up early," she said, after a short, companionable silence.

"So were you," he replied, and brushed his lips against hers. "You had a nightmare last night."

Anna tensed, then deliberately loosened her shoulders again. It was an automatic response to trauma, a perfectly natural reaction. All the same, it irked that her psyche continued to be plagued by the past, invading her sleep with flashing images of horrors long dead and gone.

"I've had worse," she said truthfully. "It's only because Seahouses reminds me of home, on the island. Then, seeing

Alex for the first time since our wedding… It isn't his fault but seeing him reminds me of his father. Or, I should say, it reminds my subconscious."

Ryan had experienced his fair share of night terrors and didn't try to offer empty words or advice; she'd heard it all. Instead, he drew her close against his body, where there was safety and warmth.

"Nobody will ever hurt you again, so long as I have breath in my body," he promised, and his arms tightened briefly around her waist.

She leaned her head back against his chest, accepting the comfort he offered, knowing she would do the same for him.

"I was thinking about Iain, too," she said. "Trying to remember anything that could help you—"

"Don't worry about that."

"It's more than just your investigation," she admitted. "It's a matter of protecting his reputation. Jasper's gunning for Iain, now that he isn't around to defend himself."

"What do you make of Vaughn?" Ryan asked, seriously. She was a reliable judge of character and, besides, the world of academia was unfamiliar territory.

Anna took a deep breath, telling herself to remain objective despite her personal dislike of the man.

"He's a good academic," she said. "But I also think he's had a lot of good fortune in life, which has helped. I suppose the same could be said of many people."

"Including Iain?"

"Actually, I remember him telling me he worked as a hospital janitor to fund his Masters' degree," she said. "Iain wasn't afraid of hard work."

"He was diligent, then," Ryan surmised. It was good to capture the small, seemingly insignificant details that made up the fabric of a person. It helped to create a picture in his mind, which would make it all the easier to track his killer.

And there had been a killer, he was sure of it.

"Yes, Iain worked long hours in and out of the university," Anna said. "He was always friendly to talk to, although he was generally a bit of a loner since his marriage broke down a few years ago."

Ryan's arms tightened around her in reaction, although she didn't think he was aware.

"As for Jasper, he's just a social climber," she said simply. "A bit narrow-minded, a bit of a bigot; the kind of man who votes Tory but tells people he votes Labour because he likes the cachet of being seen as a liberal or a socialist."

She felt the rumble of laughter pass through Ryan's chest.

"Don't hold back," he chuckled. "Tell me what you *really* think."

Anna twisted around to face him.

"I'm probably being too harsh," she admitted. "Jasper's no worse than your average ambitious academic, but I've seen his type before. They put self-interest ahead of principles and it gets on my nerves."

"Unfortunately, it's a fact of life."

"It's bad taste, so soon after Iain's death," she said. "I'm surprised Jasper hasn't been rifling through his office at the university in his desperate quest to get ahead."

"If he has, he'll have me to answer to," Ryan said, then rubbed gentle hands over her arms. "Seems like he gets under your skin. Anything I should know about?"

Anna pulled a face.

"It's not him, personally. It's what he represents," she said softly. "Jasper Vaughn is everything I hate about academia and, when I'm forced to put up with him for any significant period of time, I start wondering whether I'm in the wrong profession."

"Anna, you said yourself that Iain Tucker was a leading expert in his field. A man like that knows who he can trust, whose professional opinion matters. He didn't ring Jasper, he rang *you.* Don't you think that means you're in the right profession?"

She nodded.

"You're right. I only wish I'd been able to help him when he called me."

"You're helping him now, by helping me. I need to know what he found down there, Anna. It feels like it could be the missing piece."

"If somebody killed Iain to poach treasure, that isn't the kind of thing they can keep a secret for long," she argued. "I don't understand why it matters about the details of his find—"

"It matters because I'm starting to wonder whether Iain was killed because somebody *didn't* want the treasure to be found, not because they wanted to keep it for themselves."

"But, if that's the case, somebody would have had to know it was down there already," she said, in disbelief. "Why would they keep it hidden for so long? Why wouldn't they want to claim it?"

"That's the question," Ryan said, and then jerked his head in the direction of the kitchen as his mobile phone began to bleat out a metallic jingle from its position on the granite worktop. A quick glance at his watch told him it was almost seven-thirty, much too early to receive calls from anybody other than the Control Room.

"I think it just got harder," Anna said, and stepped aside as he crossed the room with long strides, his carefree spirit locked away once more behind a mask of indomitable strength as he prepared to face whatever challenge lay ahead.

CHAPTER 15

An hour later, Detective Constable Jack Lowerson parked his car along a side street in Seahouses and turned off the engine. He rested both hands on the steering wheel and took a moment to collect his thoughts, half expecting the old fear to return. Crippling social anxiety had been his constant companion for months; a persistent torment that preyed on his mind and reared its ugly head in moments such as these, serving to remind him that he was not ready, not capable, not enough.

It had been more than six months since Jennifer's death and six months since he'd learned his mother had been responsible. It had been a long, painful process of introspection and recovery—long, sleepless nights battling between love for his mother and hatred of what she had done. No matter how bad a person, no matter how wrong their actions, there was never any justification to kill. That was how he had been raised; it was the foundation of his belief system and the morals upon which he'd built his life. His mother had been the first person to teach him that.

And yet, she'd flouted her own rules. Coldly, and without remorse.

He'd visited her once in prison, the jury not having agreed with the defence barrister's argument that Wendy Lowerson had acted in self-defence and, the truth was, neither did he. It would take a lifetime to forgive her, not only for having taken the life of Jennifer Lucas, former Detective Chief Superintendent of Northumbria CID and the woman with whom he had once shared a bed, but for having shattered the illusion. Or to forgive her for having allowed the police to believe—even for a few days—that he had been responsible.

His mother was not the person he thought she had been.

Lowerson sat there for a while longer, mustering the strength to get out of his little blue Citroen and face the people who had, unbelievably, stuck by him throughout the ordeal. Despite all he had said and done, despite how far he had fallen in both integrity and self-respect, his friends had remained constant. They had stepped back—*pushed* back, by him—but never so far that they couldn't step forward again, to catch him when he inevitably fell.

He would never forget it, and he owed them a debt of gratitude that demanded he pitch up today and be part of the team again.

"Come on, Jack," he muttered, and looked at himself in the rear-view mirror.

He'd made a bit of an effort, deliberately wearing the clothes he'd preferred before meeting Jennifer and wearing his hair the way he liked, not the way she'd told him looked better.

Chip, chip, chip.

That was what she had done to his self-esteem.

But when he looked in the mirror, he saw a man with fewer shadows than before. It had taken strength to get on a plane and fly to Italy for Frank and Denise's wedding—he hadn't been ready to face the world, not then. And when the call had come through from Phillips late last night, asking him to return to work, he'd flown into a panic.

I'm not ready, he'd said.

I need more time, he'd said.

And yet, here he was.

Squaring his slim shoulders, Lowerson looked himself dead in the eye.

"Get out of the car and put one foot in front of the other," he told himself. "You can do this."

He emerged into the cold November morning and began to make his way towards the harbour, one step at a time.

When Lowerson reached the seafront, bright yellow road signs had already been set up to create a diversion to lead oncoming traffic away from the section of road giving direct access to the harbour, which had been designated a crime scene. He gave his name to the constable manning the police barrier, who dutifully entered it into the log book and waved him on, pointing him in the direction of a slipway leading down towards the harbourside and a series of tall stone arches. He found Ryan standing outside one of them, deep in conversation with Tom Faulkner, the Senior CSI. A wave of something like brotherly love washed over him, a profound relief at having found someone whose face he knew and recognised, one he had always looked up to.

Both men turned at the sound of approaching footsteps and broke into spontaneous smiles that were so easy, so natural, that Lowerson was embarrassed to find a lump rising in his throat.

"Hey, Jack! Long time, no see," Faulkner said.

"Hi, Tom," he managed. "Early start for you, today."

"No rest for the wicked," Faulkner winked. "Good to see you back."

When he stepped away to re-join the small team of forensic staff photographing the area where the body of Mandy Jones had recently lain, tactfully giving the two men a moment to catch up, Ryan turned to Lowerson with a searching expression.

"Thanks for coming in," he said, quietly. "I have to ask, are you sure you're up to it?"

Lowerson read patience and understanding but, mercifully, found no trace of pity. He couldn't have coped with pity from Ryan; that would have been too much to bear.

"I'm up to it," he said firmly, and realised with a soaring heart that he meant it. "What have we got here?"

Ryan gave a short nod, trusting the man to know his own mind.

"I've arranged a briefing at the Coastguard's Office in half an hour," Ryan said, getting straight down to business. "They're loaning us a room for the time being."

"Fast work," Lowerson remarked. "Considering the call only came through this morning."

But Ryan shook his head.

"There's more to this than meets the eye, Jack. First, a university professor washes up on the rocks at Longstone yesterday morning, only a few hours after he announced that he'd found an important Viking wreck. We're still in the process of unravelling whether Iain Tucker died of natural causes and, now, the Harbour Master has turned up dead too."

Ryan's eyes turned flat as he looked over Lowerson's shoulder, towards the archway where Mandy Jones had been found. A large pool of blood stained the floor, seeping into the old weathered stone cracks, and the dull glint of an earring or bracelet was just visible in the centre of it all.

"That's a lot of blood," Lowerson remarked. "She must have bled out, or nearly."

"They used an old metal hook," Ryan explained. "We found it lying on the ground, nearby. Faulkner reckons she took a single blow to the back of the head which cracked her skull, then a second blow which pierced her neck and tore an artery in the process. That would account for the heavy blood loss."

"Who was she?" Lowerson asked, deliberately blocking out the image of another woman whose head had been caved in; a woman he had once loved.

"Amanda Jones, more commonly known as 'Mandy'. Aged forty-eight, resident of Seahouses and its full-time Harbour Master, employed by the Harbour Commissioners. Phillips and I met her yesterday."

And joked about her flirtatious nature, Ryan recalled, with a small stab of guilt.

"What's the connection?"

Ryan simply shook his head.

"We don't know yet. There may be no connection but that seems very unlikely. Two deaths in as many days in a village where crime is mostly limited to shoplifting are too many to pass off as coincidence."

Just then, they heard the unmistakable sound of Phillips' voice carrying on the morning air, as he made his way down the slipway with MacKenzie.

"…I'm tellin' you, lass, that was Kevin Keegan we passed on the road back there. I'm positive it was."

MacKenzie's long-suffering Irish lilt could be heard clearly too.

"Frank, that would be a lot more interesting as a conversation-starter if I knew who Kevin Keegan was."

Phillips stopped dead at the corner of the first lime kiln, completely oblivious to the fact he had an audience, and stared at his new wife in disbelief.

"Howay, don't tell me you don't know the man who single-handedly managed the finest footballing era Newcastle United has ever known? Y'nah, KEE-GAAN, KEE-GAAN!"

He bellowed the simple football chant and several heads turned, including the CSIs, who looked across in varying degrees of confusion.

"Still not ringing any bells, Frank. I must have been busy solving murders, while this golden era of football was underway," MacKenzie replied, pointedly.

Before he had a chance to respond, she spied the young man she had helped to train and who, until recently, she had thought might never return.

"Jack," she said, warmly. "I wasn't sure if you'd come, but I'm so glad you did."

Uncaring of who might see, MacKenzie pulled Lowerson in for a hug, which he returned wholeheartedly.

All thoughts of football now forgotten, Phillips trotted up and grabbed Lowerson by the shoulders to take a good, hard look at him.

"Good to see you, lad," he said, in a voice that was suspiciously thick. "About time you came back to work; neither of these two know a thing about The Beautiful Game."

The smile that spread across Lowerson's face was so broad, and so real, it transformed him.

"If we can wrap this up by next Saturday, how about we take ourselves off to the match?"

"You've got yourself a deal, son."

CHAPTER 16

Now that the team was reunited, Ryan set about the task of organising their ranks. A brief telephone conversation with the police pathologist confirmed that they had been able to identify a deep skull fracture on the back of the man's head. There was a possibility it had been sustained post-mortem as the body had been swept back and forth against an unforgiving rock bed, but there was also a very real chance it had been the reason Iain Tucker had ended up in the water in the first place. Since Mandy Jones had been found with a similar head wound, it represented the second injury of its kind and Ryan had long since learned never to ignore a pattern, however incidental.

Leaving MacKenzie and Lowerson in charge of the crime scene, Ryan and Phillips made the short journey to the house Mandy had shared with her daughter, Daisy. Neither man relished the prospect of questioning her next of kin, especially in circumstances such as these, but they both knew that it was better to gather as much information as they could while memories remained fresh in the minds of all concerned.

"Ready?" Ryan asked, as they reached a tiny fisherman's cottage with a blue-painted door, a couple of streets back from the harbour.

"Aye, let's get it over with," Phillips said, and rang the doorbell.

DS Carole Kirby answered, wearing a solemn expression of mourning that paid no deference to her profession. The Harbour Master had been one of them, a neighbour and sometime friend, and her loss was an affront to the village and its sensibilities.

"She's through here," Kirby said, and led them along a colourful, seaside-themed hallway towards a cosy living room with an open fireplace and even more colourful décor. Trinkets, pictures and wall hangings covered every available wall space, mirroring its late owner's eclectic personal style. It took them a moment to realise that Daisy was seated amongst it all, huddled on a teal blue velvet sofa with her legs tucked up beside her.

"Daisy?" Kirby said, gently. "DCI Ryan and DS Phillips are here. You remember, you met them, yesterday?"

Daisy's turned automatically, her face haggard with grief.

"I remember," she said, dully.

Ryan nodded his thanks to Kirby, who melted away into the kitchen to make cups of tea.

"I think DS Kirby has already told you what's happened," Ryan began, drawing an easy chair closer to where Daisy sat, while Phillips perched on the other end of the sofa beside her. "We're very sorry for your loss, Daisy."

The words always sounded trite, Ryan thought. No matter how many times he said them, no matter how much he meant them, they sounded empty and clinical.

Daisy continued to stare at the wall above the fireplace with a vacant expression.

"I think there's a cup of tea on the way, but is there anything else we can get you?" Ryan asked, watching closely for signs of medical shock. "Can we call someone? Your dad, perhaps?"

Her face dissolved into fresh tears and Ryan looked to Phillips for divine intervention.

"How about a friend, love? An aunt or an uncle?"

"Josh," she managed, between great, heaving sobs. "I want Josh."

They'd rather she'd asked for a family member, but beggars could not be choosers.

"I'll make the call," Phillips murmured, and stepped out of the room.

After another minute passed and the tears had abated, Ryan tried again.

"I know this is hard," he said softly, and dug a bit deeper than he might otherwise have done. "I know, because I lost someone very close to me as well. My sister."

Daisy's eyes flickered to his, and held.

"She was murdered, four years ago," he said, and felt the usual sharp pain in his chest, somewhere in the region of his heart. "At first, it's hard to believe, impossible to take in," he said. "But whoever did this to your mum deserves to be brought to justice."

Daisy lifted a shaking hand to scrub away fresh tears, but continued to watch him with eyes that were glassy pools of misery.

"I don't know who would have wanted to hurt her," she choked.

"I can't give you any answers, yet, but I want to. I want to find whoever hurt your mother, but I need your help," Ryan said.

"I don't know how," Daisy whispered.

"I'm going to ask you some questions. Answer them as honestly as you can and that will be enough."

Daisy sniffed, then nodded.

"When was the last time you saw your mum?"

The girl raised a hand to her eyes, covering them while she tried to hold herself together.

"Before bed," she said, almost inaudibly. "We had an argument and then I went to bed."

"Alright, Daisy. You're doing fine," Ryan said, and exchanged a nod with Phillips, who slipped back into the room. "Around what time was that?"

"About eleven," she mumbled. "I got home a bit before then. We argued, and I went up to bed."

She thought of the words she had used, the names she had called her mother, and thought she might be sick.

"What did you argue about?"

Wordlessly, Daisy accepted the cup of tea that was pressed into her cold hands.

"Josh," she said simply. "Mum didn't like him."

The two men exchanged a glance.

"Why not?" Phillips asked.

"She thought he was a waster," Daisy said.

Daisy raised the cup to her numb lips, scalding her tongue in the process.

"She doesn't know him like I do."

"Alright," Ryan murmured, unwilling to find himself embroiled in matters of the heart. "Did you hear anybody come to the house, after you went upstairs to bed? Or did you hear your mum leave the house at any time?"

Daisy shook her head, dark curls swinging around her pale cheeks.

"I heard the telly go off at midnight, or around then," she said. "I suppose, I never heard her come upstairs. I didn't think about it. I didn't—I didn't check—"

She broke down again, her body wracked with harsh sobs as she gripped Phillips' hand, which he'd silently offered.

"You weren't to know this would happen," he said.

Before she had a chance to respond, they heard the front door open and close again, followed by the sound of fast approaching footsteps down the hall.

"Daisy?"

"In here," she called out, brokenly.

When Josh entered the room, Ryan's first thought was that he looked very young and, in the harsh light streaming through the living room window, very tired—as though he'd hardly slept.

"Daisy," he said again, and moved across to hunker down beside her, where she threw her arms around his neck. "I'm so sorry."

"Somebody killed her," she whimpered. "They left her, down by the kilns, as if she was nothing. Why would anyone do that?"

Josh stared at the wallpaper as she gripped him in a desperate embrace, and he made soothing sounds as his head began to spin.

First Iain, now this.

"We'll get through this together," he promised her.

The police watched their exchange and felt like voyeurs, but they had a job to do, one that could not wait.

"Daisy, I need to ask whether your mother had been concerned about anything, or anyone, lately? Had she mentioned anything that was troubling her?"

The girl let go of Josh's neck reluctantly, but continued to grip his hand as she forced herself to continue.

"I hardly saw her, really. We both work—worked," she amended. "Then, I usually see Josh in the evenings."

He gave her hand a squeeze, right on cue.

"Is that where you were, after your shift ended yesterday?" Ryan queried.

Daisy nodded.

"After I spoke to you at the inn, Josh and I hung out for a while at his mum's."

Ryan didn't bother to ask how they'd spent the time.

"And then, you came directly home?"

"I walked her home around eleven," Josh interjected.

Phillips raised a bushy eyebrow at that, heartened to find that the age of chivalry was not altogether dead.

"Did you see anyone loitering around the street or any strange cars parked outside?"

They shook their heads.

"I wasn't looking," Daisy confessed. "Besides, it was foggy last night. You couldn't make out very much."

Ryan knew that was all they were likely to get from her at present, and it was time for them to leave. They bade her farewell and offered more hackneyed words of sympathy, for which she thanked them in a small, toneless voice.

"If anything comes to mind, get in touch," Ryan said. "We'll call around again soon."

Outside, Phillips turned to his friend with sad eyes.

"Poor lass," he said, gruffly. "Doesn't seem like she's got anybody, now."

"She has Josh," Ryan replied, with a small frown. "And we have work to do. Somebody panicked last night, Frank. Killing Mandy Jones in the open like that was a reckless act."

"You said you wanted them to be nervous," Phillips pointed out. "Well, seems to me they're nervous but they're arrogant too."

"A heady combination," Ryan said. "Come on, let's find them before they take another rash decision and shatter any more lives."

CHAPTER 17

After they'd taken a preliminary statement from Gemma, Hutch showed the pair of police constables out of the *Cockle* and turned the latch-key behind them, flipping the sign to 'CLOSED'. Nobody would be venturing out so early in the morning, anyway, and he needed a moment's respite; a quiet space to reflect on what had happened in their small, close-knit community.

Gemma watched him from one of the new, expensive leather booths they'd installed a few months previously.

"How're you doing?" he asked, softly.

She looked up at him with tired, red-rimmed eyes, and simply shook her head.

"You should have seen her, Paul," she said, using his real name for a change. He liked how it sounded on her lips and wished she would use it more often; he was 'Hutch' to everybody else, but he'd rather be 'Paul' to her.

"It was awful."

"Try not to think about how she looked," he said quickly, and slid into the booth beside her. He was pleased when she didn't shift away but stayed exactly where she was.

"What's happening around here?" she said, suddenly, and turned to him in wild confusion. "First, Iain, and now, Mandy. What's going on?"

"One might have nothing to do with the other," he said, although he didn't believe it any more than she did. "Mandy was a good laugh but, let's just say, she'd lived life to the full. Who knows what she'd got herself mixed up with?"

"You mean, drugs?"

Hutch shook his head.

"I don't know. But there was always somebody new in her life, every few months it seemed. Maybe one of them wasn't all they were cracked up to be."

Gemma said nothing.

"Where's Josh?" she asked instead.

"With Daisy," he told her, and sighed when he saw hurt flicker in her eyes, quickly masked. "It doesn't mean he doesn't care about you. He knows I'm here, whereas Daisy has nobody."

She nodded stiffly, knowing he was right.

"I miss him," she admitted, and brushed away sudden tears. *Stupid,* she thought. *Stupid to cry.*

"He's growing up, finally," Hutch said, with a lopsided smile. "It took twenty-two years, but Josh is his own man and he's doing the right thing by that girl. You taught him that."

She was undone by his kindness and, when he opened his arms, she paused only for a fraction of a second before allowing herself the luxury of comfort. She nuzzled against his chest and breathed deeply of his earthy scent, enjoying the sensation of being held by a man.

They sat there for endless minutes as she let the emotion drain out and he listened, murmuring endearments, rubbing his calloused hand over her back as he would a child. She didn't know when the sensation changed and the mood shifted, she only knew that she was reaching for him, touching her lips to his, searching.

She felt his body shudder, then he was plundering her mouth, hauling her up against him with a strength she hadn't realised he possessed.

"Hutch," she said, putting a firm hand on his chest.

Immediately, he reared away, preparing himself for the rejection that would certainly follow.

"Sorry, I got carried away—"

"I was going to say, we should move upstairs," she said.

He could hardly believe it, and said as much.

"You—you're sure?"

"Are you trying to talk me out of it?" she joked, with a lazy smile. "For God's sake, carry me upstairs before I change my mind."

With a giddy joyfulness he hadn't felt in years, Hutch lifted the woman he'd loved for over forty years out of the booth and up into his arms.

At the precise moment Hutch elbowed his way into Gemma's bedroom and tumbled them both onto the bed, Ryan and his team congregated in the break room at the Coastguard's Office. Alex Walker had been true to his word and they found the area had been cleared of clutter to make way for their temporary visitors.

"We're packed in like sardines, here," Phillips said, but was mollified somewhat by a tin of custard cream biscuits that was making its way around the room.

"Just don't make any sudden movements, or we'll all fall like dominoes," MacKenzie said, and shuffled to make way for Trainee Detective Melanie Yates, who had recently arrived from Police Headquarters.

Ryan had come armed with photocopied summaries he'd produced overnight, and these were circulated around the room, precipitating a wave of rustling paperwork as its occupants began to thumb through the pages.

"Grab a seat, if you can," he called out, and tacked another image to the wall, allowing them another couple of minutes to settle in.

"You're looking well," Yates said, as she slid into a small space beside Jack Lowerson.

He turned to look at his colleague and blinked, as if seeing her for the first time. A year ago, he'd admired the young woman standing beside him—in fact, he'd spent most of his days mooning over Melanie Yates like a lovesick puppy. She'd always preferred to remain friends and, he supposed, looking back, he could understand why.

Then, Jennifer had come along and changed everything.

"You're looking well, too," he said, in friendly tones. "You've changed your hair."

Automatically, she touched a hand to her head, which had previously been capped by a mane of mid-brown hair she tended to pull back into a ponytail. Now, it was styled into a short pixie bob and had been coloured a bold, platinum blonde.

"Yeah," she said, self-consciously. "It's a bit different."

"Suits you," he said, and then turned away as Ryan began to address the room.

Yates looked at his profile for a few seconds longer and realised something very important and very, very inconvenient.

She was attracted to Jack Lowerson. The New Jack, with soulful eyes that spoke of life and loss, coated in a layer of steel that hadn't been there before. For a second, she mourned the Old Jack, then her stomach gave a little flutter as he turned to pass her the tin of biscuits that had eventually made their way past Phillips.

Damn, she thought.

"Thanks," she mumbled, and stuffed a biscuit into her mouth.

Ryan passed his assessing gaze over the other faces in the room.

Phillips, MacKenzie, Lowerson and Yates all stood at the front, with Coastal Area Commander Alex Walker completing the row beside a couple of his deputies. Tom Faulkner had discarded his polypropylene suit in favour of corded chinos and a thick woollen jumper under an all-weather coat and, at first glance, he might have passed for one of the many fishermen whose livelihoods had been disrupted in Seahouses, of late. Members of the local police had also gathered, led by DS Carole Kirby, and one of them had already been put to work manning a phone that was linked to the Incident Room number, in case of emergencies or if a member of the public had something to report. And they usually did, Ryan thought. Wasting police time with preposterous calls ranging from complaints about slashed tyres to spectres dressed as the Ghost of Christmas Future.

"Alright, let's make a start," he said, for once not having to raise his voice to be heard. "Before we get into it, I want to thank you all for pulling together on this. We're only just beginning our investigation but, if we start as we mean to go on, there's every chance we'll crack this one together."

He hoped.

Angling his body towards the wall behind him, Ryan rapped a knuckle against the first of two large images he'd stuck in the centre.

"This is Professor Iain Tucker," he said, looking into the man's harmless, slightly myopic gaze as it stared out from a photograph taken from his profile on the university website. "He was the Head of Marine Archaeology at Durham University, until his body washed up against the rocks beside Longstone lighthouse yesterday morning. He was fifty-seven, divorced with a grown-up son. By all accounts, he was a regular feature at Seahouses as well as a well-known member of the local and wider Northumbrian diving community. He'd worked on countless projects in his professional capacity, but we're most interested in his lifelong interest and possible obsession with a Viking longboat wreck he claimed to have found the night before he died."

Ryan paused, letting the information sink in.

"As you can imagine, by the time we found Iain, there wasn't too much of him left. However, I've now received a preliminary report from the pathologist, who hasn't ruled out the possibility that a deep skull fracture was sustained prior to his entering the water. It's also probable that Iain had spent up to fifteen hours in the water, given the advanced state of decomposition and distension of his body. That tallies with the witness statements we've taken from the last people to see him alive, who confirm that he was alive and well at five-thirty."

"We got the PLB data back just before," Walker interjected, correctly assuming that Ryan would want to know the update. "Turns out, the Personal Locator Beacon inside Iain's dinghy had been transmitting consistently throughout the past week. We haven't had a chance to look into it, yet, but I thought you'd want to know."

This was a major development. If, as they suspected, the dinghy had been tethered to Iain's diving boat throughout his time at Seahouses, it provided a means by which they could map his movements and, moreover, narrow down the search for the precise coordinates of the wreck he had found.

"I thought PLBs worked as emergency distress signals," Ryan said. "Don't you need to activate them before the GPS will operate?"

"Yeah, but there's a new generation of them, now," Walker explained. "Before, the battery life was so bad you couldn't keep them on all the time but now the technology's a bit better, people can leave them on and transmitting constantly, which is good news for us."

Ryan flashed a smile.

"You can say that, again. If you could start working back through the data and mapping the coordinates, it'd be a huge help. I can give you a couple of analysts to work with, if need be."

Walker waved the offer away.

"It'll be quicker if I do it myself," he said, and mentally re-shuffled his workload. It was, as Ryan had already said, a matter of everyone pulling together.

"For those of you who are just coming to the investigation today, I should tell you that Tucker's boat remains missing. The Automatic Identification System had been disabled, as had all other forms of GPS transmission, for at least a week. That would strongly suggest that Iain was responsible for disabling the AIS himself, possibly because he wanted to keep the exact location of his diving search private from other vessels, but he forgot to do the same for his PLB."

"You think somebody would kill for an old Viking longboat?" MacKenzie asked. "Seems a lot of trouble to go to."

Ryan's thoughts exactly, but he did not voice them, yet.

"Until we know what's down there beneath the water, we can't say whether it played any part in Tucker's death. All we can say for certain is that he went missing in unusual circumstances and that his behaviour was out of character."

"Any suggestion of suicide?" Lowerson asked, slipping back into his old skin with remarkable ease.

Ryan shook his head and spoke to the room at large.

"Tucker called my wife, Doctor Anna Taylor-Ryan, who happens to be a colleague of his at the university. Phone records tell us the call was made shortly after he returned to dry land, which was at ten-past-five, according to the Harbour Master's log. Tucker rang Anna to ask for a meeting the next morning. That isn't the action of a man who doesn't intend to be alive the next day and, besides which, all the witnesses agree his mood was upbeat."

Lowerson nodded.

"We've requested CCTV footage from all available businesses and private residences in the village, but it'll be a huge task to go through it all," Ryan continued. "As it currently stands, there's no footage of Iain leaving *The Cockle Inn* for the final time and no witness evidence to tell us when, exactly, that was."

"Not much in the way of forensics, either," Faulkner chipped in, from the back of the room. "I'll chase up the samples today, but we found no evidence of an altercation in the room where Iain was staying. There were dozens of separate DNA samples, as well as fingerprints in the hotel room and the same amount again in the dinghy."

Ryan held back a sigh. There were some things, he knew, that couldn't be rushed. More importantly, they *shouldn't* be rushed.

"Understood, Tom. Let's ask everyone at the inn to provide some voluntary samples, to assist the investigation."

Faulkner nodded.

"We have the opposite problem at the crime scene on the harbour," he continued. "There, we have a body, a murder weapon and a clear cause of death. We've photographed everything, and we'll bag everything up as the day goes on. We'll be working our way back over the likely route she took going down to the lime kilns, then we'll make a start on the Harbour Office and her cottage."

It was good, fast work.

"Thanks," Ryan said, with feeling. "Let us know what you find. For the rest of you, this brings me on to the second image on the wall."

He moved across to a colour photograph of Amanda Jones, taken from a frame at home provided by her daughter.

"This is Mandy Jones, the former Harbour Master of Seahouses. She was single, with a daughter, Daisy, who's twenty-two and a resident of the village. She was found dead this morning by another local resident, Gemma Dawson, who helps to run *The Cockle Inn,* employs Mandy's daughter and whose son, Josh, is currently dating the daughter, too."

"Bloody hell, it's like Cabot Cove," Phillips muttered, earning himself a sharp jab from MacKenzie.

"Without the loveable Angela Lansbury to help us to solve the mystery," Ryan lamented, choosing to see the funny side. "Mandy was found with a deep head wound and laceration to her neck, which most likely severed an artery and precipitated cardiac arrest. We're in the process of gathering statements to understand her last movements, which are unclear. Her daughter has no knowledge of when she left the cottage, except that it would have been sometime after around eleven-thirty, when she was still alive."

"What about phone records?" MacKenzie asked. "Eyewitnesses?"

"None so far," Ryan replied. "In the three hours since Mandy was found, we've made good progress, but there's a long way to go. No mobile phone has been recovered for Mandy, so we'll have to go to the telephone company for the information. Considering it's the weekend, that's like requesting the Ark of the Covenant."

There were a couple of laughs, then Ryan grew serious again.

"For the moment, I'm treating these deaths as a linked investigation, which has been cleared by the Powers That Be.

That being said, please bear in mind the possibility that there may be no link at all, so I want to know about all former spouses or partners, any recent problems or assaults, even arguments over parking spaces. You never know."

There were nods around the room.

"There's going to be a lot of footwork and plenty of long hours," he warned them. "I'm making no apologies; this is what you signed up for. However, to streamline things, I'm going to assign two Senior Investigating Officers, one to each victim. I'll oversee the Tucker case, and I'm going to ask you, MacKenzie, to oversee Mandy Jones. We'll reconvene regularly to discuss progress and see where the two overlap."

Denise nodded her assent.

"Consider it done," she said.

"Good. Phillips, you're with me. Lowerson, Yates, you're with MacKenzie. The rest of you will be assigned tasks as and when the need arises, and we're grateful for your assistance."

He drew in a deep breath and then clapped his hands together.

"Alright, let's get moving."

In the quiet of her mother's sitting room, Daisy lay on the sofa with her head resting on Josh's lap. He stroked her hair with a gentle hand and watched the dust motes dancing on the air around them.

"Try to sleep," he murmured. "You're exhausted."

"I can't sleep."

His hand stilled its rhythm and he wondered what else he could say, what else he could do to make it right for her.

Nothing, he thought. Nothing could make things right again.

"If they find out what's down there, they'll find out about *Shell Seekers*, too," Daisy mumbled, and took another shuddering breath.

Josh broke out into a clammy sweat, thinking through all the possible ramifications.

"I'll try to get out of it—"

"How?" she asked. "What if—what if they killed my mum? What if that's why they killed her?"

Josh squeezed his eyes tightly shut, trying to block out the thought.

"Thanks for not telling the police," he said.

"I couldn't," she said, and it had been hard, especially as they'd been so kind.

He rubbed a shaking hand over his eyes, trying desperately to think of a way out.

"I'll speak to them," he decided.

She sat bolt upright and faced him with puffy, tear-stained eyes.

"No!" she almost shouted. "I can't lose you, as well! What if something happens—?"

"It won't," he said, affecting some of his old confidence. "Trust me."

She said nothing, but lowered her head to rest against his shoulder.

"Do you think Iain found it?" Josh wondered aloud. "Do you think that's why he wound up dead?"

Daisy shivered in the warm room.

"I'm scared, Josh."

Me too, he thought, and checked the clock on the wall, which read twelve-thirty. Another few hours and it would be time to leave.

"We could run," he whispered, suddenly. "Leave, now."

She let out a harsh laugh that made her sound older than her years.

"And go where?" she said. "With what money?"

"I've got a bit saved," he said. "It would be enough to get away."

"What about your mum and Hutch?" she argued, although the idea was tempting, so tempting. "It would kill them if you left."

The fight drained from him as quickly as it had come. He couldn't do what had already been done by his father before him. He would not abandon the people he loved, to save himself. It was a matter of personal pride, and it was the lesson he taught new divers every time he took a boat out.

Never make yourself an island.

CHAPTER 18

Phillips stared at the diving rib with a dubious expression on his face and planted his stocky feet firmly on the pier.

"Is that thing safe?"

Pete Tawny exchanged an amused look with Ryan, who hopped onto the boat as if he'd spent his life on the water, barely needing to adjust his balance.

"Of course, it's safe," he called back to his sergeant, and chucked a life jacket in his direction, which Phillips caught as a reflex.

"Aye, I bet that's what Iain Tucker said, n'all," he muttered, and started to shoulder into the cumbersome bright orange jacket.

After a few minutes' cajolery, Phillips found himself clinging to the edge of the boat as it headed out onto the open water and steered a course for the Farne Islands. If he was able to overlook the motion of the water, which played merry havoc with his insides, he might have found the view breath-taking. The day had turned overcast as morning gave way to afternoon and thick, puffy clouds covered the sky in a blanket of steel-grey mist. Now and then, the sun broke through and glittering rays of light bounced off the water, so brightly he had to shade his eyes. To the north, a cluster of rocky islands came into view and, further still, the tiny outline of a lighthouse.

"How're you holding up?" Ryan raised his voice above the sound of the waves and the engine.

Phillips blinked the sea spray from his eyes and looked across at his friend, whose eyes were clear and shone with adventure, while his black hair ruffled in the wind. There were only fifteen years between them but, in that moment, Phillips experienced a wave of fatherly pride and found himself wondering what it might have been like to have a son. One who made him take boat rides to God only knew where, to look at rocks and speak to bird conservationists in the name of murder investigation.

"It's not as bad as I thought," he admitted, and risked taking his hand off the rail.

His stomach gave a violent lurch as his legs wobbled, and Ryan threw out an arm to catch him as Phillips made a grab for the rail again.

"Steady," Ryan said. "Think of it like riding a horse. Try to go with the natural motion of the boat, rather than against it."

Phillips rolled his eyes.

"Oh, aye, because I'm a regular equestrian, me."

Ryan laughed.

"Alright, bad example. Look, just try not to fall overboard in the next five minutes. We're almost at Inner Farne."

Sure enough, Tawny slowed the boat as they reached a narrow channel known as 'Wideopen Gut', which ran between Inner Farne—the island closest to the mainland—and its nearest neighbour.

"Bit of a gruesome name, isn't it?" Phillips remarked, as they bobbed through the Gut.

Tawny smiled, but didn't turn around. He knew better than to take his eyes off the sea at this point, even for a second.

"Aye, they've come up with some grisly names, over the years," he agreed. "Almost at the landing, now, lads."

Whinstone cliffs rose majestically from the waves, the sheer rock face spattered with the waste of thousands of birds who had nested in its crevices and circled the air during the breeding season in the summer months. But now, the island was tranquil, with only the odd, plaintive cry rising overhead. It was an eerie, beautiful place, unlike anything they'd seen before, and the three men fell silent as they passed through scenery that might have looked the same a thousand years before.

Tawny guided the boat towards the landing jetty on Inner Farne with skilful ease and, soon after, Ryan helped Phillips off the boat again, demonstrating the kind of patience he might have shown his maiden aunt. They walked carefully along a slippery boardwalk past a small, ancient building Tawny told them was deliberately mis-spelled 'The Fishehouse' and which had, apparently, been built by St. Cuthbert as a kind of miniature hotel for the monks who came to visit him during his years as a hermit on the island.

"And here's Janine," Tawny said, as a tall, grey-haired woman approached them from the direction of a squat, oddly-shaped building with a round tower painted in white which, they were told, had been a former pele tower built in the sixteenth century. "Jan's the island ranger, the one I was telling you about."

Ryan tried not to fall prey to stereotypes but, when he'd imagined the type of person who might choose to live nine months of every year on a nature reserve, cut off from the mainland with only the sea and the wind for company, he had imagined a socially-awkward recluse; somebody unable to look him in the eye and who probably kept baby chicks tucked in the pockets of her waterproof jacket. Instead, they were greeted by a friendly woman with a mile-wide smile and a ready handshake.

"Hi! Welcome to Inner Farne," she said, giving their warrant cards the once-over. "I heard about what happened to Iain, then of course about poor Mandy. I can hardly believe it."

"We're on our way to Longstone, but we wanted to stop off here and have a quick chat, if that's alright with you," Ryan said.

She nodded and began leading them back towards the pele tower.

"Of course. I don't know if I'll be able to help much, but you never know. Come on inside, out of the wind."

Her home was simply furnished but cosy, and an enormous Aga pumped out generous waves of heat as they stepped into the kitchen and began to shed their outer clothing.

"Got a nice pot of coffee on the go, if anybody's interested," she said, once they were settled around a scrubbed pine kitchen table. "Wind's picking up out there."

This last remark was directed at Pete, who nodded his agreement.

"We can't stay too long, if you're wanting to see Longstone," he told the two detectives. "The sea's been changeable the past few days, best not to risk it."

Phillips took a gulp of coffee to steady his nerves for the return journey.

"We'll be quick," Ryan promised, and was grateful when Tawny picked up his mug and tactfully left the room, allowing them some privacy to question Janine alone.

"Pete tells us you're one of the conservationists in charge of overseeing the nature reserve—is that right?"

She joined them at the table and set her cup down on an artisan coaster showing a painted image of Dunstanburgh Castle.

"Yes, I'm one of three rangers. We're based here nine months out of every twelve, usually, but this year I've stayed a bit longer. It was a warm summer," she explained. "That drew out the mating season, so I needed to hang around and make sure the birds were protected."

"What kind of birds?" Phillips asked.

"Oh, all kinds," she said. "We get a lot of Arctic terns, puffins, guillemots, razorbills, cormorants—and quite a few cuddy ducks, of course."

Ryan smiled at that, grateful now that Anna had already briefed him on the alternative name for the common eider duck.

"You must see quite a lot of tourists," he said.

She nodded and took a slurp of coffee.

"Especially during the summer months," she said. "We had to turn some boats away, this year, because the amount of footfall was disturbing the birds. It tails off towards autumn, so things have been a lot quieter recently."

"Do you keep in much with the folk on the mainland?" Phillips asked.

She made a rocking gesture with her hand.

"So-so. I see Pete quite a bit," she said, jerking her chin towards the door he'd recently used. "He runs tours and has to look out for the lighthouse up on Outer Farne, anyway. There's another lighthouse on the island here, too."

"How about Iain Tucker?" Ryan asked. "Did you know him?"

Janine nodded.

"Yes, I've known him as an acquaintance for a few years, now. He did a bit of work with MAST on their underwater projects and he does a lot of shipwreck diving, himself. He stopped off here at least once when he was in the area. I think he liked the birds," she said, and looked swiftly into the bottom of her mug. It didn't seem appropriate to add that they'd once enjoyed a memorable evening when he'd been laid up by the storm and was forced to spend the night. That had been years ago, and she would always think of Iain as a good, kind man, one whose friendship she would miss.

"Do you remember the last time you saw him?"

"Yes," she said. "I remember exactly, because it was the night before I heard he'd been found dead."

Ryan's eyes sharpened.

"Thursday night?"

"Yes, it would have been Thursday night…actually, more like Friday morning. It was around one o'clock."

Phillips made a hasty note.

"Seems an unsociable hour," Ryan said. "Do you mind telling me how you came to see him?"

"Well, it wasn't so much *him*, as his boat, the *Viking Princess*," she clarified. "I haven't been sleeping well, lately, so I was still awake watching a bit of Netflix. I saw the light from the boat reflected in the window, so I stuck my head out of the door to see if I knew who it was. It was blowing a gale, so I was a bit worried that anybody was out on the water, in the middle of it."

"How could you tell it was the *Viking Princess*?" Ryan asked.

She gave him a half-pitying look that translated roughly to 'stupid outsider', before explaining, very slowly, that all boats were not the same.

"Iain had had that boat for five, maybe six years. I've been on it, looked around it, and I've seen it plenty of times on the water or in the harbour when I've been over that way. He paid to moor it there," she added. "Anyway, the usual route through the islands goes through Wideopen Gut, past the landing point here on Inner Farne. That's deliberate, so I can keep track of the boating traffic coming through the nature reserve. It also means I get to see every kind of boat and every kind of owner, unless they flout the rules and use a different route without me knowing about it."

"All the same, it was dark, it was stormy…you're *sure* it was him?" Phillips asked.

She gave him a thin smile.

"I may not be a spring chicken any longer, but I still have my sight," she said. "I recognised the boat, I didn't say I recognised Iain."

Ryan frowned.

"What do you mean?"

She polished off the last of her coffee and set it aside, before linking her hands.

"Every time Iain passed by the landing jetty, he'd honk lightly on his boat horn. Just once, and not too loudly, as a sort of friendly 'hello'. He had his little habits and that was one of them. If it was getting dark, he'd flash his boat light a few times, too," she said. "He didn't do either of those things on Thursday night, although I might not have heard a horn above all the rain."

"You don't think it was Iain," Ryan realised.

She looked troubled, then shook her head.

"When I heard about what had happened the next morning, I realised I hadn't seen the boat coming back. I fell asleep around half-past one, so I might have missed it. That's what I told myself, anyway. But, when Pete said Iain's boat was still missing, I realised it hadn't come back through the Gut. Then I started to wonder whether he'd been the one steering the boat in the first place."

Ryan felt his heart rate quicken.

"And you're sure it passed by at around one?"

She nodded.

"I'd just started the next episode of *Making a Murderer,*" she said. "Scared myself half to death, but I never thought something would happen so close to home."

"The truth is always stranger than fiction," he said, as Tawny re-entered the room and signalled it was time to leave before conditions grew worse. Outside, the wind had begun to whistle through the old window panes of the pele tower and Phillips was looking distinctly unwell.

"One last thing, Janine. Did Iain ever talk to you about a wreck he was searching for, one in particular? Did you ever see him spending time in any particular area, diving?"

She nodded.

"Are you kidding? Iain had been going on about a Viking wreck somewhere around here for as long as I've known him...and I've been Head Ranger here for nine years," she said. "The thing is, when nothing turned up after the first couple of years, people stopped asking him about it. I suppose we didn't want to embarrass him, if he was no closer to finding it."

"How about diving spots?" Ryan said, holding up a hand to stave off any hurrying remarks from Tawny. There was more to learn from Janine, he was sure.

And there was.

"Well, to be honest, the reason I didn't worry too much when I saw his boat out so late is because Iain had been diving after dark for years," she admitted. "It's against the official rules, I know, but he was a very experienced diver. Besides, once you're down to a certain level underwater it's dark regardless of whether the sun's shining above water, especially since there's a lot of coal slurry on the rock bottom."

You should have said something, Ryan thought.

"Anyway," she continued. "Iain had been spending a lot of time way past Knivestone, or at least that's what he said the last time I saw him."

Ryan came slowly to his feet.

"Thanks for the coffee," he said. "If you think of anything else, please get in touch."

She nodded.

"Did I—should I have called the Coastguard, when I saw the boat out that late?" she asked, the words rushing out of her mouth before she could snatch them back.

Ryan gave her a long, level look.

"I think you know the answer to that, already," he said. "But there's no reason to think it would have made any difference to what happened to Iain."

With a polite nod, he stepped back outside and into the driving wind.

CHAPTER 19

As Phillips prepared to face another ordeal on the high seas, MacKenzie banged on the door to *The Cockle Inn* and peered through the window alongside.

"Nobody home?" Yates said.

"The light's still on," MacKenzie replied, and knocked on the door one last time, to be sure. "And it's only two-thirty."

Thirty seconds or so passed, then they heard the rattle of the heavy door being unlocked and it swung open to reveal Hutch standing in the doorway, looking a bit dishevelled.

"Sorry, we're closed," he told them, politely enough.

"Mr Hutchinson? We're from Northumbria CID. I'm Detective Inspector Denise MacKenzie and this is my colleague, Trainee Detective Constable Melanie Yates. We're sorry to disturb you, but we wondered if we could ask you some questions?"

"No—you're not disturbing me, not at all. We were just—ah—just having some quiet time, after the news this morning," he said, and showed them both inside.

Once inside, he fell back into the role of the accommodating host.

"Can I offer you a soft drink or something warmer?"

"That's very kind of you, but no, we're fine," MacKenzie said, taking in their surroundings. The inn was upmarket, she thought, with good quality furnishings and not a bar fly in sight. "We were hoping to be able to speak to Gemma Dawson?"

"Gemma already gave a statement this morning," he said.

Both women gave him bland, meaningless smiles. *Cop smiles,* he thought.

"I can go and get her," he amended, with a slight edge to his voice.

"That would be so kind, thank you," MacKenzie said, and watched him hurry upstairs to find his co-manager.

"I seem to recognise that guy," she said, after a moment. "I wish I could remember where I've seen him before."

"I ran background checks on all the residents here," Yates told her. "Ryan requested it, yesterday. Paul Hutchinson's got no previous; none of them have, apart from Gemma's son, Josh, who accepted a caution when he was eighteen for possession of marijuana."

"Hardly a capital offence," MacKenzie was bound to say. "Fairly standard eighteen-year-old behaviour, not that I'd know much about it."

Before she could take measures to prevent it, she found herself imagining what it might be like to parent a teenager, one who got himself into scrapes with the law.

She wondered what it might feel like to carry a baby in her womb, or to worry about their first day at school. She'd seen approximations on television, in films, in the books she'd read and from the friends she'd spoken to, over the years. But she'd never known motherhood, with its highs and lows, its simplicity and complexity.

It did no good to dwell on things she couldn't change, MacKenzie told herself. She was too old to be thinking of children; much too old.

When Yates spoke again, she was glad of the distraction.

"I wonder why Josh didn't take his father's name?"

MacKenzie dragged her eyes away from a large wooden sign above the bar which read, 'NO RIFF RAFF' in fancy painted gold letters, and faced the younger woman.

"What do you mean?"

"I mean, why doesn't he go by 'Josh Hutchinson'?" she said, keeping her voice low. "Do you think they don't get on?"

"He's the boy's uncle, not his father," MacKenzie replied. "It was in Ryan's summary."

Yates flushed. It wasn't like her not to be diligent in her work; then again, she'd been distracted, mostly by her newfound attraction for DC Lowerson. It was galling to know she could be so affected, and she had a firm word with herself about it.

"Sorry," she muttered. "I must have missed it."

But MacKenzie shrugged it off, and a moment later they were re-joined by Hutch and a woman they presumed to be Gemma Dawson. From the photos they'd seen of the various persons of interest and material witnesses Ryan had tacked to the wall in their temporary Incident Room, their first thought was that she did not resemble her son at all. Where Gemma was blonde—albeit, helped a little by the hairdresser, nowadays—and blue-eyed, her son had curly dark hair, almost as dark as Ryan's, and brown eyes of a different shape to his mother's.

"Sorry to keep you waiting," Gemma said, a bit breathless from her mad rush to pull on some clothes and run a brush through her hair. "Paul told me you're from CID?"

"Yes, we wanted to ask you some questions about the late Mandy Jones."

Gemma walked across to the bar, where she busied herself making coffee, which they politely refused.

"How long had you known Amanda Jones?"

"We were at school together," Gemma said. "We all were," she added, with a smile for Hutch who was hovering protectively nearby.

"Was she a friend of yours?"

There was an almost imperceptible pause, then Gemma shrugged.

"We rubbed along," she said, not wishing to speak ill of the dead. "She came in every now and again, especially since Daisy works for us."

"I see. I'm sorry to ask you to go over everything again, Ms Dawson, but can you tell us how you came to find her body this morning?"

Gemma's eyes became clouded and the buoyant mood she'd enjoyed for the last couple of hours began to fade away.

"I'm trying not to think about it," she said.

"We understand, but it's part of our job to go over the facts. It would help us if you could try."

Gemma nodded.

"I was up early today. I couldn't really sleep, last night, because I was thinking about poor Iain. It's awful, having all this happen on your doorstep," she said, and they nodded sympathetically. "Anyway, since I was already up, I decided to take the dog for a walk."

As if he had overheard her last few words, the dog nosed its way around the edge of the bar and looked up at the newcomers with a quizzical look in its eyes.

Yates tickled the dog's ears, obligingly.

"Around what time was that?" MacKenzie asked.

"It was just as the sun was coming up—maybe, seven, seven-fifteen? It's all in the statement I gave—"

"We appreciate it," MacKenzie murmured, and gave her an encouraging smile. "It must have been a beautiful sunrise. We miss that, living in the city."

Gemma smiled in return. There was nothing more flattering than when a stranger complimented your home and the patch of sky she had claimed as her very own.

"It was lovely," she agreed. "All reds and yellows, after the storm the night before. I strolled down towards the harbour with the dog and I thought I'd waste some time before the bakery opened."

"Where did you go?"

"It was the dog who led the way, really," Gemma said, with a grimace. "He kept tugging me down towards the lime kilns. I don't usually walk down that way but since I wasn't in a hurry, I let him choose the direction. I can't help thinking I wish I hadn't, then somebody else would have found her."

MacKenzie understood what she meant; discovering a body wasn't usually included on anyone's Bucket List of life experiences.

"Mandy's family are grateful that you found her and reported it," was all she said. "Did you call the police right away?"

Gemma nodded.

"There was nobody around that I could see, so I rang Carole."

"That's Carole Kirby," MacKenzie repeated, for Yates' benefit. "The local sergeant in charge of Seahouses Police Station?"

"Yes, we sometimes do pilates together, so I just rang her landline number."

While MacKenzie was focused on Gemma, Yates' eyes had strayed towards the man standing quietly beside her.

"We have to ask a number of routine questions as part of our enquiries," she said, in the kind of no-nonsense tone that made MacKenzie proud. "Could you tell us where you both were during the hours of nine p.m. last night and seven o'clock this morning?"

There was an awkward pause.

"Ah—do we need a solicitor or anything?"

Yates' eyes strayed towards MacKenzie, who waited for her to see it through. There would be many times during her time as a murder detective—once she passed the exam—where she'd have to ask difficult, uncomfortable questions. Questioning a witness—who might also be a suspect—about where they were during the relevant timeframe was the least of it.

"No, Mr Hutchinson, you don't need a solicitor unless you feel you would like one," Yates replied, in even tones. "As I say, these are routine questions we're asking of everybody who knew or came into contact with the deceased."

That seemed to satisfy him, and Yates breathed a sigh of relief.

"Um, well, we had a bit of a long day, yesterday, didn't we?" he asked of the woman next to him, who nodded. "Your colleagues were here until late in the day, questioning us about Iain Tucker, and I spent a bit of time getting together the CCTV footage. Then, the bar and restaurant were pretty full all evening."

"Nothing like a bit of juicy murder to bring people together," Gemma said, sarcastically.

"True enough," he said. "The kitchen was busy right up until final orders, and it took forever to get people out at closing time."

"Which was?"

"Well, we closed a bit earlier last night, around midnight. Everyone was exhausted. Josh and Daisy left a bit before then, after her shift ended—"

"About eleven," Gemma put in.

"Yes, around then, and Gemma and I spent a bit longer tidying the place up. We locked up and went straight to bed, afterwards. Josh has his own key," he added.

MacKenzie looked across at Yates, waiting to see if she'd ask another difficult question, and was pleased when she did.

"Ah, this is a bit delicate, but can I ask whether you, ah, co-habit?"

The pair looked at each other and giggled like schoolchildren. There was no other word for it.

"I suppose we do, don't we?"

"I hope so," Hutch murmured, smiling down into her eyes.

"So, just to be clear, you went up to bed together?"

"Since you're so interested, *no*, we didn't go to bed together last night," Gemma almost snapped. She was a woman who valued her privacy and always had done. It stemmed from being the butt of so much local gossip after Kris left, she supposed, but the thought of being the topic of other people's conversation was abhorrent.

"I went up to my flat on the first floor, and I heard Hutch going up to his flat directly above ours not long after."

"Thank you," Yates murmured. "Is that your recollection too, sir?"

He seemed surprised that she would check.

"Yes, I went upstairs not long afterwards. I heard Josh come back in around twenty-past twelve, too."

While Yates made a note, Hutch turned to MacKenzie.

"Do you have any leads?" he asked.

"We're pursuing all lines of enquiry."

After the two women left, Hutch turned to Gemma.

"I've been thinking, we should ask if Daisy wants to move in with us here, for the time being."

Gemma thought of her son and his girlfriend under the same roof—and of all the 'bumps in the night'—and opened her mouth to reject the idea.

"They're grown adults," he reminded her, before she'd had time to utter the first syllable. "Now that our relationship is…*different*, you could bunk in with me and let them have your apartment, or vice versa, whatever you prefer. They'd have their own space and she'd have company around her."

She looked up into his bright blue eyes and any further argument died in her throat. It made sense, what he suggested, and it was the right thing to do.

"Alright," she said, feeling a weight settle against her chest. "We can speak to Josh when he comes home."

Hutch pressed a kiss to the top of her head.

"There, that wasn't so hard."

CHAPTER 20

Waves rocked Pete Tawny's boat as they navigated their way through Staple Sound, a rough channel of water separating the two main clusters of islands which together made up the Farnes. Closest to the mainland was Inner Farne, where they had left Janine Richardson to her bird-watching, while Outer Farne lay further out to sea and, even further beyond, the tiny islet known as Knivestone.

To understand the life Iain Tucker had lived and to get a better feel for the terrain, Ryan and Phillips placed their trust in the capable hands of the lighthouse keeper and watched with frank admiration as he guided the boat through strong currents, all the while singing a bastardized version of the late, and great, David Bowie's *Starman.* In other circumstances, it might have made them laugh, but they were otherwise occupied in clinging on to the safety rail for grim life.

"See over there!" Tawny called out, pointing to the port side. "That's Gun Rocks. If you dive down a few metres, you'll see old cannons lying under the water. Nobody knows which wreck they came from, but the seals love 'em!"

Ryan grinned, momentarily forgetting the reason they were there.

"You can understand how Iain got into all this, can't you?" he called out to Frank, not minding as another wave sprayed salty water into his hair and eyes. "It's an adventure."

Phillips looked at him as though he'd sprouted three heads.

"You've gone daft, that's what," he declared. "The sooner we get you back on dry land, the better. This isn't *Pirates of the Caribbean*, y'nah."

Ryan grinned fiercely and, for a moment, had the look of a pirate about him.

"Doesn't it make you feel *alive*, Frank, being out here on the water?"

Phillips nearly lost his footing.

"I'll tell you what makes me feel alive, son. A night in with the missus and the phone switched off."

Ryan laughed again and, with some small sense of achievement, Phillips realised it was starting to become a habit.

"Lighthouse up ahead!" Tawny called back to them and, as they rounded another rocky outcrop, Outer Farne appeared with its pretty red and white striped lighthouse which had once been home to Grace Darling.

Ryan leaned forward to speak to Tawny more clearly.

"Whereabouts did you see Iain?"

"Over there," Tawny replied, pointing in the direction of the deceptively flat rocks spreading out beneath the lighthouse.

Ryan had thought Longstone lighthouse stood on the most easterly island of the Farnes, but he remembered what Janine had told them about Iain exploring the waters even further out to sea and looked around the wider vicinity.

"Is that Knivestone, over there?" he asked, and peered through the rain towards an isolated rock that must have been a bane to sailors for centuries.

"Aye, that's it," Tawny replied. "The diving schools do tours to Knivestone to see the *Abyssinia.* It was a German steamer which sank in 1921. Go down about twenty feet and you'll find her broken up all around the gullies."

"Not today, mate," Phillips called out, and Tawny chuckled.

Ryan looked once more towards the slippery, aptly-named hunk of rock lying in wait for unsuspecting seafarers and felt the hairs on the back of his neck prickle. He could hardly imagine a young girl and her father braving weather much worse than this, risking their own lives against the overwhelming power of the ocean. It was just as difficult to imagine a quiet, introverted marine archaeologist pitting himself against the tides in the dead of night, no matter how much he'd loved diving.

Someone, or *something*, had driven him to it, and ultimately onto the rocks, too.

Back at the Coastguard's Office, MacKenzie and Yates returned to find Lowerson hunched over a laptop computer with a half-finished cheese toastie sitting forlornly at his elbow. Across the room, a police constable was reading a dog-eared glossy magazine as they manned the telephone, while a small electric fan heater whirred away in the corner and circulated the musty air.

"Talk about staff shortages," MacKenzie said. "Did the rest of the team call in sick or something?"

Lowerson looked up and stretched his arms above his head to ease out the kinks, an action which drew Yates' reluctant attention.

"Ryan and Phillips should be on their way back," he said. "They went out on Pete Tawny's boat to speak to one of the rangers on Inner Farne. Alex Walker's still trying to map the last movements of Tucker's boat to see where it ended up and, as for the rest of them? I haven't got the foggiest."

Yates laughed a bit too loudly and MacKenzie gave her an odd look.

"Have you heard from Faulkner?" she enquired, turning her attention back to Lowerson.

"Yeah, I had a word with him earlier. He says they've finished going over Mandy Jones' office and they're making a start on her cottage, soon. Ideally, they'll need the place to themselves, so one of us will probably need to have a word with Daisy and see if she has anywhere else to stay, for the time being."

MacKenzie reached for the tin of custard creams and was alarmed to find it completely empty.

"What happened here?" she demanded, all thoughts of murder momentarily cast aside.

"Take it up with your husband," Lowerson replied, holding his hands out, palms facing in the universal sign for peace. "I had nothing to do with it—well, I had three biscuits to do with it."

"The man's a menace," she muttered, and stalked across to dump the tin into the large plastic bin in the corner of the room. "Did Faulkner tell you anything else?"

"All he told me was that the blood pattern and general trace evidence suggests Mandy died where she fell, inside the lime kiln. There's no sign of any other murder weapon, either, so they've bagged the iron hook up for testing. He's waiting for approval to put a rush on it, guv, otherwise it'll take days."

"Approve it," she said, and almost clapped a hand over her own mouth. That was Ryan's call to make, not hers.

"Approve what?" the man himself asked, as he entered the room rubbing a towel over his slick wet hair. Phillips trailed behind him looking like a bedraggled cat and, for the life of her, MacKenzie couldn't say why she found it so appealing.

"Ah, we were just talking about approving the resources to allow the CSIs to hurry along the testing of the samples they've taken today," she said. "I was saying we should approve it."

"Good thinking," Ryan said. "Would've done the same thing, myself. What's next on the agenda?"

MacKenzie stared at him for a moment and he raised a single, dark eyebrow.

"What?"

"I—nothing."

"Good. For a moment there, I thought you were going to tell me you doubted your own good judgment," he said, with his usual insight. "We had a bit of luck out on the water today—"

Phillips let out an eloquent snort, which Ryan chose to ignore.

"We believe Iain Tucker's boat entered Wideopen Gut at around one in the morning, on Friday. Working backwards, it takes thirty or so minutes to get from Seahouses to Inner Farne, which is where he was seen entering the Gut, so that tells us he set off from Seahouses at around half-past midnight or a bit before. Assuming for now that he was still alive and piloting the boat, that gives us a window for time of death of between roughly one a.m. and ten-fifteen a.m., which is when he was discovered, albeit the pathologist thinks he'd been dead for up to fifteen hours prior to that."

"Sea exposure makes it hard to settle on a time of death," Phillips put in, and dabbed a towel over his balding head.

"Agreed. If Iain died around one a.m. or thereabouts, it may still be consistent," Ryan agreed. "That's all presuming our witness, Janine Richardson, is reliable."

"At our end, we still haven't located any eyewitnesses or managed to narrow down Mandy's time of death,"

MacKenzie said, then turned to Lowerson. "Unless you happened to get hold of any CCTV?"

He nodded.

"I've been in contact with a few of the businesses on the high street and down by the harbour," he said. "They were expecting the call, since Frank had already been in touch with them about Iain, yesterday. The footage is starting to come through but, given Mandy's probable route from her home to the harbour, I'll hazard a guess there'll be very little except maybe a couple of cameras near the traffic lights which might have picked her up. Even then, everyone agrees the fog was heavy last night, so I'm not holding my breath for good visibility."

Ryan listened with only half an ear, far more impressed by the way Lowerson was settling back into his work after so long away from the office than by his ability to drum up CCTV footage. Work wasn't everything, but it was a step in the right direction and, after all he'd been through, Jack deserved to get his life back on track.

"Did you manage to do those background checks, Mel?"

She nodded.

"We were just talking about it earlier, sir. I ran standard checks on Paul Hutchinson, Gemma and Josh Dawson, Daisy Jones and the people who were listed as being present at the time Iain Tucker made his announcement about the wreck. The lists provided by Gemma and Paul were almost identical, making twenty-eight people in total, thirty-two, if you count the Shaeffer family who stayed overnight at the same time as Iain."

"And? Anybody currently on the run for multiple murders?" Ryan asked, hopefully.

"Unfortunately—or, *fortunately*—not, sir. None of the permanent residents at the inn had anything worse than a caution for possession of marijuana between them. Other than that, there was a smattering of speeding tickets and low-level assaults for a couple of the locals."

"All very law-abiding," Phillips said, perversely disappointed. "What about Tucker's ex—and Mandy's too? Anybody come into their lives lately who might have held a grudge?"

"Iain Tucker's ex-wife and son went into Newcastle yesterday afternoon to identify his body and I took a statement from each of them," Yates said. "They were both devastated, for one thing, and both very much alibied during the relevant timescale. There's no way either of them could have been responsible."

Phillips clucked his tongue.

"As for Mandy Jones, we're still having trouble finding any record of Daisy's father. There hasn't been anybody but the two of them listed on the electoral roll since Mandy's parents transferred the cottage over to her, so it's hard to get a steer on whether there was anybody significant in her life, other than her daughter. Should I ask Daisy?"

Ryan thought of the young woman and felt a stab of concern. If Mandy had been the only family Daisy had known and her father was no longer in their lives, it would rub salt into an open wound to quiz her about his absence now.

"Try to find a record of Daisy's birth certificate, instead," he suggested. "If you still come up empty-handed, we'll ask her then."

Yates nodded.

"We're still trying to get hold of Mandy Jones' financials, her bank statements and all that. Faulkner's taken her laptop and iPad into the lab for testing and he'll work with the tech team to see if there's anything interesting on the hard drives. We'll look at her e-mail history and social media accounts but that'll take another day, at least," Lowerson said, and made a grab for the stale toastie, before thinking better of it.

"What about her employer?" Phillips thought aloud. "You'll probably need to have a word with the Harbour Commissioners before Faulkner can go over the computer in her office, anyway, since it's their property."

MacKenzie nodded.

"It's a bit of a convoluted set-up," she explained. "The harbour is held on trust for the benefit of the community by a board of Commissioners, which is made up of local bigwigs. I contacted the general number on the website and left a message, but I'll chase it up later today and see if I can get hold of one of them."

Ryan hitched a leg up onto the edge of the table in the Break Room-cum-Incident Room and folded his arms as he considered the woman who had been Mandy Jones.

"I'd chase the bank again," he said. "The position she held made her a bribe-risk. I want to see her financial statements."

MacKenzie nodded her agreement.

"Will do. How's the Tucker investigation coming along?"

Ryan heaved a meaningful sigh.

"Let me see, now. We've got no conclusive autopsy report, no eyewitnesses other than Janine Richardson, no interesting mobile phone records, no meaningful CCTV footage or forensic evidence and definitely no handwritten confession to the man's murder. In all honesty, I'd be struggling to justify keeping this one open, if it weren't for Mandy Jones turning up so soon afterwards."

As if somebody upstairs had heard his plight, Alex Walker rushed into the room at that very moment brandishing a rolled-up map of the Farne Islands.

"I've done it," he announced, a bit smugly. "I've mapped Iain Tucker's last known PLB locations."

They crowded around the table as he spread out the map, which had been annotated with a series of multi-coloured dots and arrowed lines which must have taken him most of the day to plot.

"Each of the colours represents the PLB's movements over the past four days," he explained. "I haven't gone back any further than that because I reckon this tells us all we need to know."

The room fell silent as they studied the regular journeys Iain Tucker had made in the days leading up to his death.

Sometimes, the route diverged, but at least two things remained consistent each time. First, that he always left Seahouses and headed towards Wideopen Gut and past the landing at Inner Farne, corroborating what Janine had told them. Second, that he had consistently travelled to a specific coordinate roughly five-hundred metres off the rocky edge of Knivestone before continuing onward in an almost straight line back to Seahouses.

"He went the roundabout way so that people wouldn't follow him," Ryan murmured. "He wanted to lose himself in the islands before heading up to Knivestone."

"The GPS records show these same coordinates every day, always after four o'clock," Walker said.

"As dark was drawing in," MacKenzie murmured.

"After the other diving vessels finished for the day, too," Ryan pointed out. "He didn't want spectators."

"If only he'd kept his mouth shut," Phillips said, sadly. "The poor bloke might've still been alive."

Ryan straightened up and put a hand on Walker's shoulder.

"Thanks, Alex. This is a huge leap forward and I'm grateful."

Walker gave an embarrassed shrug.

"Don't mention it. Look, I've got to get back to my day job but let me know if there's anything else I can do."

"You might as well let the others know that they'll be inundated with marine archaeologists tomorrow morning," Ryan said, then immediately thought better of it. "On second thought—"

He strode across to the door and closed it with a soft *click*.

"Iain Tucker probably lost his life because he knew these coordinates," he said, turning around to face them. "Because of that, this information goes no further than these four walls. Agreed?"

There were nods around the room.

"Whoever it is will realise soon enough that we're searching for the wreck," Lowerson pointed out. "What difference does a few hours make?"

Ryan turned to him with serious eyes.

"In some cases, it's the difference between life and death."

CHAPTER 21

While Ryan talked his Chief Constable into spending a portion of the Constabulary's already strained resources on a jointly-funded expedition to find a Viking wreck, on the tenuous basis that it may provide answers relevant to Iain Tucker's death, another man made the journey from Seahouses to the stately town of Alnwick, fifteen miles to the south.

The streets were quiet by the time Josh arrived and a light drizzle coated the windscreen of his car, giving the passing scenery a general sense of gloom. He found a parking space and hurried towards his destination, conscious that he was running exactly on time but couldn't afford to be late.

The little Indian restaurant was a quiet, inconspicuous place that tended to attract visitors from all walks of life. The staff were discreet and asked few questions other than what their patrons would like to eat or drink, which made it the ideal place for a private meeting.

The door jingled above his head to announce his entry and Josh glanced around the room to see if the other member of his party had arrived.

Yes, unfortunately.

Josh headed over to the little two-seater table and slid into the unoccupied chair, feeling his heart begin to thud against his chest as he came face to face with the person he believed to have killed Mandy Jones and who might choose to kill again, if he wasn't careful.

Next time, it could be a member of his family—or Daisy.

"You're right on time."

Josh nodded as the waiter poured two glasses of tepid water, then retreated.

"I needed to talk to you."

"So I gather."

Josh struggled to contain his frustration as the waiter returned again, this time with poppadums and a selection of chutneys. He didn't want any food; he wanted to get the words out quickly, before he lost his nerve.

"Did you—have you heard what happened to Mandy Jones?"

"Of course. Very inconvenient, for all concerned."

Josh stared in horrified disbelief, then lowered his eyes. He was always the first to look away.

"You remind me a lot of your father," came the unexpected remark and it slid like a deft arrow between his ribs and into the soft, vulnerable centre of Josh's heart. He felt it keenly, the longing to know every scrap of information about the man who had left them before he was born. He'd found old pictures of his father, ones taken around the same age he was now, and they might have been twins. He wished he had known him, even a little, if only to tell him what a useless, self-serving coward he'd been to run away.

Anger followed on the tails of sadness. Anger at himself for being so predictable and so easy to manipulate.

"I'm nothing like him."

"How would you know?" came the sly rejoinder. "You're remarkably similar, not only in looks but in temperament. You both prefer to take the easy road."

Josh felt a red mist descend and his fingers gripped the table.

"You think this is *easy*? You think I like having to—"

"Quiet."

The word was rapped out like a single gunshot and Josh rocked back in his seat, as if he'd been slapped. There, in a crowded restaurant surrounded by strangers, it was easy to forget the danger of speaking too loudly. It was a precarious balance he needed to find, if he wanted to avoid ending up like Iain Tucker or Mandy Jones.

The sound of a poppadum being broken in half intruded into his thoughts.

"I don't want to be involved anymore," Josh whispered. "I want out."

There was no immediate reply; only the sound of another poppadum crumbling. Tension strummed on the air between them and Josh shuffled in his seat, wishing he had the nerve to get up and walk away.

But, of course, he didn't.

"I'm afraid that won't be possible."

"Wh-what do you mean? I've done everything I was supposed to. I don't want to be a part of it anymore," Josh repeated, hating the desperate sound of his voice.

The waiter hovered again, asking if they'd like to order their food.

"We'll have another few minutes, please."

It was not a request.

"You can have the money back," Josh said, once the waiter had gone, then wondered where the hell he'd find the cash to replace all that he'd taken. It didn't matter; he'd take out a loan against the business, if need be. Anything to extricate himself from the living hell that was, at least in part, of his own creation.

"I don't think you heard me the first time, Joshua. There is no severance clause to our relationship; no option to buy me out. I suggest you come to terms with it or there will be consequences."

A moment later, Josh found himself sitting alone at the table, his dinner partner having departed. He drew in several long breaths and then fumbled in his wallet for some notes to pay the meagre bill.

"Thank you, sir," the waiter said, and had already forgotten Josh's face by the time the door jangled shut behind him.

"Need a lift?"

Yates jumped slightly as Lowerson appeared behind her chair.

"Sorry, didn't mean to startle you," he said. "I wasn't sure whether you brought a car this morning, so I thought I'd check in case you needed to hitch a ride back into the city."

"Is it that time, already?" she asked, and swivelled around to look up at the clock on the wall. Unlike the cheap plastic time-keeper which graced the interior of the Criminal Investigation Department, this one was an antique made of polished burr walnut.

Its ornate dials read *five-forty-five.*

Ryan was seated across the room with his mobile clutched in one hand while his other flew across a notepad as he made intermittent remarks concerning budgeting and resources. He caught their eye, looked at the clock himself, then made a waving signal to indicate they should go home.

"Take the opportunity, while you can. There isn't much more you can do here tonight, so you may as well get a good night's sleep," MacKenzie said. "It'll be another long day, tomorrow."

"Alright," Yates said, and turned back to Lowerson. "Um, I brought my own car, but I can walk with you."

She felt her neck redden with embarrassment.

"Sure, let me grab my coat."

After they headed out into the darkened streets, Phillips waited for a respectable ten seconds before passing comment.

"D' you think it's been long enough, then?"

MacKenzie looked up from her inspection of Mandy Jones' social media accounts, which seemed mostly to have consisted of heavily made-up 'selfies' and videos of cute-looking animals performing tricks for their human owners.

"Long enough for what?"

"For Jack to be thinking of other lasses, that's what."

Her eyebrows flew into her hairline.

"Who are you, now, the Town Matchmaker?"

Phillips spread his hands.

"All I'm saying is, Mel's a nice girl. He could do a lot worse."

"That may be true, Frank, but the heart doesn't always follow what the head says. If it did, I'd be Mrs Liam Neeson, by now."

She grinned at his affronted face.

"Aye, well, he'd have to fight me off, first," Phillips muttered.

"Who'd be fighting who off?" Ryan asked, having finally finished negotiating terms with the various parties to a shipwreck salvage operation that would begin the very next morning.

"Never mind," MacKenzie told him. "Did you have any luck with Morrison?"

Ryan ran his fingers through his hair as he replayed the conversation he'd just had with their Chief Constable.

"Yeah, eventually. She's given the go-ahead to join forces with MAST to do a sweep of the area around the coordinates Alex has mapped out," he said. "She hasn't authorised much but it's enough to fund a morning, maybe a full day. If we're right about those coordinates, hopefully it won't take longer than that because we'll be in the right place already."

"X marks the spot?" Phillips said.

"Let's hope so," Ryan said. "I spoke to Ursula Tan from the MAST team and she says they've got the equipment they'll need, since they're already working on a long-term project further down the coast at Beadnell. I got the strong impression she'd drop that one like a sack of hot coals if she finds something on the seabed over here," he added. "I also spoke to Iain's former colleague and everybody's favourite Big Shot, Jasper Vaughn, too."

And that had been a tiresome conversation, made more so by the man's natural propensity to speak rather than to listen.

"He might not be at the top of my Christmas card list but there's no denying the man knows his onions when it comes to marine archaeology," he said. "We may need him to find Iain's wreck."

"And, what if there's nothing down there, after all?" Phillips was forced to ask.

"Then, we'll have a bunch of very disappointed archaeologists, an angry Chief Constable and an even bigger mystery on our hands," Ryan said. "Because, if Iain Tucker and Mandy Jones didn't die because they knew about a Viking shipwreck, it means they died because they knew about something else."

He paused, thinking of a time, not so long ago, when a dangerous cult known as 'The Circle' had operated in these parts; where unscrupulous people with psychopathic tendencies had bribed, coerced, threatened, assaulted and often killed in a cycle of greed and blood-lust that had permeated even the uppermost ranks of Northumbria CID. It was possible that it had reconvened, that another group of like-minded narcissists had banded together, springing up again like weeds.

"Keep your eyes and ears open," he told them. "In small places like this, people tend to close ranks. Yesterday, Mandy Jones looked us in the eye and claimed she had no idea why Iain Tucker had died, but now she's ended up meeting with the same fate. If she'd spoken out, things might have ended very differently for her."

"Fear is a great motivator," MacKenzie murmured, thinking of her own personal history. A phantom pain shot up the leg where a long white scar reminded her every day that a knife had once torn cleanly through the muscle.

"Let's hope the tide turns, tomorrow," Ryan said, and meant it in more ways than one. Unless the stormy weather moved on, they would not be able to find the answers they so desperately needed the sea to reveal.

CHAPTER 22

"I remember where I've seen him before."

Much later, back in the little house they shared in Newcastle, MacKenzie paused in the act of brushing her teeth in their en suite bathroom and called out to Frank, who was unbuttoning his work shirt.

"Eh? What's that, love?"

She spat out the toothpaste and walked back into the bedroom.

"I said, I remember where I've seen Paul Hutchinson before. When I was doing a search on missing persons recently, a name flagged up as a possible match for like crimes. He didn't fit, as it turned out, but I had a quick look at the file, anyway. I'm sure it listed Paul Hutchinson as the man's brother. It was covered in the local press, too—there was a picture of Paul taken from when he'd given an interview."

"You've got a memory like an elephant," Phillips said.

"And don't you forget it," she joked.

"Well, at least that explains why Josh's father seems to be such a taboo subject," he said. "No pictures, no casual references. It makes you wonder."

"Let's see if I can find anything on it," she muttered, snatching up her mobile phone from the bedside table to run a quick Google search.

Phillips climbed onto the bed beside her and leaned back against a stack of cushions, wondering why in the world anybody would need more than two at any one time.

"Here we go," she said, after a moment. "Paul's brother, Kristopher Reid, was reported missing on 21st October 1995. There doesn't seem to have been much of a police appeal, but there's a bit in the *Northumberland Gazette* about it."

"Different surnames," Phillips remarked. "Must be half-brothers."

MacKenzie passed him the phone so he could look at a grainy photograph of Kris Reid that filled the screen.

"He's the spitting double of his son," he said, moving the screen closer to his eyes, then further away again to accommodate his ageing vision. "Even down to the curly hair."

MacKenzie nodded.

"It says here there was no suggestion of foul play and no evidence of suicide or suicidal intent. His car was found abandoned in the long-stay car park at Newcastle Airport a week after Kristopher went missing and the police concluded he'd gone off the grid of his own accord."

"It happens," Phillips said, scrolling through the article.

"I wonder what he was like," MacKenzie murmured, thinking of a little boy who had never known his father.

"No bloody good, if he'd bugger off and leave his pregnant girlfriend high and dry," Phillips said, with simple logic.

"Plenty of people agreed with you," she said, scanning the old article. "*Local sources who wish to remain anonymous have told this paper that the missing man was known to have an unreliable temperament*."

"There you go," Phillips sniffed. "I tell you what, if my old Da had ever caught me trying to do a runner on a lass, he'd have given me the hidin' of my life."

"We'll not argue about the way to ensure a long and happy relationship," she said dryly. "But I'll venture to say that nobody would really want to spend their days with somebody who was only there out of a sense of obligation."

"Depends how much they love them," Phillips argued, and MacKenzie fell silent because he was right.

Love knew no reason, sometimes.

"Do you have everything you need?" Gemma asked, and reached out to stroke a gentle hand over the girl's hair.

"Yes, thanks," Daisy replied.

She felt utterly drained, her tears having dried up during the course of the day to be replaced by a dull, burning sensation at the back of her eyes. Her head felt fuzzy and unreal, as though she were swimming underwater, and she couldn't quite remember how she'd come to be at the inn, only that Gemma had tucked her into the big double bed that had been hers.

There was still no sign of Josh.

"I wonder where Josh could be," Gemma worried, as if she'd read her mind. "It's getting late."

"I think he was visiting a friend or something," Daisy said, lamely.

Gemma wondered how her son could flit off meeting friends when his girlfriend had just suffered the loss of her mother, but kept her thoughts to herself.

"Well, try to get some sleep now. I'll tell him to be quiet when he comes in."

As she turned away, Daisy stopped her.

"Thanks for looking after me," she whispered, and Gemma's heart wept at the broken sound of her voice. She said nothing but leaned down and pressed a kiss to the girl's head.

"Try to sleep," she repeated.

Downstairs, Hutch still hadn't re-opened the pub, but he had stoked up the log-burner until it roared with cheerful flame.

"I've put Daisy in my room," Gemma told him, coming to settle in a chair beside the fire. "The police are planning to go through Mandy's cottage tomorrow, so it's best that she's here."

"How's she doing?"

"She seems calmer than before."

"Aye, it'll get worse for her before it gets better," he murmured, closing the stove door again and straightening up. "Why didn't you just put her in Josh's room?"

She huffed out a sigh.

"Paul—"

"Gemma, they're in their twenties, for goodness' sake. This isn't the eighteenth century; they'll want to be together."

When she said nothing, he moved across to frame her face in his hands.

"Just like *we* want to be together," he said, hardly believing it was true. "Soon enough, all this nasty business will be behind us and it'll just be you and me again."

She nodded, watching a hunk of paper curl and burst into flame inside the log-burner.

"I hope so," she said. "And, for the record, there's nothing wrong with being old-fashioned. I threw myself into a relationship, once, and look where it got me."

Hutch wouldn't allow his happiness to be dimmed.

"That was a long time ago," he said, firmly. "Kris has gone and he's not coming back."

Just then, a key turned in the outer door and it seemed, just for a moment, as though Kris Reid had come back to prove his brother wrong.

Josh looked between their shocked faces.

"You look as if you've seen a ghost," he said, wearily. "Night."

In the silence that followed, they heard his quick steps as he jogged upstairs and thought of another man who'd moved with the same energy, the same zest for life, and wondered where he was now.

When Ryan returned home after eight o'clock, he found Anna immersed in a volume of Bede's *Ecclesiastical History of the English People.* It was not what he might have described as light bedtime reading, but he supposed she might say the same of the forensic reports and case summaries that made up the majority of his reading material.

She tilted her chin up as he leaned down to give her a kiss.

"Have you eaten?" he asked, and was unsurprised when she shook her head.

"I got a bit engrossed in all this," she said, gesturing to the books spread out across the kitchen table.

"Just as well I stopped off for a take-away," he smiled, and held up a couple of brown paper bags. "Feel like some sweet and sour pork?"

Her stomach gave a timely rumble.

"Have I ever told you how much I love you?"

"Because I keep you in egg fried rice?" He grinned.

"Mostly, it's for your body," she said. "But sometimes it's because you think of me, even when your mind must be full of all kinds of other, more important things."

Ryan paused in the act of unpacking the food and walked across to hunker down beside her chair.

"I always think of you," he said, covering her hands with his own. "Even when I'm neck-deep in a murder investigation, I think of you and of how wonderful it'll feel to come home to you. I'm never happier than when I'm with you, Anna."

She leaned in to kiss him.

"Thank you," she murmured, then walked her fingers up his chest. "You know, I was reading about a Viking warrior today who quite reminded me of you."

"Really?" he said, as his hands snaked around her waist. "You'll have to tell me how similar we are, later."

"Later?"

"I'd say around an hour."

She raised an eyebrow.

"Didn't think you'd have the energy," she said, sticking her tongue in her cheek.

"Never underestimate a Viking warrior."

CHAPTER 23

Sunday, 4th November

The following morning, Ryan entered the Coastguard's Office with a definite spring in his step, whistling *Rudolph the Red-Nosed Reindeer* under his breath, a fact of which he was entirely unaware.

"Thought you said it was too early for Christmassy stuff?" Phillips called out, with a wink for Lowerson. "Seems to me you're as cheerful as Santa's favourite elf."

Ryan looked at the amused faces around the room.

"Nothing wrong with enjoying one's work," he said, haughtily. "Besides, I was whistling *Bohemian Rhapsody*."

"If that was *Bohemian Rhapsody,* I think I just heard Freddie Mercury turning in his grave," Lowerson chipped in.

"Alright, alright," Ryan said, and started to dish out the cups of coffee he'd picked up from a little artisan shop on the way in.

"Lifesaver," MacKenzie told him, and took the first greedy sip. "That's almost better than sex."

Phillips looked across with an accusing eye.

"I said *almost,* Frank."

Ryan checked his watch.

"It's just coming up to eight o'clock," he said. "The marine team will be here any minute now. Phillips, I'll take a wild guess and say that you'd rather not come out on the boat again, so why don't you stick around here?"

"There is a God," his sergeant declared, pressing his palms together. "I'll make myself useful from the comfort and security of dry land."

Right on time, there came a brief knock at the door before it opened to reveal Ursula Tan and a couple of her colleagues from MAST.

"I think Jasper's parking his car outside," she told them. "We managed to rope in a couple of additional divers from the local British Sub-Aqua Club who've been working with us down at Beadnell. We've got a limited window since you can only see Knivestone at low-water and, according to the tide forecast, that means we've got around three hours this morning and possibly another two hours this evening."

"What difference does the water level make?" Phillips asked the obvious question the non-divers amongst them had undoubtedly been thinking.

"It makes visibility easier, for one thing," she replied. "There's a shallow gully which bisects Knivestone island—that's where you'll find the *Abyssinia* wreck. Judging from the coordinates you sent through last night, our theory is that the gully spreads out much further than originally thought, past the intersection through the island and into open sea to the east. With long-term tidal changes and strong water currents, our best guess is that it's altered the silt on the seabed, revealing more of the gulley and perhaps that's what Iain found, the other day. But it's much harder to find and explore gullied areas at high tide."

She paused as the door opened again to reveal Jasper Vaughn, who had returned with his own assistant, a mousy-haired young man he introduced only as 'Michael'.

Ryan looked around at their motley crew and smiled roguishly.

"Let's get this show on the road."

Although they had the coordinates provided by the GPS tracking on Iain Tucker's Personal Locator Beacon, they were only accurate to within five-hundred feet in any direction. A search of his home, office, hotel room and car had not turned up any notes or charts to help narrow their search any further, which Ryan suspected had been a deliberate move on the part of Tucker's killer. It was therefore necessary to use sonar and magnetometry to locate what had come to be known as 'Tucker's Wreck.'

The team of experts from MAST had brought their own dive boat named the *Jolly Roger*, which came equipped with all they would need for a prospecting excursion, including a top-of-the-range magnetometer. However, this was no substitute for local knowledge, so they enlisted Coastal Area Commander Alex Walker to navigate them through waters he knew like the back of his hand.

"Handles differently to the lifeboat," he said, testing the wheel. "Nippy on the water, too. Wouldn't mind something like this, myself."

"Test driving a new one?" Ryan asked.

"Always in the market," Walker grinned. "I've never been on a prospect mission before. Shipwreck diving isn't really my thing, usually, but that could change after this little excursion."

"How come?"

"Just never got into it." He shrugged. "It can be a bit like a gambling addiction, or so I hear. Once you get bitten by the treasure-hunting bug, you keep coming back for more."

Ryan thought of Iain Tucker's obsession and nodded.

"What's that?" he asked, pointing towards a huge, twenty-foot cliff face as they rounded the southern edge of the islands.

"That's 'the Pinnacles,'" Walker replied, and slowed the boat a little so Ryan could get a better look at the jutting rocks which looked to have sprung from the sea like kryptonite. "That's where you'll see thousands of birds nesting during the summer, puffins mainly. It's even more impressive underwater; the rock goes down much further below."

As Ryan listened, a thought struck him quite forcefully: he was *happy*. There were always snatched moments of happiness in his life, mostly thanks to Anna and the friends he had around him, but lasting contentment tended to elude him. He supposed that was understandable; it had been an eventful few years, filled with loss and trauma, and he was only human after all. A person needed time to heal.

He didn't know what the future would hold or what fresh trauma awaited him around the corner but, standing there on the dive boat with the wind blowing against his face, he could say he felt truly happy knowing he was doing what he'd been born to do, living where he felt most at home, learning the land that had adopted him as its own.

"Anna not coming along today?" Walker asked, and then glanced over his shoulder to make sure they wouldn't be overheard. "I thought maybe Jasper had put her off."

Ryan smiled at the unlikely prospect of Anna being put off her passion for local history by anyone or anything.

"No, nothing like that. She's teaching today," he said. "Marine excavation isn't her forte anyway; she said she'd swing by if we bring up any artefacts, though. I was speaking to Vaughn this morning and, say what you like about him, the man's useful to know. He's a dendrochronologist as part of his archaeological repertoire which, he told me at length, is the analysis of tree rings to help date the wood used to build a vessel."

"All the way back to Viking times?"

"Let's see if we can find anything at all, first," Ryan said.

Alex slowed the boat as they approached the northern edge of Knivestone, fully visible since the water was at a low level, as Ursula had said it would be. Jasper Vaughn stepped inside the cabin armed with a nautical chart, presumably to make sure that Walker hadn't suffered an amnesiac episode and was no longer able to read a chart for himself, nor operate the high-tech navigational deck the boat had fitted.

"Bear north, north-west," he said, without any pleasantries.

"Aye, aye, Cap'n," Walker replied, with a heavy layer of sarcasm.

"What happens when we get there?" Ryan asked, to pre-empt any forthcoming argument.

"We'll try the sonar and the magnetometer," Vaughn replied. "There are several different kinds but, to keep things simple, Ursula and I have agreed to use synthetic aperture sonar, or SAS. It's more expensive but it gives a higher resolution."

"How does it work?" Ryan asked, as they left Knivestone rock behind them and motored into open waters.

"It's a sophisticated form of post-processing sonar data," Vaughn replied, with an air of condescension Ryan might have found irritating if he hadn't been in such a good mood. "Very simply put, you move the sonar device, which is attached to the boat, in a straight line to illuminate the same spot on the seabed with a series of acoustic pings. Those sounds bounce off any large, foreign entity that might be lying on the seabed. It's integrated with a navigation system and motion sensor to help process the data and should provide a good quality image of anything that's down there as well as being able to tell us the distances between here and the seabed."

"And what about the magnetometer?" Ryan asked. "I wouldn't have thought there'd be much metal on a Viking wreck."

"Why don't I show you?"

Vaughn led Ryan to the back of the boat and pointed to what looked, at first glance, like an enormous blue fishing rod with a long PVC nose cone at the end of it.

"It's attached to the boat by this retractable cord," he explained, and gestured towards what looked like a bright yellow hosepipe. "You lower it into the water and drag it through the area you're interested in. It detects anomalies in the Earth's magnetic field which occur when new, alien magnetic fields are superimposed, the kind created when ferrous materials gather on the seabed."

"Like old warships?" Ryan asked.

"Exactly. We don't expect to find anything new on that score," he said. "The more modern wrecks around this area have already been catalogued and we know their positions."

"If we were prospecting for something more recent, we'd use ultraviolet light," Ursula said, joining their conversation. "Most metals, apart from gold, disintegrate over time and the ions dissipate into the water. That shows up under UV, which helps to find wrecks from the First and Second World Wars."

"Or a hoard of silver coins," Ryan suggested.

"Never happened yet," she said. "When I first got into this business, I thought I'd be bringing up pieces of eight in no time, but it's mostly been chunks of old wood and metal."

"Never say never," Vaughn muttered, and walked away to join Walker at the front of the boat without another word.

Ryan considered the man's retreating back and, in the awkward silence that followed his abrupt departure, Ursula spoke up.

"You know, he's always been that way," she said, looking out across the sea. "Zero social skills; always looking for the next win, the next thing to make him famous. He's the most ambitious man I've ever met."

Ryan said nothing, long experience having taught him that people tended to speak much more freely without interruption.

"That's where we always differed," she continued, brushing her fringe out of her eyes. "He's interested in legacy for his own sake, whereas I'm interested in it for all our sakes."

Realising that she might have said too much, she gave a nervous laugh.

"I should know," she said, in a brittle voice. "We were married for about five minutes, when I was young and stupid. Now, we're very distant work acquaintances."

She turned up her collar and gave Ryan a sad smile, while the boat's engine sputtered and then rumbled to a stop beneath their feet.

"Funny how life goes," she said. "I think we're here."

Ryan looked around at the unremarkable spot in the ocean, which looked exactly the same whichever way he turned. Knivestone was half a mile behind them, appearing much smaller than before.

It was time to see what lay hidden beneath.

CHAPTER 24

On the mainland, MacKenzie and Yates entered the pristine foyer area of Vernon Salvage Inc., a company responsible for marine salvage operations following incidents at sea. Their offices were based out of an old Victorian building in South Shields where, the placard in the entranceway told them, the family business had been founded in the early part of the twentieth century.

"Mr Vernon will be with you in a minute," the receptionist told them. "Please help yourselves to coffee or tea."

Never likely to refuse the offer of caffeine, the two detectives headed over to where an antique table had been set up with a coffee machine, its little pods arranged artfully in an antique porcelain bowl next to a miniature cooler that held jugs of milk and cream. Having fortified themselves, a more detailed glance around the room confirmed that there was money to be had in marine salvage, judging from a series of gilt-framed oil paintings depicting each successive generation of the Vernon dynasty, right up to the present incumbent, Hugh Vernon, whose jowly face stared down at them from the wall.

"You can see the family resemblance," Yates remarked, and almost dropped her cup when the man himself materialised from one of the carpeted corridors to her right.

"Hello," he said, warmly. "I understand you're from the police?"

He was a short man—shorter than his painting would suggest—with thinning hair that was a suspicious shade of brown and complemented his year-round tan. He wore a smart, three-piece suit over a pristine white shirt and neck-tie, an outfit which might have been worn a hundred years before and served to give the impression of an unchanging, generational business.

"Yes, I'm DI MacKenzie and this is DC Yates, of Northumbria CID. We're here in connection with the death of Amanda Jones, the harbour master at Seahouses."

Immediately, his face fell into lines of concern.

"Of course, you are. It's a terrible tragedy; I was shocked when I heard the news of what had happened," he said gravely. "Please, come through to my office and I'll give you whatever help you need. Kerry? I'm not to be disturbed."

"Yes, Mr Vernon."

They followed him along a plush hallway until they reached a wide oak door, which he opened for them.

"After you, ladies."

It was strange, MacKenzie thought, how an act of chivalry could be charming in the hands of one person and creepy in the hands of another.

"Please, take a seat," he said, as he ushered them inside.

MacKenzie came straight to the point.

"Thank you for responding so promptly to my message yesterday," she said. "I understand you're one of five members on the board of Harbour Commissioners?"

"That's right, yes. I'm afraid a couple of our board members are out of the country at the moment and the others lead very busy lives."

MacKenzie didn't bother to argue that, when it came to a murder investigation, that was hardly a valid excuse for failing to respond to police enquiries.

"I see. Well, we're especially grateful for your time, Mr Vernon. To begin with, could you tell us the extent of your relationship with Ms Jones?"

He tapped a manicured finger against the edge of his desk.

"The Commissioners hold their quarterly meetings here, which Mandy attended," he said. "Of course, I remember interviewing her for the position a number of years ago and, naturally, I stopped in whenever I was in the area to say 'hello.'"

"And, how would you describe Ms Jones?"

He puffed out his cheeks as he pondered the right thing to say.

"She was a very able harbour master," he said, generously. "She was very easy to get along with, very bubbly."

MacKenzie paused, allowing Yates to pick up the conversation. It was good practice.

"Ah, did you know of any reason why Ms Jones might have been unhappy or upset? Had she told you of any recent trouble she'd been having at work?"

"Well, we had our last meeting in September and she seemed very pleased with how things were ticking over," he said. "There were the usual rumbles about needing more staff, of course, but that's a constant gripe. Nothing I'd have said she was worrying about."

MacKenzie changed tack.

"Can I ask who manages the harbour accounts?"

He didn't bat an eyelid.

"The Commissioners employ an accountant and once a year we're audited externally."

"May I have the name of the accountant?"

A slight pause.

"Ms MacKenzie—"

"Detective Inspector."

"I beg your pardon. Detective Inspector, I'm afraid I don't know what our accountant could possibly have to do with Mandy's unfortunate death."

"That will be for us to determine," she replied, in the same genial tone. "May we have his or her name?"

His face morphed, just for a second, into something ugly. Clearly, he was not a man used to being thwarted, and especially not by a woman.

"His name is Andrew Simmons," he snapped. "He's one of the managing partners of Simmons' Chartered Accountants. They have an office on the high street."

"Out of interest, Mr Vernon, do you also employ Simmons in your capacity as Managing Director of Vernon's?"

"That's a matter of public record," he said. "Yes, I do. I was the one who recommended Andrew's firm to the Commissioners."

"Small world," she said, with a bland smile.

Vernon remained silent, but his finger continued to tap against the edge of the old Chippendale-style desk that was far too large for his small, rounded body.

"Is there anything else I can do for you?"

"It's good of you to be so accommodating," MacKenzie said, assuming correctly that she'd get more from the man if she employed a deferential tone, however insincere it may be. "There is one more thing. Could you tell us when you last saw Ms Jones?"

He leaned forward and linked his hands together.

"Am I a suspect in the case, detective?"

She feigned surprise.

"These are standard questions, Mr Vernon. There's no need to feel defensive."

He smiled, but there was no mirth to it.

"Look, I'm sure you'll find out sooner or later. Mandy and I had an affair, which lasted about eighteen months. It happened at a vulnerable time in my marriage and

I regret it very much. My wife doesn't know," he said, candidly. "Mandy took advantage of this from time to time and asked for little presents. I have no doubt you'll see a few cash deposits listed in her account, which must be why you were asking about our accountancy arrangements."

The two women exchanged a glance.

"I assure you, the money was taken from my private account and not the business one here, or the Harbour Commissioners' fund, which is something I don't have access to in any event. As I say, I regretted my relationship with Mandy and was concerned that my wife would be hurt and upset, if she were ever to find out."

He paused meaningfully.

"I hope, since I've been so honest with you about this, that you'll exercise a modicum of respect for my privacy and agree not to tell my wife under any circumstances. The shock of it would be likely to make her ill, again."

While Yates might have fallen for the lost look in his eye, MacKenzie was made of sterner stuff.

"I'm afraid we can't give you that assurance," she said. "As a matter of good practice, we don't reveal what a witness may or may not have told us while in conference with another witness unless we feel the information is likely to elicit further useful intelligence. I can tell you that your private life is of no concern to us, Mr Vernon, and we appreciate your honesty."

Much later, they realised Hugh Vernon hadn't answered their question at all.

CHAPTER 25

Having drawn the proverbial short straw, Lowerson left a fresh tin of biscuits in Phillips' dubious care and made the journey back into Newcastle to the Royal Victoria Infirmary. He had mixed feelings where the hospital was concerned, having lost six months of his life in a coma and thereby becoming a semi-permanent fixture on one of its wards. He'd been relieved to see the back of the place when he'd awakened, but he felt a deep sense of gratitude towards the doctors, nurses, consultants and every other healthcare professional who'd seen him through what had been—until recently—the worst time in his young life.

Now, he was returning in a professional capacity to meet with the police pathologist and, though it came with the territory, he wasn't altogether sure his stomach was prepared for the sight of a cadaver so early in the day. It was an unusual contradiction that he could look upon the sight of violent death at a crime scene but found it much harder in a clinical environment; he supposed it was the fact that the mortuary reminded him inappropriately of a butcher's shop which, as a vegetarian, he found repellent at the best of times.

Lowerson took the lift down to the basement level and, almost as soon as the doors swooshed open, he felt the temperature rise as a series of narrow fans pumped warm air out of the mortuary to keep it constantly cold. He made his way along the corridor to a set of metal-coated double doors operated by a security key-pad and, thankfully, he remembered the code after the third attempt.

"Morning!"

The senior police pathologist was a man named Jeffrey Pinter, who was possessed of an unfortunate, lanky frame that tended to reinforce the morbidity of his profession and today was no exception. He seemed to glide across the room, which was blessedly empty apart from one of the mortuary technicians whose hand rose and fell as they stitched up a Y-incision in the chest of the unfortunate Mandy Jones.

Lowerson's stomach gave a violent lurch and he looked away, busying himself by entering his name in the log book and selecting a visitor's lab coat. He took a bit longer than necessary to do up the buttons and then, when he felt he could trust himself, looked back to find Pinter waiting with a patient look on his mildly condescending face.

"Ready?" he asked.

"Of course, I was just—ah, so, what can you tell me about Amanda Jones?"

"I was sorry to see her, when she came in," Pinter said, leading him to the far end of the room where the body had been laid out on one of the long metal tables. "Ryan said it looked as though she'd suffered a severe blow to the head, followed by a second blow to the neck or vice versa, given the visible injuries and the presence of what appeared to be the murder weapon—correct?"

"Yes, we found a heavy iron hook, the kind you'd see on a fishing trawler or something like that."

"That would be consistent," Pinter said. "We found traces of rust in her wounds."

They came to stand at the side of the table and Lowerson cleared his throat.

"Ah, so there was no—no, ah, signs of anything in her toxicology to suggest another cause of death?"

At heart, Pinter was a decent man. That being the case, he angled his body in front of Lowerson in a subtle move that obliterated the worst of the view, to give the younger man some time to gather himself.

He had his pride, after all.

"No, nothing untoward. Her blood showed a very low level of alcohol consumption and nothing more sinister than that," he said. "No, I'd say this one's straightforward as far as cause of death is concerned. The carotid artery was severed in the neck, either before or after the wound to the parietal bone."

"The pari—?"

"It's just here," Pinter explained, tapping the upper back portion of Lowerson's skull. "I'd say both blows came from behind, too. The direction of the neck wound is revealing, when you take into account the shape of the weapon."

He stepped aside again, and produced a retractable pointer.

"The tear is to the right section of her neck, here," he said, pointing to the affected area. "If you look at the direction, it appears to drag down towards her shoulder, which would be very hard to do if one were standing in front of her. Much easier to inflict a blow like this from behind."

As he forced himself to look upon the sad, stiff form of what had once been a woman, Lowerson's stomach settled. For a moment, he'd worried that the sight of Mandy Jones might have reminded him of Jennifer, of what had happened to her.

But it had the opposite effect, entirely.

It hardened him.

"Nobody deserves to die that way," he said, echoing the words he'd heard Ryan say, so many times before. He thought he'd understood them, but he realised he hadn't, not deep down. He'd seen the victims as numbers, but none of them were. They were the shells of what had once been humans; mothers, fathers, friends, lovers, enemies. Their lives had mattered, to at least one other person, which was enough.

"What about time of death?" he asked softly.

If Pinter noticed a change in his demeanour, he said nothing.

"The report says she was found at around seven a.m. on Saturday morning and by the time the body was transferred to me, here, it was ten-past-nine. Her core temperature had fully acclimatised to the surrounding environment and she had lost pints of blood; whatever remained had begun to suggillate as she was clearly in the throes of advanced livor mortis," he said. "Taking all of that into account, I'd say she'd been dead at least six hours by the time she was found, more, obviously, by the time she came here."

Lowerson nodded.

"That puts her time of death at shortly after midnight on Friday night," he said, thinking of the victim's timeline. "Her daughter thinks she left the house around midnight, so it wouldn't be too far outside the estimate you've given."

Pinter tried to look humble but failed miserably. He was one of the finest pathologists in the country, and he knew it.

"Any defensive marks?" Lowerson asked, more as a box-ticking procedure than anything else as he had a feeling he knew what the answer would be.

"None," Pinter replied, and looked down at Mandy's body. "She didn't see it coming, or she might have thrown up an arm, might've done something... well, there you have it."

He seemed embarrassed by the unusual display of emotion and Lowerson changed the subject.

"What about Iain Tucker—any update on him?"

Pinter thought of the man who was presently tucked inside one of the drawers above Lowerson's shoulder and decided not to mention he was in such close proximity.

"That was sheer waste," he said, shaking his head. "Two in as many days, as well. Still, it's no different to the homeless, the addicts, the lonely…everybody comes through those doors, at some stage or another. As for Iain Tucker, I can't tell you anything you don't already know. His injuries were such that it was impossible for me to say whether he died following accidental drowning, or he drowned following a blow."

"It's a case of which came first, the chicken or the egg, you mean?"

"Exactly," Pinter said. "But the egg is definitely scrambled now."

Lowerson pulled an expressive face and thanked the pathologist again, before heading back out and into the fresh air of a crisp November morning. He stood for a while outside, leaning against his car while he took a few deep breaths in and out. Strangers came and went, hurrying towards the main entrance, focused entirely on their own problems. That was the way of the world, he thought; it was easy to wake up each day and think only of your own small world but, when you were faced with death in all its multi-coloured glory, it tended to bring you up short.

"You need to stop listening to those mindfulness podcasts," he told himself, and stepped back inside the car.

Death might come to us all, but it hadn't come for him just yet.

CHAPTER 26

Josh hadn't been able to sleep for most of the night and, when sleep finally had come, it had been disturbed and full of nightmares. When he awakened, he'd found Daisy missing from his mother's double bed and was disorientated for a moment, trying to remember how they had come to be there.

Then, it all came rushing back.

Mandy.

He scrubbed a hand over his face and stumbled out of bed, a tall, wiry man with dark eyes and rumpled hair a couple of shades darker than his uncle's. He caught himself in the long cheval mirror which hung on the back of the bedroom door and hurriedly looked away, not needing to see the fear in his own eyes, nor the shadows beneath them.

"Daisy?"

He found nobody in the Manager's Apartment, so he pulled on a sweatshirt and padded downstairs, careful to mask any signs of stress before he faced his family. As it turned out, he needn't have worried about hiding his anxiety, for all emotions were trumped by the surprise he felt when he walked into the kitchen to find his mother locked in a passionate embrace with his uncle.

He must have made some small sound because they jumped apart like a pair of guilty teenagers.

"Oh! Josh! I'm sorry, we—ah, we didn't see you there."

"Yeah, I get that."

Gemma exchanged a worried glance with Hutch.

"We were going to tell you, love. We just felt it was a bit thoughtless to talk about relationships when Daisy's just lost her mum."

Once he managed to block out the mental image, Josh made a quick assessment of his feelings on the subject and found that he was happy for them both.

He folded his arms and affected an air of disapproval.

"Just how long has this been going on?"

Hutch stiffened a bit, ready to step back and do whatever was necessary not to hurt the boy.

"Not long—"

"About forty years—"

They spoke at the same time and then looked at one another; she in confusion, he with a sad smile of understanding. He had been under no illusion that Gemma had loved him in the same way he had adored her for more years than he could count.

"I've loved your mother ever since she was the new girl at primary school when we were kids."

The words were spoken softly and with such devotion, Josh couldn't keep up any kind of pretence.

"I'm happy for you both," he said. "It's about time you stopped tip-toeing around each other, anyway."

Hutch walked across to look at the boy who was his brother's son, the son who might have been his.

Should have been, his mind whispered.

"You really don't mind?"

In answer, Josh drew him in for a hard embrace and squeezed his eyes tightly shut, thinking of all the times this man had been there, filling his father's shoes. He let himself imagine what it might be like to confide in him about the nightmare he was living; to purge himself and seek help. It was tempting, but he couldn't be the one to ruin this moment in their lives. They'd waited so long to be happy after his father had taught them both never to trust and never to love again. How could he disappoint them? How could he confirm their worst fear, that the apple hadn't fallen far from the tree?

He drew back again, a ready smile on his face.

"Where's Daisy?" he asked, injecting a false brightness into his voice.

"The police needed to ask her a few more questions," Gemma told him. "They're down at the station, now."

Josh felt his heart skip a beat, imagining the worst.

"I'll head down to meet her."

After he left, Hutch smiled across at Gemma.

"He's a caring lad, isn't he? Always thinking of others," he said. "He's a credit to you."

She reached across to grasp his hand.

"And you," she corrected him. "There's more of you in Josh than you know."

Such simple words, he thought, but they made his heart soar.

At Knivestone, the process of geophysical surveying was already underway. For all their personal differences, Ursula Tan and Jasper Vaughn worked well side by side, huddled over their calculations as the sonar data began to roll in. Ryan had completed a beginner's diving course a few years earlier, but his skills did not stretch to the kind of experienced scuba diving that was required should they strike lucky and discover a wreck. He therefore had to be content with observing the process from the cabin via an array of computer screens and video monitors that had been linked up to the sonar and magnetometer, learning as much as he could about a world that was entirely new to him. He had imagined, somewhat naively, that it would be a fairly straightforward process to find a ship but, as it turned out, there was a very specific science to confirming the existence and accurate position of a wreck.

Time and again, the *Jolly Roger* was turned around and the process repeated. The air was bitterly cold, but the crew didn't seem to notice, taken as they were with the task in hand. There was a thrum of excitement amongst divers and archaeologists, police and coastguard as they waited for the verdict from the expensive machinery that was trawling the sea floor.

"Pulls you in, doesn't it?" Alex Walker said, from his position at the wheel. "For some people, all this water and sky is a bit overwhelming, but I love it."

Ryan nodded.

"It's a reminder of your own insignificance in the grand scheme of things. I guess some people would prefer not to be reminded."

"I'd rather people were cautious than just plain stupid," Walker said, and adjusted his sunglasses. "You wouldn't believe the number of people who get caught on the causeway on Holy Island, or who find themselves in a bit of bother out here in the Farnes. City folk—they take a few boating lessons and, suddenly, they fancy themselves as Captain Jack Sparrow."

He paused, listening to Ursula calling out for him to bring the boat around one more time.

"Not exactly glamorous, is it?" he complained, but did as he was bid. "Pity they didn't use side-scan sonar and send a few people down, instead."

"Apparently, this will give them a higher resolution image."

"Aye, well, any time this year would be good. I'm freezin' my balls off, out here."

Ryan laughed.

"Seems a long time since you last visited us, Alex. Don't be a stranger," he said.

The coastguard gave a self-conscious shrug.

"For a while, there, it seemed like I was under a dark cloud," he replied. "I s'pose I didn't want it to rub off on anyone else."

Ryan shook his head and thought of how similarly their minds worked, leading them to seek isolation in order to protect those they cared about.

Just then, there came a commotion from the other end of the cabin.

"Ryan!"

He hurried across to join the small crowd who had gathered around one of the monitors.

"What is it? Have you found it?"

Vaughn drew him forward and pointed towards a multi-layered image of what appeared to be two separate entities on the sea floor.

"Is that *two* ships?" he said, incredulously.

"We don't know yet," Ursula cautioned him. "It could be two parts of the same ship."

"But it's a ship," Ryan said.

They looked amongst themselves, like children who'd just discovered Santa's Grotto.

"It's a ship, alright," Vaughn said. "Looks like Iain was right, after all."

It served as a poignant reminder of why they were here, and Ryan shut down any boyish excitement about a shipwreck, turning his mind back to murder instead.

"How soon can we get a diver down there, to see for ourselves?" he asked.

"The water level is already much higher than before," Ursula said. "Soon, the current will pick up and I can't send divers down in such bad conditions. We need to wait until the next period of low-water slack tide."

Ryan told himself to be patient. They had just found a shipwreck, after all.

"When will that be?"

"Later this afternoon, according to the tidal forecast," she said. "We can control plenty of things in life, but the tides aren't one of them."

A thought struck Ryan and he pointed towards one of the monitors.

"This one's linked to the magnetometer, right?"

They nodded.

"That wouldn't pick up a wooden vessel, would it?" he asked. "That would rule out a Viking longboat, surely."

"The magnetometer's picked up one of the objects on the seabed, but the sonar has picked up two," Ursula explained, and tapped a different screen. "There's no record of any shipwreck on existing charts for these coordinates. They're both new."

"We could send down one of the AUVs," Jasper suggested.

"AUV?" Ryan queried.

"He means an autonomous underwater vehicle," Ursula explained. "They're a lot like drones. They're able to navigate themselves, so you can use them independently of the boat without having to tether them. But they're very expensive to use and—"

"A bit above our pay bracket?" Ryan guessed.

"Yes, but surely now that we've found two independent structures on the seabed, that warrants further exploration," Jasper argued.

"Why don't you call the university and ask them to pay for it, then?" she snapped. "MAST can't be expected to fund the entire expedition; even with a little help from the police, it's not enough to justify that kind of prospecting, especially not when we only have to wait a few hours and we can dive ourselves."

Ryan judged it the opportune moment to step in.

"The wrecks aren't going anywhere after all this time and, besides, all good things come to those who wait. If we're lucky, we'll be getting two shipwrecks for the price of one."

Reluctantly, Jasper agreed, and their faces broke into silly grins.

"We've really found something, this time, Jasper," Ursula said, their private history forgotten in a shared moment of victory.

They broke into a jig, laughing around the boat deck like a pack of lunatics, and Ryan moved to stand at the edge of the boat. He looked out across endless gallons of water and wondered if Iain Tucker had danced around the deck of the *Viking Princess,* wherever she was laid to rest now.

"No wonder somebody wanted this for themselves," he murmured.

CHAPTER 27

At the Coastguard's Office, Phillips celebrated the news of a shipwreck having been found by christening a fresh tin of biscuits.

"The Receiver of Wreck won't be happy," he remarked, twiddling his fingers as he mulled over his selection. "The poor bloke's only just flown back home. He'll have to get straight back on the plane again."

"If they find a hoard of treasure for Her Majesty's coffers it'll soften the blow," MacKenzie replied.

"That remains to be seen," he said, making a grab for a chocolate wafer before the tin was confiscated by the Biscuit Police. "How's the Mandy Jones investigation coming along?"

"Mel and I went to see Hugh Vernon this morning," MacKenzie said, moving the tin firmly out of reach. "He's the only one of the Harbour Commissioners who wasn't out of the country or otherwise uncontactable. He's the current MD of Vernon Salvage, a marine salvage company based out of South Shields. It's a national operation that takes care of salvage operations around the British coastline, making sure a load of oil drums and lost cargo doesn't clog up the ocean floor when a tanker goes down."

"What does he have to do with anything?" Lowerson asked, tipping back his chair with the toe of his shoe.

"The Harbour Master is employed and supervised by the board of Commissioners," Yates explained. "Technically, he was Mandy's boss."

"He says he was a lot more than that, too," MacKenzie added. "The account statements came through yesterday afternoon from Mandy's bank. It didn't take much to notice a regular £150 weekly deposit being made every Saturday morning or thereabouts. It made us wonder, so we asked Mr Vernon about his accounting arrangements—at the company and in his capacity as a Harbour Commissioner. He didn't like it, did he, Mel?"

Yates chuckled.

"The bloke's got classic Small Man Syndrome," she said. "I think he was bothered about the fact he was being asked awkward questions by two women, more than anything else."

"You could be right," MacKenzie said. "Anyhow, he ended up telling us he'd been giving Mandy Jones cash hand-outs, so she wouldn't tell his wife about an affair they once had. He didn't go into any further detail about how regularly he gave her money or where the exchange took place—"

"That's weird, isn't it?" Lowerson cut in. "Why wouldn't he just arrange a bank transfer and save himself the hassle of a personal exchange?"

"Maybe he wanted the personal exchange," Phillips suggested. "Or maybe his wife checks his account statements, so he wanted to keep it cash only."

MacKenzie gave him the beady eye.

"I'm choosing to overlook the way your mind immediately came up with both of those suggestions," she said.

"Aye, probably for the best, love."

The other two were still chuckling when the door opened to admit the missing member of their small team.

"Oho! Blackbeard 'imself has returned," Phillips cried out, and spread his hands in a wide, theatrical gesture. "Howay then, m'hearty, where's the booty? Divn't tell us you walked straight past the fish shop without picking up a bag of chips."

Ryan rubbed his chilled hands together.

"Remarkably, I managed to walk past a food establishment without feeling compelled to make a purchase," he said. "I just came in off the boat—"

"It's been said many a time before," Phillips quipped.

"—and we have to wait for the water level to reduce before we can send the divers down," Ryan finished, with a glare. "Even then, we'll have to move quickly to make the most of the light. I've got about an hour before we need to head back out again, so I thought I'd pop in for an update while they're refuelling."

"We were just talking about Hugh Vernon," Yates said, helpfully.

"The salvage guy?" Ryan said, pulling up a chair.

"That's the one. He's claiming responsibility for a series of small but regular cash payments made to Mandy Jones, but he says they were hush money, so she wouldn't tell his wife about an affair they had."

"What does he look like?" Ryan enquired.

"What?"

"It's a serious question," he said. "Let's not try to pretend that people aren't just a teensy bit superficial when it comes to matters of the heart. Mandy Jones was a good-looking woman and she wasn't shy, either. From what we've heard, she had boyfriends who tended to be younger than she was. No judgment," he added. "But that's a pattern. I don't remember seeing his Facebook profile and thinking that Hugh Vernon would win any beauty contests, or that he was particularly young, either."

"He's neither," MacKenzie confirmed. "And I agree, it's a strange match. But stranger things have happened."

But Ryan wasn't buying it.

"Have you come across a single scrap of evidence to suggest that she'd had an affair with him, other than what Vernon told you himself? And what about the dates of this alleged affair—do they tally with the dates he claims he began paying Mandy hush money?"

Yates flicked through her notebook, then shook her head.

"He didn't tell us the date the affair was supposed to have started, he only told us that the affair lasted around eighteen months."

"Could be pure fabrication," Ryan said, crossing one long leg over the other. "Let's look at this thing objectively. The Harbour Master is a bribe-risk, simply by virtue of their position. Now, I'm not trying to cast aspersions on the late Mandy Jones, but it wouldn't be the first time somebody accepted a kick-back for looking the other way, would it?"

"You're thinking our pal Vernon might have slipped her a few bob to keep quiet about something she'd seen down on the harbour?" Phillips asked.

"I'm thinking Mandy saw—or *didn't* see—things on a regular basis," Ryan replied. "This wasn't a one-off payment; it was an ongoing arrangement. There had to be a reason for that."

"There's something else, too," MacKenzie said, pulling up a report on her laptop. "The tech team say that her recent internet browsing history included frequent searches on 'how to get a work permit or visa', property searches on the south coast as well as in Spain, plus flight comparison websites. What does that tell us?"

"She was planning to get away," Lowerson said.

"Exactly."

"What about forensics?" Ryan asked. "Any other suspect items down at her office, or at home?"

"They're still going over her electronics," MacKenzie replied. "But Faulkner did find a burner mobile, pay-as-you-go, in the pocket of one of her jackets. The messages had all been deleted but there was a record of recent numbers dialled. We're in the process of trying to identify each of those."

Ryan nodded his approval.

"I don't recall any mention in Daisy Jones' statements of her mum thinking of emigrating," he said.

"Perhaps she didn't know," Phillips said. "Or maybe she thought it wasn't important."

"Perhaps." Ryan was unconvinced. "I'll tell you something else, though. You don't often see *Shell Seekers* open for business."

The others were surprised.

"You mean, Josh Dawson's business?"

"That's the one. I've never seen that diving school open, not once during the time we've been here. I know there's been a lot of upheaval in the past few days, but other diving companies have remained at least partially open."

"Do you want to question him?" Phillips asked. "We could bring him in for a chat, if you like."

But Ryan shook his head.

"Let's see how things pan out with Vernon," he said. "We don't have enough to throw at Josh Dawson, yet, but I wouldn't mind a look at his business accounts down the line."

MacKenzie nodded her agreement.

"What about Iain Tucker?" she asked. "How's that side of things coming along?"

Ryan rolled his shoulders and rearranged himself in the uncomfortable wooden chair as he ordered his thoughts.

"We might have found a wreck, but there's still no sign of the *Viking Princess*—unless we discover that's the wreckage we all thought was a Viking longboat," he added, wryly.

"I had a word with the pathologist earlier today," Lowerson said. "He had nothing much to add on that score. Faulkner found a bunch of unidentified samples in Tucker's car, but that's completely normal considering the number of people who would've been in and out of it, over the years. There was nothing useful in the dinghy, no prints or useable substances since it'd been exposed to the weather and the rain would've washed anything juicy away."

"What about his hotel room?" Ryan asked. "Anything come back on that?"

Lowerson just shook his head.

"There were numerous prints found in the room—some they've identified as belonging to Tucker himself, others they've identified as Paul Hutchinson, Gemma Dawson and Daisy Jones. Any of them might have been in to clean the room, since they tend to do it all themselves. There were numerous old, partial prints we can safely assume belonged to previous hotel guests, too."

Ryan sighed, running through his mental checklist.

"Alright, so we didn't hit lucky, there. How about phone records from his mobile? Any sign of his electronics, yet?"

"Naht, the phone company still haven't come back with anything, probably because it's the weekend. I'll chase them up first thing tomorrow," Phillips said. "There's still no sign of any papers or electronics, either at Tucker's home or his office."

"Yeah, they're long gone," Ryan surmised.

"It doesn't matter so much now," MacKenzie pointed out. "If our perp was hoping to prevent you from finding the wreckage by disposing of Tucker's charts and records, then they've failed miserably, haven't they?"

Ryan smiled grimly and glanced at his watch.

Time to go.

"Wish us luck," he said. "We're about to find out why somebody went to all that effort."

CHAPTER 28

"What the hell are you doing?"

Daisy walked into the bedroom to find Josh stuffing clothes into a holdall. He worked quickly, as he packed a meagre selection of his worldly belongings into the bag he'd been given as a teenager, on his first day of secondary school.

"We need to leave," he said urgently, his voice bordering on panic. "I can't sit around here waiting any longer, wondering if you or me, or somebody else I care about will turn up dead."

"That isn't going to happen!" She reached for him, but he shrugged her off.

"Look, you can come with me or stay here, it's up to you," he said. "But you need to decide now."

"For God's sake, Josh—"

"Are you *listening* to me?" he said, grasping her arms in a bruising grip. "I told you last night, there is no way out except to run. I offered to pay the money back, but that was refused. I don't know what else I can do."

"You can speak to Gemma, or Hutch," she said desperately. "Please, Josh. You can't leave."

Her face was a pale mask, her eyes enormous and filled with hurt.

"Please, don't leave me."

Something triggered in his mind, a memory that was not his own but had been planted inside his mind ever since he'd been old enough to understand.

Kris left them, they'd say. *How could he leave them?*

He remembered his mother's polite mask as another old woman from the church committee came to call, bearing second-hand toys or clothes she neither needed nor wanted. But she'd accepted them with good grace, had smiled and nodded as they stayed to coo over her baby boy, the one who looked so like his wayward father.

Shameful, they'd whispered.

How will he cope, growing up without a father?

He recalled the proud tilt of his mother's chin, the regal silence she'd employed until it was an acceptable time to show them the door. Then, once it had closed, he'd heard her soft tears behind the bathroom door; muffled sounds she'd tried to hide from him and from the world.

Mummy? Mummy, are you in there?

I'll be out in a minute, sweetheart. Go and play.

He saw his mother's tears in the face of the woman standing before him and the clothes fell from his numb fingers. He sank down onto the edge of the bed and held his head in his hands.

"Do you really think there's nothing else we can do?"

He brushed the sleeve of his shirt over his eyes and looked up.

"This isn't your problem, Daisy, it's mine. You're not a part of it."

"Of course I am," she said, angrily. "We're in this together, Josh."

Her breath hitched as tears clogged her throat and she struggled to contain them, imagining the terrible loneliness of a life without her mother as well as the man, who was still a boy, sitting in front of her.

"If we go, we go together," she told him, firmly.

They heard the creak of the stairs and Josh rose, thrusting the holdall into a cupboard before somebody could see.

"Nothing's changed," he told her quietly. "And, if you're serious about coming with me, start packing a bag, because I'm leaving tonight."

At the wreck site, Ryan stood on the deck of the *Jolly Roger* and watched the small crew of MAST divers alongside Jasper Vaughn, as they prepared their tanks to enter the water. The sun was spectacular as it slowly descended towards the horizon, throwing beams of light across the rippling water as the tide changed and Knivestone appeared once again from the depths of the sea to the west and, beyond it, Longstone lighthouse and civilisation.

"Nearly there," Ursula said, coming to stand beside him. "I've agreed to stay up here for the first run. Next time, it'll be my turn to go down."

Ryan smiled at her enthusiasm, thinking it was a rare person who actively missed being able to dive into the freezing water of the North Sea.

"Jasper's got a camera fitted to his cap," she said. "That'll be linked to the monitor here, so we'll be able to watch things unfold."

"You said the wrecks were lying between forty-five and fifty metres below," he said. "That makes it a deeper dive than usual, doesn't it?"

Her face sobered.

"Everybody here is an experienced professional," she assured him. "But I won't lie to you, it'll be a difficult dive. The currents are very strong around here—added to which, it's likely there'll be poor visibility as they go down, partly due to geophysical factors and partly due to the fact we're rapidly losing daylight."

Ryan nodded towards the group of men and women who were strapping on tanks.

"I'm not telling you how to do your job," he said, simply. "But I have my own due diligence to take care of. I'm here representing an investment made by the Northumbria Constabulary and, put simply, we've already lost two people because of whatever's lying down there. I don't intend to lose any more."

Ursula nodded.

"We'll do our best."

She moved off to oversee the dive lift, which was fitted to the back of the boat and was designed to make it easier for professional divers to enter deep water. As the mechanism activated, Ryan joined Ursula and Alex Walker in the cabin area, where their eyes were glued to the television monitor that would feed real-time video images from Jasper's camera back to the boat.

As the footage began to roll, Ryan's first thought was that the underwater world was an opaque, mossy-green landscape where it was impossible to see further than a couple of feet in any direction. But then, it was as if a veil was slowly lifted and the underwater panorama revealed itself.

"Incredible," he murmured.

While they remained in the shallows, the vastness of the ocean spread out before the divers and the three who remained on board watched as their powerful searchlights shone white beams through the murky water to guide their way, deeper into the unknown.

Suddenly, Jasper's camera jolted, and the footage bobbed as something darted in front of him. Time was suspended for a moment until the whiskered face of an Atlantic grey seal swept into view. Inquisitive and charming, the five-hundred-pound animal wriggled its nose into Jasper's face, no doubt trying to work out what had invaded its home.

"If only I could see Jasper's face," Ursula said, with a snigger.

"They're like Labradors," Walker said, with a chuckle. "There's a colony of thousands of seals around the Farnes. If you go into shallower waters, you can pet them like puppies."

"I don't believe it," Ryan said.

"I wouldn't tell a lie," Walker said, crossing his heart. "They're great big soppy beasts; that's why divers keep coming back here, to see the seals as much as the shipwrecks."

They fell silent again as the divers moved on, entering a different realm that was alien to them, deeper and deeper into the darkness of the ocean floor. Above sea level, the boat crew waited with bated breath; unable to look away from the monitor, transfixed by the slow progress of Jasper's camera. Now and then, they caught a hand signal or gesture from one of the other divers as they moved in formation, lowering themselves by degree as they drew closer and closer to their destination.

"Can't be far now," Ursula muttered. "They've been down there for ten minutes."

No sooner had she spoken than the wreck was upon them, rearing up towards the monitor as if from nowhere. It emerged from the shadows like a ghost ship, its metal lines standing face-up and intact, its port-side wedged forever against the underside of a long shard of whinstone rock which had been there for centuries and had, for reasons best known to its creator, decided to reveal itself. Centuries of tidal currents had swept tonnes of silt and sand from the seabed, creating a steep ridge against its outer edge which might have concealed the wreck for centuries to come, had a twist of fate and the turn of the tide not decided otherwise.

"That's only the first," Ursula said. "It looks fairly small; maybe a naval trawler of some kind. Look, they're splitting up into teams."

Sure enough, the divers fanned out in two teams, with Jasper leaving the less exciting military vessel behind in favour of the more prestigious offering that might await him.

"How long do they have left?" Ryan asked, never losing sight of the practicalities.

"Around forty minutes. It'll take them twenty to get back up, so they've got around twenty minutes left to explore."

They watched as Jasper passed through a jungle of trailing sea kelp that had made a home around the first wreckage, trailing its slimy fingers against the edge of his camera as he swam through it. The camera panned out again and shifted to the same murky grey-green nothingness as before and Ryan felt a certain disquiet as he watched the two divers braving the deep.

"There," Ursula whispered, reverently. "Oh, my God."

The three of them were silent as the underside of a long wooden ship came into view, nestled beneath the same protective shield of rock and silt as its younger neighbour but significantly older.

"Do you think—?"

Walker began to speak, then came to an abrupt stop as an elaborately carved bow and stern of a Viking warship came into view, its clinker-built hull still showing the seamless lines of overlapping wooden craftsmanship that had been the stuff of Nordic tradition.

"It's beautiful," Ursula said, and Ryan glanced across to find she was weeping. Tears of silent joy fell down her face and he realised something that she had not, perhaps, realised herself. The joy she displayed at the second-hand experience of seeing the wrecks couldn't possibly compare with seeing it first-hand and so, for her to have foregone that pleasure to allow Jasper the opportunity instead, spoke volumes of her latent feelings for the man.

He fished out a small packet of tissues, which he offered to her.

"Thanks," she muttered. "You must think I'm ridiculous."

"No," Ryan said. "I think you're dedicated."

She nodded.

"I've dived around the Farnes for nearly fifteen years," she said. "In fact, I've dived all over the world, from the Pacific to the Indian Ocean. I've seen the *Oseburg*, which was the best-preserved example of a Viking longship. But even just by looking at the fleeting images on Jasper's camera, I can see it doesn't compare to what we've found here."

She turned to look at the two men beside her.

"This—it's the stuff marine archaeologists dream of," she said, sniffling again. "Iain was right," she added. "He was absolutely right, and I laughed at him. I'm so sorry."

Ryan only shook his head.

"You had a natural scepticism, which is different."

He was about to say more when Walker tapped his shoulder to draw their attention to the monitor again. Reluctantly, Jasper was now making his return journey towards the surface with his dive partner, retracing his route through the artificial reefs, past anemone and Dead Man's Fingers, past rows of crab and kelp. But he had paused to meet the other diving team, who had been exploring the first wreck.

And who were now making furious, panicked hand gestures.

"Get the diving lift ready," Ryan muttered. "Something's wrong."

CHAPTER 29

Word of a shipwreck had spread like wildfire amongst the villagers, who gathered down by the harbour to greet the *Jolly Roger* as she made her triumphant return. They lined the harbour wall, waving the colourful diving boat in and expecting to hear its horn blast once, twice, three times to acknowledge the moment. But it remained silent as it entered Seahouses, as neither boat nor crew brought any glad tidings for the people who lived there.

"Howay, let's get moving," Phillips said to Lowerson, and began to usher the crowd back from the slipway to allow better access for an unmarked black-painted ambulance vehicle that had been called out in readiness.

Whispers began to spread, rumours of a police presence that was not normal for a happy event such as this.

Where were the local camera crews? Where was the pomp and circumstance?

The locals, who had already felt the impact of two deaths in their community, began to grow restless and a strange hush befell the proceedings. They watched the diving boat slow as it came alongside the northern pier, watched as the tall, dark-haired chief inspector leapt onto the pier to tie off the ropes and began to feel a prescient kind of dread for what was to come.

Amongst them were Hutch and Gemma.

"I wonder what's going on?" she said. "I thought they'd be…you know, a bit more excited about it all."

Hutch said nothing and watched Ryan stride along the pier, where he was met by a couple of members of his team.

"There could have been an accident," he said, in an odd, faraway voice.

"Maybe," she said. "If that's the case, we should leave them to it."

She started to walk off, then realised he wasn't following.

"Paul? Aren't you coming? What's wrong?"

"I—I get a funny feeling." He placed a hand against his chest. "Let's wait a minute longer."

He began to move slowly towards the barrier; closer to where Ryan stood talking to one of the technicians who would transfer the body to the mortuary. In his hand, he held a clear evidence bag and, inside that, a diver's knife he recognised instantly.

Kristopher's diving knife.

"Gemma."

She rubbed a hand across his back, worried by the look on his face.

"What's the matter?"

But he wasn't really listening. Hutch muscled his way forward, making directly for the group of police.

"*...unidentified remains. This was the only personal effect we could find.*"

He heard Ryan's well-spoken voice over the din of the surrounding crowd and surged through them, desperate to see the thing up close, to see if he was right.

"Whoa there, lad. Where d'you think you're going?"

He came up against an immovable object in the form of DS Phillips, whose mild-mannered expression belied a core of pure iron.

"I-I need to see. It's the knife. Kris had that knife."

Phillips followed Hutch's eyeline, but the evidence bag was no longer in view.

"What're you on about, son?"

"The *knife*! I saw it!"

His raised voice attracted Ryan's attention and he turned, moving across to join them with an unreadable expression in his misty blue eyes.

"Hello, Mr Hutchinson. Ms Dawson. I'm afraid we have a barrier in place for the moment. We'll lift it as soon as we're able."

He was about to turn away again, to oversee the sad business of transferring the liquid shell of what had once been a person, when Hutch grabbed his arm.

Ryan's eyes turned to steel.

"You don't want to do that, Mr Hutchinson."

But the man was not himself.

"I saw a knife. In a plastic bag. You were carrying it, just now."

"Hutch, I think we should leave the police to it—" Gemma tried again, her eyes full of apology.

But Ryan's focus had changed.

"What about it?" he asked him, softly. "What about the knife?"

Hutch's throat bobbed, and his eyes were wide and frightened as he forced himself to say what he needed to say.

"It belonged to my brother. It belonged to Kris."

Gemma's hand fell away, and she took an involuntary step backwards.

"What do you mean? What are you *talking* about?"

Ryan saw panic and denial, horror and hope mingled all into one. He gestured for them to come forward, and they stepped away from the crowd.

"Describe the knife to me," he said. "What did your brother's knife look like?"

Hutch rubbed his chest as he spoke, in a dull, flat voice Gemma hardly recognised.

"It was dark blue, about this long," he said, using his index fingers to estimate the size. "There was a little black octopus symbol at the hilt and it was engraved with the word, 'KRAKEN.'"

"How can you be sure?"

Hutch swallowed painfully.

"Because I was the one who bought it for him, nearly twenty-five years ago."

Ryan reached inside his inner jacket pocket and withdrew the evidence bag, watching the man's eyes register shock and pain.

The little navy-blue diving knife was rusted over but, on one side of its handle, they could clearly see a single word engraved: 'KRAKEN'.

Two technicians wheeled a gurney from the boat towards the ambulance, its wheels grating against the old asphalt slipway and the crowd fell silent as they spotted a black body bag strapped to the top, little more than a pocket of air, so decomposed were the remains resting inside the diving suit they had recovered.

"It can't be," Hutch managed, and his chest closed up so tightly he could hardly breathe. "It can't be him."

Gemma's eyes rolled back, and her legs buckled. There was a shout and then she was falling, falling into sweet oblivion where nothing and nobody could hurt her.

The inn had re-opened in time for the lunchtime crowd but, since most of their customers had made their way down to the harbour to greet the *Jolly Roger*, it remained empty except for a couple of passing cyclists who'd stopped in for an orange juice on their way to Berwick-upon-Tweed. As the minutes ticked by, Josh manned the bar and watched the clock, waiting with increasing levels of anxiety for Daisy to return with her bags packed so they could leave, once and for all.

When the main door opened, he turned immediately, expecting to see her standing there. Instead, his mother entered with Hutch close behind her wearing an expression of utter devastation.

For Josh, all thoughts of escape melted away in the face of his mother's obvious distress. He imagined who else might have turned up with a shattered skull and thought immediately of Daisy.

"Mum? What's happened? Is it Daisy?" He abandoned his work and hurried around the bar.

Gemma stopped and looked up at him, her face a pale mask of fragility and exhaustion.

"No, Josh. It isn't Daisy," she said at length.

"What is it then?" he demanded, looking to Hutch for the answers but finding only a hollowed-out version of the man he'd been that morning.

"I need to sit down," Gemma whispered, and didn't wait for a response before making her way through to the dining area, which was completely empty. She slumped into the first chair she found and stared at the crackling fire with eyes that were bone dry.

She'd cried so many tears for Kris; oceans and rivers of tears over the years, so that now the worst had been confirmed, there was nothing left.

"It's your father," she said, in a curiously detached tone, as Josh and Hutch joined her at the table. "They think—the police think they've found his body."

"It's him," Hutch muttered softly.

Josh looked between the pair of them and then let out a short, angry laugh.

"If this is a joke, I'm not laughing."

"Look at your mother, boy, and tell me if you think we're joking," Hutch's voice cracked like a whip.

Josh could feel the emotions rising, all the anger he'd buried since childhood.

"Are you sure?" he asked. "You have to be sure."

"The police will confirm the identity by the morning," Hutch told him. "But I'm telling you, I know it's Kris. They found his diving knife inside the zipper pocket of his diving gear and he never went anywhere without it."

Josh tried to compute the information, his face revealing very little of the turbulent emotions running beneath.

"Years ago, when I asked…you told me they found his car at the airport. The papers reported it, at the time," he said. "That's why the police closed their investigation. They concluded he was missing but didn't want to be found."

"That's what we thought," Hutch agreed, in a low voice. "That's what everybody thought."

"There has to be a mistake, then. It has to be somebody else."

Gemma listened to them both with a deepening sense of detachment as the years rolled back in her mind. She thought of the woman she had been, pregnant and heartbroken, with very little money. She remembered the kindness Hutch had shown her, all the quiet, unstinting support as she'd come to terms with a future without the man she had loved and the father of her child.

Now, that child was a man, one who'd spent his whole life believing the father he'd never met to be selfish and unkind; someone who hadn't cared enough about his child to get in touch or come back to visit, not even once during his lifetime.

To find out that everything he'd believed about his father might have been wrong was life-altering news.

"What if we're right?" she said quietly. "What if it's Kristopher?"

"I'll need to contact mum," Hutch said, taking comfort in practical things that he could control. "I only hope the news doesn't kill her all over again."

The first time, when she'd heard of her younger son's disappearance, had been enough to precipitate a minor stroke that had left her needing years of physiotherapy. Now that she was older still, the outcome might not be so rosy.

"What if it is him?" Josh repeated slowly, turning the notion around in his mind. "Everything changes, if it's him they found trapped inside that wreck."

Gemma's eyes sharpened.

"What do you mean, love? This doesn't change what we've always known: that he's gone."

Josh only shook his head.

"It changes everything," he said, clutching his hands together to stop them trembling. "All these years, I believed he was a certain kind of person, one who'd let everybody down. I saw pieces of him in myself, all these years, and every time I messed up it was as though I was hurting you all over again," he said.

"You didn't, sweetheart. You aren't the same person he was—"

Josh held up a hand to reject the comfort she wanted to give him because he was not in any frame of mind to accept it. He was angrier than he'd ever believed it possible to be, filled with the need to understand and avenge a man he'd never truly known, whose character had been muddied and maligned for over twenty years.

"Did the police say how they found him?"

Hutch shook his head.

"They only said that they discovered the remains of the body inside one of two wrecks they discovered over near Knivestone. We aren't supposed to tell anybody our suspicions—not until they can check their records and try to make a positive identification. Otherwise, the press will go mad."

"So what if they do?" Josh snarled, surprising him. "I've read all the old local tabloids with their nasty, gossipy little quotes. It's there, in black and white, for anybody to read and, thanks to the internet, it'll be there for a long time to come. What if they were wrong? What if you were all *wrong*? He deserves to have the record put straight, doesn't he?"

Gemma's head was pounding, and her throat felt scratchy and sore when she spoke.

"Your dad was…Kris wasn't a bad man. I loved him," she remembered. "But he was no angel, either."

Hutch didn't bother to argue with the truth.

"He loved the sea and, maybe for a while, he loved me. But he didn't choose to share with me whatever took him out all that way to Knivestone," she said. "He had secrets."

Josh looked between their faces and thought, for the first time, that they looked *old*. His mother, who normally appeared smooth and unlined despite her years now looked faded, as though she'd aged decades since he'd last seen her.

"He never left us," she said brokenly, as the tears finally came. "He never left us after all."

She buried her head into the warmth of Hutch's chest, seeking a safe harbour, not sure she could withstand the hurt and upheaval of another police investigation. It had taken years to recover from the last time.

Hutch ran a gentle hand over her hair while he watched his nephew's face across the table, reading the anger and the confusion in his eyes.

His brother's eyes.

It had taken twenty-three years to try to overcome the long shadow Kris had cast over their lives and to earn his own place in the affections of the woman whose head now rested against his heart. He'd wanted to believe Gemma's son might become his son, in all the ways that mattered.

But he realised he'd been naïve.

Naïve to imagine he could ever replace his brother, even in the eyes of one who had never known him. It had been devastating and touching, all at once, to hear Josh forgive a man who had been reckless, stubborn and self-centred, in life. But then, even as a young boy, Josh had created all manner of imaginary tales about his father, preferring to think that Kris was a hero or an international spy, rather than accept he'd been lacking. Even as he'd grown up, a small part of Josh had always hoped to prove them all wrong one day and show the world that his father had been everything a boy could dream of, and it was a hard pill to swallow.

Where had Kris been, while he'd taught Josh to ride his first bike? Or, when Josh had asked about girls and what the hell to do with them?

At the bottom of the sea, his mind whispered. *Dead, at the bottom of the ocean, while you led the life he was supposed to have.*

CHAPTER 30

While the marine archaeological team dealt with the tedious administration that went alongside discovering not one, but *two* shipwrecks, Ryan got down to the business of opening a third murder investigation. The circumstances were highly irregular, the bureaucracy was off the scale and they were still no closer to understanding who might be responsible for some or all the deaths clustered in that tiny corner of the world.

"Alright, settle down," he snapped.

Police and forensic personnel buzzed around the tiny Incident Room in far greater numbers than before, word having spread far enough to entice volunteers who were clearly energised by the glamour of finding a body in such unusual circumstances. Ryan waited for the noise to die down before disabusing them of that notion.

"Before we go any further, I want to remind you that murder is murder regardless of the setting," he said. "You don't get extra brownie points for solving this one over the death of a local gang member found inside a flop house. Their deaths are equally important and should be treated as such. Is that understood?"

He saw a couple of faces fall.

"If any of you have suddenly realised you have other places to be, there's the door," he said, pointing to the back of the room. "As for the rest of you, let's get down to it."

Outside, darkness had fallen and the lights inside the room were reflected in the window panes. Ryan turned down the blinds to block it out, unwilling to allow something as prosaic as tiredness to interfere with the job in hand.

"Two of the divers belonging to the local British Sub-Aqua Club discovered the remains of another diver during their initial exploration of the first of two shipwrecks discovered off Knivestone. It hasn't been named, yet, but it appears to be a British naval trawler, dating back to the First or Second World War," he said. "Photographs were taken, and they'll be circulated at the first opportunity. In the meantime, this is what we know so far."

Ryan paused to ensure he had their full attention, then continued.

"Six divers went down at around three-thirty this afternoon, splitting into two teams once a second, much older wreck was discovered nearby. A video link had been set up with one of the members of the second team, which was fed back to a monitor on the boat and which I followed throughout the dive. Unfortunately, no video footage was recorded of the first naval wreck and so we're relying on the statements given by the underwater team, for now."

He held up a photocopy of each statement he'd taken during the journey back to the harbour, earlier in the day.

"You'll find copies of these statements in your packs," he said, referring to the summaries he'd created in the past hour. "You'll note that the accounts of the three divers belonging to the first dive team are virtually identical," he said, while papers rustled around the room. "The naval trawler is wedged in an upright position with its port side against a long sill of whinstone rock which has gathered silt during the intervening years, leaving the starboard side of the boat visible and intact. After a brief risk assessment, the divers judged it to be stable and safe enough to explore. They approached what was the captain's deck, photographing their progress, before proceeding along an accessible gangway leading towards what looked to be a cabin area. The door to the starboard cabin had been wedged closed from the outside using what appeared to be a metal rod, which they were unable to move because it was covered entirely by sea and plant life and had rusted itself to the surrounding metal."

Ryan leaned back against the wall and folded his arms.

"The presence of the rod appeared out of place and gave the team some cause for concern. By swimming back out and around to the side of the ship, they were able to see through to the interior of the cabin, where they saw the remains of a diving suit and helmet, including a set of tanks which appeared to be much newer than the boat itself. At that point, the team returned to the surface to report the find. After refilling their tanks, the divers—one of whom is also a voluntary member of the Northumbria Police Underwater Search and Marine Unit—were able to safely remove the starboard window and recover the remains from that direction."

Ryan thought back to what had been a risky, time-pressured operation as the water level continued to rise with the changing tide. He'd been ready to call it off, not willing to risk lives in the process, when they'd managed to break through.

"Do we have any idea who it is?" Yates asked.

Ryan nodded.

"We have the tanks and helmet and, of course, the remains of a skeleton inside what was left of the diving suit," he replied. "They've been transferred to the lab for testing and any DNA they're able to extract will be cross-checked against missing persons."

"There's only one missing person from around these parts who would've had the know-how to dive around Knivestone," DS Carole Kirby spoke up. "A man called Kristopher Reid, who went missing back in '95."

Ryan nodded and produced a photograph of Reid taken from a newspaper article, the same one MacKenzie and Phillips had discovered the previous evening, which he stuck on the wall behind him.

"This is Kristopher Reid," he said, for the benefit of the others in the room. "His brother, Paul Hutchinson, was present on the harbour when we transferred the remains. He witnessed me carrying an evidence bag containing the only other piece of physical evidence we recovered from the zipped pocket of the diving suit: a small, engraved knife. He claims the knife belonged to Kris and his description matched the knife in our possession."

There were murmurs around the room.

"Kris Reid did a bunk, years ago," Kirby argued, not quite able to see that the local rumour mill might have been wrong. "He left Gemma Dawson pregnant and it was the talk of the town. She doesn't have much in the way of family, so it was a bad time for her."

"I'm sure," Ryan agreed. "The fact remains, we've got a dead diver in possession of a knife belonging to Kris Reid—the only diver reported missing in the past twenty-five years who is still unaccounted for."

"As soon as we can extract some DNA, we'll compare it with the samples already provided by Josh Dawson and Paul Hutchinson and see if we can find a familial match," Faulkner said, from the edge of the room. "It's highly unlikely there'd be any DNA record on file for Kristopher Reid from the mid-nineties; the DNA database was still in its infancy, back then."

Ryan nodded.

"The upshot is, we've had two unexplained deaths in the past week. At first, we thought somebody out there wanted to claim the victory of discovering a Viking shipwreck for themselves," he said, and thought of the academics who were, no doubt, arguing the toss over who would manage the excavation of today's find, their interest focused entirely on the relics of the past rather than the loss of human life. "I think we were wrong on that score. I think somebody killed two people to prevent the discovery of an older murder, one they hoped would remain undiscovered."

"You're sure it's murder?" MacKenzie asked. "It couldn't have been nitrogen narcosis or an air tank failure of some kind?"

Ryan's lips twisted as he shook his head.

"Nobody bars themselves into a room from the inside, unless they're Houdini," he replied. "Somebody else did this. Somebody in this village knew about the body and they've killed to protect it."

"If it is this lad, Kris Reid, who'd have wanted to kill him?" Phillips asked.

Ryan pointed to his sergeant, as if to capture the thought.

"That's the question, Frank. If we crack this murder, we crack them all."

Later, after the briefing ended and Ryan was packing away his things for the evening, there came a knock at the door.

He looked up to find Josh Dawson hovering by the doorway.

"Can I come in for a minute?"

Ryan's eyes flicked across to the murder wall, which contained a number of colour photographs, including one of the man's father.

"Let's talk outside," he offered, but it was too late.

Josh stared at the image on the wall, recognising it as one from a newspaper article back in 1995. He could remember the name of the newspaper, too, since he had copies of all the clippings stored safely in the folder he carried beneath his arm.

"People say I look like him," he said.

Ryan glanced back at the image on the wall, then into an almost identical pair of deep brown eyes.

"You look very much like him," he said, honestly. "Does it bother you?"

Josh was surprised by the question, never having asked it of himself consciously before.

"It did, until today."

Ryan picked up his bag and closed the door to the Incident Room, forcing them both outside and into the Coastguard's workspace with its humming computer monitors and mounted digital radar.

"Is it raining outside?" Ryan asked.

Josh shook his head.

"First night this week we haven't had any rain."

"Good. Let's take a stroll around the block, and you can tell me what's on your mind."

The younger man nodded, surprised to find Ryan so easy to talk to. He supposed an air of authority could be deceptive.

They headed out into the cold evening and began to walk away from the centre of the village, both men seeming to need a break from its claustrophobic streets in order to think clearly. They passed by the *Cockle* but Josh didn't pause, keeping pace with Ryan as they headed further north towards St. Aidan's Dunes, which swept along the beach that ran all the way to the base of Bamburgh Castle, further up the coast.

"All my life, people told me I was better off not knowing my father," Josh began, after a few minutes' companionable silence. "But, today, for the first time, I've been given a reason to believe they might be wrong. Can you tell me whether the body you found today is my father?"

He stopped at the foot of the dunes and looked Ryan in the eye, man to man.

"I know you can't discuss your case," he qualified. "But I need to know if you believe it could be my da—That it could be Kristopher Reid."

It helped to call him by his full name, Josh realised. If he used the word 'father' or 'dad' too often, he wouldn't be able to see things through.

Ryan swore softly beneath his breath, wanting to brush him off and trill out some standard words about procedure and confidentiality but, as he looked at the young man's face, he couldn't bring himself to do it.

"Yes," he said. "We believe the diver we found today may be your father, Kristopher Reid. I've asked our forensic team to analyse the samples you've already given us, so we can compare the DNA profiles and come up with a more definitive answer."

Josh's lips trembled and he turned away, staring out to sea while he brought his emotions back into check. Ryan didn't rush him, nor would he have expected him to hide his feelings; he couldn't imagine what it would have been like to grow up believing that one of the people to whom you owe your very existence was so unworthy, although it happened more often than anyone would like to admit.

Nobody was perfect, after all, so it came down to a question of degree.

"You know, my father spent most of his career working overseas," he said, conversationally, as they listened to the waves crashing against the sand further below. "He led a very busy life, he and my mother, and they travelled a lot. To create some stability for me and my sister, they put us into boarding schools. Separate boarding schools," he added. "We saw them during holidays and for the odd weekend but, for the majority of my childhood, my dad was a stranger to me. I couldn't claim to know him well and I felt abandoned, most of the time. Still, not knowing him as well as I'd have liked didn't prevent me from loving him, then, or now."

Josh nodded, his face in profile.

"And the fact he sent you away?"

Ryan gave a slight shrug, recognising that personal confidences didn't come easily to him at the best of times, never mind in the middle of a triple murder investigation.

"We've had long discussions about it, but the short version is that my father made the decision he felt was right at the time, just as your father took decisions that made sense to him at the time. At the end of all this, Josh, you may find that your dad wasn't a perfect paragon. You know why? Because none of us are. We're all human, trying to make the best we can of life."

Josh remained silent for long minutes while Ryan's words ran through his mind, then came to a decision.

"I have a confession to make."

CHAPTER 31

After Gemma had taken herself off to bed, no longer able to keep her eyes open despite it being only a shade after seven o'clock, Daisy sought solitude and escape in the television set in the sitting room upstairs and Hutch found himself manning the bar alone. Luckily, it wasn't a busy night, the recent spate of deaths having driven people into their homes after dark, for safety. All the same, one or two die-hard drinkers remained, ambling up to the bar every now and then to refill their glass of ale, their ruddy complexions thrown into harsh focus by the nautical lamps Gemma had fitted overhead.

Gemma.

Looking around the bar area he thought of another time, years before, when she'd kissed his brother in the middle of it all. Closing his eyes, he could still see them locked together, as if nothing and nobody in the world existed but them. He remembered the pain of unrequited love, even all those years ago, and the ecstasy of having finally claimed her for his own.

She isn't yours, his mind whispered.

His eyes flew open again.

"Stop it," he mumbled.

"What's that, son?" one of the regulars propping up the bar called out to him.

"Nothing, Alan. Get you a refill?"

"Still got a half here, lad."

With a pleasant smile, Hutch turned away, hiding his face from the world. Twenty years ago, he'd wondered how he would survive, living with the pain of loving someone who looked at him like a brother; just a faithful friend who was always there to pick up the pieces. He'd never expected that to change—not even when Josh was born or during all the years that followed. If anything, Josh had filled the void in Gemma's life, a perfect miniature of the man she'd lost, only better.

After all, Josh would never leave her. Sons never abandoned their mothers.

What room had there been in her life for him?

None, until lately.

He thought of their night together and smiled wistfully, but his smile turned down at the edges as he thought of how distant and cool she had been this evening. He knew the reason for it, as well.

Kris. Always, Kris.

He saw his brother's memory floating in her mind and behind her eyes, he heard his brother's name spoken softly on the air as she tried to comfort Josh while he battled to come to terms with the fresh blow. He saw his shadow around every corner and heard his laughter on the wind whenever he stepped outside his front door. He'd carried the guilt of living for twenty-three years, at times almost going mad with the notion that his brother might return to punish him for stealing his woman and his child; for surviving.

And now, in his happiest moment with Gemma, Kris had returned. His body being discovered was the reason why she couldn't think of him now, and he didn't bother to wonder whether she ever would again. Now, with the ghost of Kristopher between them, he would always find himself relegated to third place, behind Josh.

As the dog snuffled at his feet, Hutch gave a harsh laugh.

Fourth place, he amended.

"Full moon tonight," one of the men complained.

The midnight sky was littered with a thousand stars, illuminating the small salvage boat as it crept along the coastline towards the Farne Islands. Its AIS had been deactivated, as had all other tracking devices, to ensure its movements would remain undetected.

"Ten minutes and we'll be there," the skipper told the short, portly-looking man who stood beside him, watching the waves with an eagle eye for any other vessels on the water.

"You can do better than that," he said, and the captain increased the speed with a frisson of alarm. The money was appealing, but he still planned on coming out of their venture alive at the end of it.

"What happened to Dawson?" he asked.

"That isn't your concern," Vernon replied. "I don't pay you to ask questions."

The captain fell silent and concentrated on navigating through a tricky current.

"According to my mate, it's around a mile north-north-west of Knivestone."

"Your mate better be right."

Vernon peered out at the dark water, listening to the slosh of the waves as they fell against the hull of the boat. The waters were protected around here, more so than usual, by virtue of the many thousands of birds, seals and other wildlife that had made it their home. People came to gawp at them and take pictures of themselves so they could upload it onto social media and outdo their less adventurous friends. They oohed and ahhed over the birds and took their kids on boat tours before heading back to play crazy golf and eat battered fish. People looked at the islands in wonder and with reverence, but all he saw was another opportunity.

The salvage boat was part of a fleet he kept in a private facility, separate from the usual fleet he sent out to take care of legitimate business. His father and his grandfather before him had always told him that a man should have a hobby and, he supposed, his hobby was illicit marine salvage. He'd converted the beam trawler to operate heavy salvage equipment, including a mechanical grab, side-scan sonar, several floodlights, magnets and airlifts as well as a freefall steel chisel weighing over eight metric tonnes which he had used several times before to break into stubborn wreck sites.

"Coming up alongside Knivestone now, sir," the captain said, with a deference Vernon found pleasing.

"Keep a lookout."

From his position on the uppermost level of Longstone lighthouse, Pete Tawny put an urgent call through to the jetty landing at Inner Farne, where Janine Richardson was waiting to take his call. After a brief exchange, she ran outside to relay the message to the Coastguard and Police boats moored by the Fishehouse.

"They've just passed Knivestone," she told the Coastal Area Commander.

Walker checked the scanner on his boat, which registered nothing in the vicinity.

"Ryan was right," he muttered. "They're sailing beneath the radar. Thanks, Janine."

"How did he know?"

"Tip-off," he replied.

With that, they set off in a fan formation, with one of each of the three boats circling through the islands to approach their target from different sides and reduce the chance they'd need to give chase.

"Let's surprise the bastard," Walker said, and grinned. "Easy as she goes."

Shortly afterwards, HM Coastguard boarded the ghost salvage vessel and Hugh Vernon was handed over to the local police to be charged with fraud and blackmail, as well as numerous contraventions of the Merchant Shipping Act and the Protection of Wrecks Act. With Josh Dawson as their star witness, it wouldn't take them long to unravel Vernon's various illicit activities, including the illegal looting of shipwreck sites and the criminal disposal of dangerous salvage by Vernon Salvage Inc. into the protected waters off the North-Eastern coastline.

While Vernon shouted for his—no doubt expensive, no doubt dirty—lawyer, Ryan enjoyed the comfort of hearth and home with his wife, Anna.

"I can't believe I'm the historian in the family, yet you're the one who's uncovered a thousand-year-old Viking warship," she declared, clicking through the digital images taken by the diving crew once more. She made appreciative noises as she reached the close-up images of the carved prow which had been fashioned into the curling body of a snake with its face jutting outward, no doubt to strike fear and panic into the heart of any sailor brave enough to take her on.

"We can do a job-swap if you like," Ryan said, not altogether jokingly. "You can come and solve these murders and I'll pore over the textbooks to figure out who those ships belonged to."

"I think I'd have the bad end of the bargain," she said, happy to admit that investigating these particular murders was a much more challenging task than trying to determine the origin of a few planks of wood. Well, perhaps more than just a few planks of wood, she amended, as she flicked through some more of the images.

"Has the team managed to secure a license to excavate, yet?"

"Getting itchy fingers, are we?" Ryan joked. "They're working on it. Ursula says you'll be the first one they call once they can make a start on bringing up some of the junk."

Anna looked at him as though he'd said a naughty word.

"What?" he asked.

"Priceless ancient relics are not 'junk,'" she said, and wondered how she had managed to fall hook, line and sinker for a man who'd seemed to have been born without any passion for the past. She supposed it came from seeing death at such close quarters and being reminded of his own mortality on an almost daily basis. That was bound to give him a strong impetus to look forward, rather than back.

She turned off the screen and leaned back in one of the comfortable armchairs in their sitting room, enjoying the last embers of the fire and the way its glow polished Ryan's hair to a blue-black shine. He lay on the sofa opposite with his feet crossed at the ankles, a file still open on his lap.

"It's after midnight," she murmured. "I'm surprised you're still awake, after the day you've had."

"There's always more to do," he replied, but took the hint and closed the file. There wasn't much more he could do before the morning.

"Do you know who might have killed him? The man you found today, I mean."

Ryan nodded.

"Yes, of course. I can't prove it, yet, unfortunately."

Anna raised an eyebrow when he gave her a name.

"You'd have to be very sure," she said. "Nobody would believe it, otherwise."

"Wouldn't they? I don't know. People have done so many appalling things, in the name of love."

"Even so, it's extreme."

"I've seen worse," Ryan said, without irony. "People never fail to impress me with the extravagant and imaginative ways they find to kill other people but, when it comes down to the nitty-gritty, their reason for doing away with someone usually boils down to love, sex, jealousy, money or revenge."

"How are you going to prove it?"

He sighed, swinging his legs down from the sofa to lean his forearms on his knees.

"Honestly? I'm not sure," he said. "The killer's been smart, even at short notice and in some of the worst conditions imaginable. I've gone over and over the evidence we have so far and there's no obvious connection to any of the deaths; nothing that would hold up in court."

"What are you going to do, then?"

"I'm going to do what I always do," he said. "I'm going to follow all the lines of enquiry until I can't go any further and I'm going to work the crime scene. The principle doesn't change just because the crime scene happens to be forty-five metres underwater."

"You're not going to dive down yourself?" she asked, a bit worriedly.

Ryan laughed and held out a hand to tug her upwards and into his arms.

"I might enjoy a bit of holiday scuba diving but that isn't the same as diving in the middle of the North Sea, in one of the most dangerous diving sites in the world. I like adventure, but I don't have a death wish."

She leaned up to plant a kiss on his lips.

"Be careful," she told him. "You don't have to dive to be in danger. There's enough of it on land."

CHAPTER 32

Monday, 5th November

Guy Fawkes' Night

When Ryan's team arrived in Seahouses the following day, the morning had not yet broken. It had been agreed with the marine archaeological team that their work would focus on the Viking shipwreck for the time being, pending full arrangements for funding, licensing and registration with Hector Sayer, HM Receiver of Wreck, who had been positively gleeful upon hearing the news the previous day. In the meantime, police divers would convene in time for an early morning dive to enter and conduct a more thorough search of the cabin where the diver's body had been discovered, alongside a wider search of the naval trawler, on the off-chance there might be some surviving evidence to provide a clue as to who had been responsible for barring the unfortunate man inside what would become his underwater coffin.

Unfortunately, fate was not on their side.

"Detective Chief Inspector Ryan?"

Ryan turned in the process of boarding the *Jolly Roger* to find a tall, straight-backed man in full naval uniform approaching him along the north pier. He was flanked by two junior naval officers, and they all wore serious expressions on their clean-cut faces, in varying degrees of severity.

"Lieutenant Commander Nicholas Smythe-Weston," he said, in the crisp, rounded tones of one who had spent his life in service to the Crown. "A word, please."

The small team from the police Underwater Search and Marine Unit cast wary glances amongst themselves. The unannounced arrival of Her Majesty's Navy did not bode well. If Ryan was concerned, his face betrayed none of it, and he stepped lithely back onto the pier with a smile fixed firmly in place.

"DCI Ryan," he said, extending a hand. "How can I help?"

The briefest of handshakes was exchanged before Smythe-Weston spoke.

"I'll come straight to the point," he said, stiffly. "It's come to our attention that you've uncovered a trawler belonging to Her Majesty's Navy. Given her location and size, we believe the trawler to be the HMS Bernicia, which was sunk on 14th May 1940. Twenty-three men were lost when she went down, and the site is therefore protected as a designated war grave. That being the case, you have no legal right to enter or interfere with any aspect of the wreckage."

Ryan listened to the man's spiel with mounting disbelief.

"Are you aware that we found the body of a diver, yesterday?" he asked, in even tones.

"I'm aware that you found a body following an illegal entry to the war grave, yes," the man said, silkily. "We are willing to overlook the transgression on the understanding there will be no further interference."

"I don't believe what I'm hearing," Ryan muttered. "Are you seriously telling me you're more concerned with an eighty-year-old underwater mausoleum than with an active murder investigation?"

"Under the Protection of Military Remains Act 1986—"

"Don't start spouting legislation at me," Ryan snarled. "The man we found yesterday had a home and people who loved him. They deserve to know how he died. The same goes for the other two people who died this week."

"I can't comment on that," the man said, and jutted his chin towards the *Jolly Roger* and the men and women who watched with frank curiosity to see how the discussion would pan out. "Please ask your team to stand down."

"I'll do no such thing," Ryan shot back. "That wreck might be a war grave—and I have every sympathy for the families of the seamen who lost their lives—but it's also a crime scene and that takes precedence, in my book. If you've got a problem with that, take it up with my superiors."

The man's jaw almost dropped at the audacity of Ryan's response; it was rare to come across anyone who would argue with a naval officer, and rarer still to find rebellion in the *lowly* ranks of the police. But then, he knew very little about the man standing before him, especially not the fact that Ryan had grown up around diplomats and military types and was therefore completely unfazed.

"I warn you again, Chief Inspector, we have the capacity to impound your boat."

"Then do it," Ryan said, taking a step closer so they stood toe to toe. "All I'm hearing from you is a lot of hot air. If you plan to stop me from fully investigating a crime scene, you'll have to impound that boat because I'm going back to the wreck of HMS Bernicia, whether you like it or not."

Smythe-Weston couldn't help admitting a measure of respect for the man who was prepared to stand his ground and, as it happened, Ryan was right. Unless he called up one of Her Majesty's warships, he couldn't prevent the boat leaving the harbour.

"I strongly advise against it," he blustered, conscious of losing face in front of his staff.

"What civilian jurisdiction do you have?" Ryan asked him, and then answered the question for him. "You have no powers of arrest or prosecution. In fact, all you're doing is wasting our time. Now, if you believe a crime has been committed here in Northumberland, report it through the usual channels or, even better, call the Incident Room," he drawled, slapping one of his business cards into the man's unsuspecting hand. "In the meantime, I've got a triple murder to investigate."

With that, Ryan turned and climbed back onto the boat, without looking back.

On land, Phillips and MacKenzie made their way to *The Cockle Inn* for the stroke of nine o'clock, finding it open to the breakfast crowd which consisted of two fishermen and a Dutch family who'd been staying at a holiday cottage by the beach nearby. They found Gemma serving in the dining room, moving with practised efficiency despite the fact she'd hardly slept the previous evening.

"Morning, Ms Dawson," Phillips said, and she barely held back a sigh. It seemed her family would be subject to a never-ending cycle of questions and interviews and she wondered if they would ever be free of it.

"Morning," she said, with as much feeling as she could muster. "Let me get the last of these breakfasts out, then I'll come and join you. Would you like a coffee?"

"That'd be very kind," MacKenzie said, and watched the woman slip back into the kitchen.

They had just settled on a table in the corner when Josh came in, pausing only briefly before walking across to join them at the table.

"Do you need to speak to us again?" Josh asked, and Phillips cleared his throat.

"Have a seat, lad. We wanted to wait until—ah, here they are."

Gemma and Hutch emerged from the kitchen, the latter drying his hands on a tea towel as he walked out, and they realised he must have been standing in for the chef.

"Gemma says you need to see us?" he said, with none of his usual friendly charm.

"Why don't you have a seat," Phillips replied, pulling out the chair beside him. What they had to say was best said face to face.

MacKenzie lowered her voice, so that her words wouldn't carry across the room.

"Our laboratory worked through the night to extract DNA from the bone marrow in the remains we found on board the naval shipwreck yesterday afternoon," she said. "Once they had a profile, it was a simple exercise to compare it with the samples Josh and Paul kindly volunteered previously, in connection with the death of Iain Tucker."

"Is it him?" Josh asked, through lips that were bone dry. "Please, just tell me."

MacKenzie nodded.

"Yes, we believe the man we found on board what we now know to be the HMS Bernicia was your father, Kristopher Reid. I'm very sorry for your loss," she said, to all of them.

Hutch stared, while Gemma simply rested her head in her hands.

Only Josh remained clear-sighted, his eyes blazing with unshed tears.

"Are you sure?"

MacKenzie's eyes pricked with sudden emotion, taking her by surprise. She'd given news of this kind to countless families before; in fact, she'd delivered much worse than the message she'd just relayed, but there was something about the vulnerability in the young man's face that wormed its way behind her defences.

Underneath the table, Phillips put his hand over hers and that simple gesture almost tipped her over the edge.

"We're as sure as we can be," she said briskly. "There was a familial match between the diver's DNA, yours and your uncle's profile."

They did not include Gemma in that analysis, given that there would be no genetic link between her and the late Kristopher Reid.

Josh nodded, then scrubbed both hands over his face.

"That's it, then," he said, with false cheer. "Now we know."

"Yes, now we know," Hutch repeated, in a funny sort of voice.

"How did he die?" Gemma forced herself to ask, though part of her didn't need to know. "Did he drown?"

"The cause of death cannot be established definitively at this stage, although it's most likely Mr Reid suffocated by drowning, yes."

MacKenzie thought of the conversation she'd had with Jeff Pinter, the police pathologist, who'd worked overtime to provide a preliminary assessment of the pitiful remains they'd found inside the diving suit. It had taken him half the morning to lay out the parts of Reid's skeleton in the correct formation, but the process had confirmed one thing: there were no puncture marks or indentations to the bones that spoke of a knife assault, nor any clean knife tears to the diving suit.

Nevertheless, the man had been trapped inside the cabin space, an underwater tomb that would have been the last thing he ever saw. She didn't like to think of the kind of terror he must have felt knowing he would die alone, in darkness, beneath the oppressive weight of the sea.

"We'll be re-opening the old files relating to your brother's disappearance," Phillips was saying. "It may be a distressing time for all of you, having to re-live the trauma all over again, but I'm afraid we need to look at the lines of enquiry that were relevant back in 1995."

"We understand," Gemma said, when Hutch remained silent.

"In that case, we need to ask you and Mr Hutchinson a few questions which, I think, would best be done in private," Phillips added, sparing a thought for the young man who couldn't possibly have any answers relating to his father's disappearance.

"I'll see how Daisy's getting on," Josh murmured, and excused himself from the table.

Once he'd left and was well out of earshot, MacKenzie and Phillips exchanged a glance. They had more news to impart and, in some ways, what they had to tell this family now was worse than before.

"Ms Dawson, Mr Hutchinson, during the course of our DNA enquiry we came across another familial link between an existing DNA profile and the one we now have for Kristopher Reid."

MacKenzie paused, waiting for that to sink in and readying herself for the backlash.

"Another...I'm sorry, I don't understand. Do you mean you have a profile for our mother—Kris's mother, on record, which matched? Or Kris's father?"

Phillips shuffled in his chair, wishing himself anywhere but there at that precise moment.

"No, I'm afraid it's neither of them. The fact is, we found an extremely high probability of a familial link between your late brother's DNA and that of Daisy Jones."

Gemma felt the blood rush into her ears, pumping oxygen around her body to keep her from collapse.

"That—that's not possible," she whispered. "Daisy's the same age as Josh; they were born less than a month apart."

The two detectives fell silent, considering it to be a more tactful approach.

Gemma clasped a hand over her mouth to stifle a cry. Thoughts of Kris having been unfaithful to her paled in comparison with the implications it had for the relationship Josh had with Daisy, and hoped to have in the future.

She felt sick, and rose quickly from her chair, hurrying towards the bathroom.

"I'll see if she's alright," MacKenzie murmured, and dashed after her.

In the residual silence, Hutch stared at a deep scratch on the table where they sat.

"Pity, that," he muttered, running his finger over the wood. "It was only new last year."

"I know this has come as a shock," Phillips said quietly. "We had the lab check the results again, to be doubly sure."

"I knew he had someone else on the go," Hutch said, in a voice so small Phillips strained to hear him. "Mandy wasn't half the woman Gemma is."

Phillips frowned, thinking it was hardly a fair comparison to make now that the woman was dead and, besides, what happened in the past didn't matter half so much as the future of the two young people who had fallen in love with one another but for whom a future would never be possible.

"I don't know how to tell them," Gemma gasped, once she returned from the ladies' room. "It'll shatter them both, all over again."

"We can do it, if you'd rather," MacKenzie offered.

Gemma shook her head.

"It can't come from a stranger," she said, and reached across for Hutch's hand only to find it clasped in his lap.

"Daisy won't have anyone, once she finds out," he said, sadly. "What'll she do?"

Gemma drew in a trembling breath, hardly knowing what to think or how to feel. Only yesterday, she'd lamented her grown-up son entering a relationship with another woman in his life and, now, this had happened.

It was too much to take in.

"Please," she said, looking between Phillips and MacKenzie. "I want to give them one last day. We'll tell them, I promise, but not until the morning. She's just lost her mother and he—he's just lost a father, all over again."

MacKenzie inclined her head.

"How you tell them will be your decision, Ms Dawson, but we're obligated to share this information with Josh and Daisy at the earliest opportunity. We'll call by again in the morning."

Gemma closed her eyes and nodded, wondering how she was ever going to find the words.

CHAPTER 33

Despite his best intentions, conditions at sea had been too dangerous to dive that morning and Ryan had been forced to call off the trip to HMS Bernicia until the high winds died down sufficiently to allow them to proceed. He was honest enough to admit that it was disappointing to find himself in compliance with the Navy's high-handed command, albeit due to forces outside of his control, when he'd rather have been out there doing his job. The weather had been changeable all week; smooth and calm one minute and violently stormy, the next. He and the archaeological team had hoped for a few days' grace to allow them to begin the first stages of an excavation that was already making headlines, no doubt thanks to Jasper Vaughn's own PR machine that had secured him several newspaper and television interviews before their work had truly begun.

Ryan knew what Vaughn was doing, just as he felt certain the rest of the team would know: he was cementing his position as the foremost expert on the project, a move that was both sad and degrading to the highly-qualified team that surrounded him—and to the memory of his former colleague, Iain Tucker. For his part, Ryan had never cared who was given the credit for a collar, preferring to believe that another criminal off the streets wasn't just a triumph for one person, it benefited them all.

Horses for courses, he supposed.

Ryan set aside a copy of Kristopher Reid's old missing persons file which, he'd been sorry to note, was scant at best. The nineties had been Gregson's era, he recalled, and their corrupt former Detective Chief Superintendent had spread his poison far and wide, infiltrating all echelons of the police hierarchy and debasing the standard of workmanship to be expected of the staff in his employ. Gregson might be languishing behind bars now, but his disease could still be felt; echoes of past misdeeds leaving their mark in many of the old case files they stumbled across during the course of routine enquiries.

"It says here that Kristopher Reid had a few pops for D and D," Lowerson remarked, from his position at the other end of the conference table in the Coastguard's Office. "Petty arguments, mostly; nothing that looks malicious. Sounds like the bloke had too much to say for himself when he'd had a few, and it rubbed some of the other punters up the wrong way."

"He was expelled from secondary school," Yates put in, and stood up to stretch her legs for a moment. "Sounds like he was a bit of a tearaway."

"What was he expelled for?" Ryan asked.

"Setting fire to a toilet roll in the boys' locker room," she replied. "Standard dumb thing to do."

Ryan thought of his own regimented upbringing and idly wondered what it would have been like to be the class tearaway. Dangerous and fun, most likely, in equal measure.

"We need to get down to that wreck," he muttered, feeling all kinds of frustration.

"There won't be anything left after all this time," Lowerson said. "The water would have washed it away."

Ryan huffed out a laugh. There was a saying, he thought, about teaching your granny how to suck eggs. Clearly, Lowerson wasn't familiar with it.

"I realise that," he said, and reached for a photograph of the diving knife they'd found tucked into the pocket of Kris Reid's suit. He shoved a copy of the image across the table and pointed a finger towards it. "Look at the blade on that thing."

Lowerson and Yates both looked again.

"What about it? The rust?"

"Carry on at this rate and you'll be on the first available refresher course," Ryan said, darkly. "No, the rust isn't the interesting bit. The blade is almost completely blunt, and the tip has broken off. What does that tell you?"

The penny dropped.

"He tried to use it to get out," Yates suggested.

"Or to leave a message," Lowerson said, at last following the train of Ryan's thoughts. "You think he might have carved a message on the wall down there?"

Ryan leaned back in his chair.

"I started thinking about this, last night. If I was trapped inside that cabin underwater and I knew I'd die there once my tanks ran out, what would I do as a final act?" he asked. "How could I punish the person responsible for bringing about my death, trapping me inside a metal room full of water, nearly fifty metres beneath the surface, without any means of escape?"

"You'd implicate them," Lowerson realised.

Ryan nodded.

"Bingo. Now you know why I want to get down there as soon as possible."

Just then, his phone began to jingle a loud rendition of *Rockin' Around the Christmas Tree* which he had not been responsible for, and Ryan swore affectionately.

"Frank," he muttered, before answering.

"Ryan?"

He came to attention as Chief Constable Sandra Morrison's voice came down the line.

"Yes, ma'am."

"I've just received an extremely irate complaint from a Lieutenant Commander Smythe-Watson or Weston, or something," she said irritably. "He tells me there was an altercation at Seahouses Harbour earlier today and that you're refusing to respect a designated war grave, in direct contravention of the legislation and, I might add, the standards of morality and integrity I expect of my staff. Got anything to say?"

Ryan breathed a sigh of relief and switched the receiver to his other hand while he poured himself a cup of bad coffee from the ancient filter.

"Is that all? I thought you were calling about something serious," he replied. "Yes, I had a conversation with Lieutenant Commander Smythe-Weston, although I'd hardly call it an altercation. He wanted to stop me investigating a crime scene within the wreckage of the HMS Bernicia, the naval trawler we uncovered yesterday, and I told him where to get off."

Back at her desk in CID, Morrison had to smile.

"I'm afraid it doesn't work that way," she said, severely. "I'll admit it's a grey area as far as jurisdiction goes, but don't you think it might have been better to seek a compromise, or to ask him to grant a license to enter the wreck for the purposes of your investigation?"

Ryan pulled a face and took a fortifying sip of coffee-flavoured sludge.

"Frankly, ma'am, I don't. They're the ones who charged down to the harbour this morning, bandying around rules and regulations. He was trying to scare me off and I called his bluff. They have no jurisdiction and he knows it."

"You told him to call 999 if he had a crime to report!" Morrison burst out. "Ryan, there's a bit more to this than you realise. The HMS Bernicia was sunk in 1940 by friendly fire. Official Secrets might have expired but they're still touchy about that kind of thing getting out and they're trying to keep the coverage low-key."

And instead, Jasper Vaughn was running around doing interviews with every paper and glossy magazine within a fifty-mile radius, Ryan thought.

"The *Bernicia* was found within a couple of hundred feet of the Viking wreck," Ryan said. "They can't hope to keep its existence a secret any longer, not when it'll forever be associated with its famous neighbour."

Morrison sighed.

"Look, I've had a word with Smythe-Weston's Commander," she said. "He's agreed to make an exception on this occasion to allow the police to enter the wreck for the sole purpose of continuing our investigation."

Ryan could have argued further, but he was a firm believer in picking one's battles.

"Whatever helps them to sleep better at night," he said. "I don't care which hoops I have to jump through to get down there, so long as I can do it sooner rather than later."

"What's stopping you?" Morrison asked.

"Right now? Gale force winds," he replied, taking another sip of coffee as he watched the rain driving in from the sea. "It'll be a miracle if we can get a diving team down, today."

A few minutes later, he ended the call and slipped the phone back into his pocket, thinking about the person he believed to have killed three people. There was malice in each case, a kind of vicious spite that revealed itself in the manner of their deaths and served as a useful insight into the mind of the person responsible.

The killer had acted swiftly and without remorse, their own needs ranking far higher than those of the people around them. A person like that was volatile.

As the rain began to ease off, Ryan turned back to his team.

"Jack? Get Phillips on the phone and tell him there's been a change of plan. I want Daisy Jones brought in for questioning. Tell him to think up some pretext."

Lowerson blinked.

"I thought we had everything we needed from her, for the time being? And isn't that contrary to the PACE guidelines?"

"We do," Ryan said. "And it is. I'm bringing her in for safe-keeping, Jack, but I don't want her to know that, just yet."

"Or anybody under the same roof," Yates realised.

Ryan turned back to watch the sea, willing the storm to pass.

CHAPTER 34

"Can you tell us about your relationship with your brother, Mr Hutchinson?"

Hutch had elected to be questioned first, waiving his right to a lawyer in the hopes of speeding things up a bit. They were seated in his cubby-hole office once more where, Phillips happened to note, he had scaled back his photographic shrine to the woman they would be questioning next.

"He—Kris was my younger brother. You can imagine what that's like."

"Not really," MacKenzie said. "Why don't you tell us?"

"He was—"

Selfish.

Unreliable.

"Kris was very outgoing," he said, after a second's pause. "Very gregarious, with a lot of charm. Women loved him."

"Women, or one woman in particular?" MacKenzie asked, so easily he almost missed it.

"I—you mean Gemma."

They waited patiently for him to elaborate.

"It's no secret that I've loved Gemma for a long time," he said, lifting his chin. "But if Kris had been alive, I'd have put her out of my mind, or tried to."

"Did you argue over Gemma?" Phillips asked. "Wouldn't be the first time a woman had come between two brothers."

"No, we didn't argue." *I never told him, and Kris was too egocentric to notice.*

"All the same, it must have been hard seeing the pair of them together, in the old days," Phillips pressed.

Hutch clenched his hands, then deliberately unclenched again. He needed to remain calm.

"I was too busy to notice," he lied.

"Come on, mate. When a man loves a woman the way you love Gemma, there had to be moments when you felt like fate was against you, eh? Especially when he went missing. You must have felt mixed emotions, then."

"I—I felt worried, obviously."

"And?"

"And nothing. I felt worried for my brother, especially as I knew by then that Gemma was expecting his child. I was angry he would leave her at such an important time and I was worried something might have happened to him."

MacKenzie made a murmuring sound.

"It's funny, you know, when we looked back over your brother's file something struck us: there was hardly any coverage. Nothing on the evening news or in *The Evening Chronicle.* Can you explain that?"

Hutch swallowed and reached for the glass of water sitting on the desk beside him.

"I can hardly control what the newspapers choose to print," he said.

"No, but you could have kicked up more of a fuss. You could have shouted a bit louder, Paul, when your kid brother disappeared."

Hutch went red and then a deathly white as the blood drained from his face. They were right, he thought. He could have done more but he didn't because…

"Did you see an opportunity, Hutch?"

His eyes dropped away from the woman's face, unable to maintain eye contact any longer.

"I wanted to help, that's all."

"Aye, and maybe if she was grateful, that wouldn't be such a bad thing would it, eh?" Phillips prodded. They needed to see how angry this man could get, and this was the best way they knew how.

"*No,*" Hutch snarled. "I was a friend to her, an uncle to Josh…"

But they were right, he thought. He had coveted his brother's partner and child, wanted them for his own. Nothing had changed, just because time had passed and that child had grown. When Josh succeeded, he felt all the pride of a father, and when he was knocked down, he felt the same deflation.

"Yes," he admitted, with a harsh sob. "I wanted Gemma and Josh. I was glad Kris had gone. God forgive me, I was *glad* he had gone. I hated him for having everything I wanted and for squandering it, when I'd have given anything for even a look from her."

Gemma had composed herself by the time Phillips and MacKenzie caught up with her again. Her hair and make-up had been refreshed and she was making a note to stock up on certain drinks in the bar. At first glance, they might have thought she'd never heard the news about Daisy, which must surely have come as a severe blow, not merely to her family but to her own self-esteem.

They followed her into the kitchen, which was empty now. It was a modern affair, with big stainless-steel range cookers and countertops that gleamed. They took their trade seriously, MacKenzie thought, and hadn't scrimped on the costs.

"Can you tell us about your relationship with Kris?" she asked, as they settled on three stools.

Gemma cast her mind back, all the way.

"Kris was…well, he was gorgeous," she said. "Good-looking but with a twinkle in his eye, you know?"

"I know," MacKenzie said, with a smile for her husband.

"He was the sort of person who could command all of your attention," Gemma recalled. "When he spoke, people listened. When he gave you his attention, it was his full attention. He made you feel special."

"But?" MacKenzie prompted her.

Gemma gave a wry smile.

"He didn't have much of a work ethic, and that could be stressful. We started up *Shell Seekers* together and it was mostly my money that went into it, money I'd saved working as a barmaid for years. It was mostly me who did the work, too," she admitted, with a sad shrug. "It didn't change how I felt about him. I knew what he was like, when I first met him while we were at school. If there was a way to get out of something, or a shortcut he could take, Kris would take it."

"Were you happy?"

Gemma opened her mouth, then shut it again as she thought back. *Yes,* she thought. *She had been happy.*

"He was my world," she admitted. "We made each other happy. I couldn't understand it when I thought he'd left me; it made no sense. At the time, I thought it was a reaction to the news about the baby…it wasn't planned, you see."

They nodded, without any kind of judgment.

"Most babies aren't, or so I hear," MacKenzie smiled.

Gemma nodded.

"From the moment I found out I was expecting Josh, I wanted to build a home, to get our lives on track. But Kris…" She shook her head slightly. "He just wasn't built that way. He was a risk-taker, a man who liked to live a bit on the edge. He hated 'normality' whereas I think I've always craved it."

"You'd have found that with Hutch," Phillips remarked.

Gemma nodded.

"I agree. At the time, I just didn't see him as anything other than a friend who happened to be Kris's brother. As more time passed…well, I realised he might have had feelings for me. I felt empty after Kris left, or after I *thought* he'd left. I wasn't ready to love anybody else or even to try. It's taken me this long to take a gamble again."

She smiled.

"All's well that ends well?"

"I hope so."

CHAPTER 35

Hours ticked by until the weather finally changed, and the police divers took their chance to head out to Knivestone and seek out the answer Ryan needed. The tides meant there would be only a short window of time to search the cabin inside *HMS Bernicia*, and there was every possibility its walls might be so thickened by kelp and algae that it would be impossible to find anything beneath.

But they had to try.

Ryan stood with Alex Walker in the Coastguard's Office, watching the progress of the *Jolly Roger* across the marine radar shown on a large monitor.

"You're confident you've got the right one?" Walker asked, after a few minutes had passed.

Ryan blew out a noisy breath.

"It's a fifty-fifty chance," he said. "Not bad odds." *And he had a favourite.*

The outer door opened to admit Phillips and MacKenzie, both of whom looked as though they'd been through a car wash.

"Enjoy your swim?" Ryan asked, with a grin.

"Aye, very funny," Phillips said, shouldering out of his raincoat. "Got caught in a rain shower on our way back from the inn."

"How did it go over there?" Ryan asked.

"As well as can be expected," MacKenzie said. "We told Gemma and Paul about the DNA match between Kris Reid and Daisy Jones—they joined up the dots quickly enough."

"How did they react?"

"Both of them seemed to be floored by the news," Phillips replied. "If their shock wasn't genuine, they're two of the finest actors I've ever seen. Both seemed more concerned about how the kids would feel, once they found out."

"And how did *they* take it?" Ryan asked.

"They don't know yet. We agreed to give the family until the morning to lay it out for Josh and Daisy, in private," MacKenzie said. "It'll be better coming from one of them than one of us."

"Not necessarily," Ryan muttered, but let it go. "It'll be a hard knock, however they hear about it."

"Daisy was none too happy about being dragged in again for questioning; Carole Kirby came up with some old blarney about Mandy knowing some people connected to Vernon's Salvage, so she had Daisy looking through mountains of known-person files to see if she recognised any, the last time we checked."

"Tell Kirby to keep her there as long as she can," Ryan said, watching the little illuminated dot on the radar flash from a stationary position as the *Jolly Roger* reached the dive spot. "Another half an hour should do it."

Ryan's radio crackled into life.

"Receiving, over."

He held a brief conversation with the police sergeant in charge of the Underwater Search and Marine Unit, a team they had worked with on several cases before, and then settled down to wait for news.

After the police had gone and Josh had retreated upstairs, Hutch went in search of Gemma. It was time, he realised, to lay his cards on the table; to open himself up to the woman he loved and hope she would accept him once he had. It was risky, the kind of gamble Kris might have taken, but not him. He felt giddy with nerves, unsure of how much to say or whether to say anything at all.

"Gem?"

He found her stoking the fire in the main dining room ahead of the dinner crowd, such as it was. Their door hadn't been opening so frequently since news of the murders had got around and, even though nobody had died at the inn, they were tainted by association.

Hopefully, it wouldn't last. These things never did.

"Hi," she said, with a smile that didn't quite reach her eyes. He wondered if it was because of the news about Kris, about Daisy…or because she *knew*.

"I thought we could sit for a while," he said, and indicated a comfy-looking sofa they'd arranged near the fire for those visitors who preferred to have a coffee and catch up on the daily news.

He sat down on the sofa and waited for her to join him, taking her hand when she did.

"We've known each other a long time, haven't we?"

Gemma looked down at their hands, sensing what was to come.

"Yes, we have."

"You know how much I love you, Gemma. Everything I do…everything I've *done*, I've done for you."

Tears filled her eyes, but she managed a short nod.

"I know," she said heavily.

"I hope…I hope after so long, you know I'd never do anything to hurt you," he said and, again, she nodded.

If her hand tensed beneath his, he chose to ignore it.

"When the police first came around to talk to us about Iain Tucker—you remember?—you told them I'd come upstairs not long after you had, on Thursday night."

She nodded, turning to him with wide eyes that shone with fear.

"But I didn't come straight up to bed, Gemma. I didn't do that, at all."

A full twenty minutes had passed since the last communication and, when the radio signalled again inside the Coastguard's Office, Ryan snatched it up.

"Ryan, receiving. Over."

"Sir? We found a name. Over"

The room fell silent as the disembodied voice of the police sergeant came down the line, describing the task of checking all the walls of the cabin inside the HMS Bernicia, only to find that Kristopher Reid had a touch of Michelangelo in him and had written the name of his killer on the ceiling, instead.

When they said the name, spelling it out clearly so there could be no misunderstanding, Ryan turned to his team with blazing eyes.

"Let's move."

CHAPTER 36

When Ryan entered *The Cockle Inn,* he found Paul Hutchinson seated alone at a sofa in front of the fire. He didn't bother to turn around but continued to stare into the flames, mesmerised by the flickering light. His neck was bent and, for the first time, he looked defeated.

"Where's Gemma?" Ryan asked him, moving carefully so as not to startle him. "Where's Gemma, Hutch?"

"She left," he said, his heart broken. "Josh, too."

"Her car isn't in the car park," Phillips said, joining them via the side door. "Should I put out an APB out on it?"

Ryan lifted a shoulder.

"May as well," he said, and Phillips spoke swiftly into his police radio. "But it isn't the car I'm concerned about. Where's Gemma's boat, Hutch? Which one is hers?"

He didn't answer.

"She knew that I—she knew that I suspected," he said, swiping away tears. "I tried to ignore it but the feeling kept niggling away at me, until I couldn't think about anything else. It was when she told the police that she'd heard me coming up to bed just after she had. It was a lie, because I'd stayed up for another hour in my office after closing time. I couldn't understand why she told them that...then it struck me that she needed me to agree with her. She needed them to think she'd been tucked away in bed and that somebody else had been the last person awake, the last person to lead Iain Tucker astray."

"Where is she now, Paul?" Ryan wasn't interested in the man's introspection and he needed to move quickly.

"I couldn't understand why she hated Daisy so much," he muttered. "Even before Josh started showing an interest, she was so hard on the girl and it wasn't like her. I realised today, when you told me about Kris being Daisy's father, I realised she knew all along. She never breathed a word because she'd have had to admit she knew Kris had been having an affair with Mandy."

"She couldn't have killed Mandy because of that," Ryan said. "If jealousy were the reason, she could have killed Mandy Jones at any point in the last twenty-three years."

Hutch shook his head.

"She didn't tell me. But I think Mandy must have seen something. Maybe she wanted money."

Ryan thought of Mandy's internet history, her plans to move away. She hadn't said anything about Daisy's parentage, either—but when things developed between her daughter and Josh, she knew she needed to move them apart.

"Neither of them spoke out," he said, disgustedly. "They let their children fall in love, knowing they shared the same father."

Hutch pressed his lips tightly together, thinking of how Josh had looked when they'd told him, less than half an hour before.

"I told you, she's gone. I don't know where."

"If you're lying to us now, you'll be prosecuted for perverting the course of justice," Ryan warned him. "You knew she'd lied and you said nothing. You did nothing."

He didn't bother to deny it. He'd live with the knowledge for the rest of his days, wondering when and how Gemma had changed, how he'd failed to make her happy.

"She found out about Mandy, didn't she?" Ryan realised. "That's why she killed your brother."

"They found those wrecks twenty-three years ago," Hutch said softly. "She told me before she left. They'd hit the jackpot and it would set them up for life. They'd planned to report it, register it all and go on to run the biggest diving school in the country. It didn't work out that way. The same night, Gemma heard him speaking to Mandy, arranging their next meeting. So, when they went down to the wreck site the next day, she left Kris there to rot."

Even saying the words made him feel sick. All these years, he'd lived and worked alongside her and, all the while, she had blood on her hands.

Phillips' radio sounded, and he moved away to speak to his colleague.

"They've picked up Gemma's car travelling southbound on the A1," he said. "Josh was driving."

Ryan set aside the automatic feeling of disappointment; the woman was still his mother and it was a hard bond to break, even when that mother was a stone-cold killer.

"Have him arrested," he snapped. "This one, too."

But Hutch had different ideas.

"If she's taken a boat, you should bring me with you. I might be able to talk some sense to her," he said. "Make her come in, of her own accord."

Ryan was sceptical.

"Why should we trust you? You're blinded by her."

"The blinders are well and truly off, now."

"If you mess us about, I won't hesitate," Ryan said, and then turned to his sergeant. "Phillips? Get in touch with the others and tell MacKenzie to set up a command centre. Put the Coastguard on alert to intercept a diving vessel by the name of—"

He looked towards Hutch and the other man knew he'd reached a crossroads. Speak now, or be cast out.

"She'll have taken Josh's boat," he said. "It's the *Misty Morning*."

Gemma steered the boat parallel to the shoreline, dodging all the rocks and islets she knew were scattered across the water like pebbles, holding the wheel firm against the wind and rain which came down in a sheet and had almost soaked through her clothing. She hadn't brought much; no supplies, no practical clothes and she'd broken a cardinal rule of boating by failing to wear a life jacket.

Perhaps because, in her heart, she knew she wasn't really going anywhere.

At first, she'd had some crazy notion of using the islands as camouflage; of dipping in and out of the shallow, narrow channels she'd grown up with and waiting until the coast was clear before making a break for Scotland or just sailing towards the horizon and hoping for the sea to envelop her.

She thought of her son and of the look on his face as he'd overheard the conversation with Hutch. He'd looked so lost, so forlorn, as though she'd crushed the last vestiges of his boyhood; that sweet, innocent core of idealism that had somehow endured was now gone.

You killed my father.

Murderer.

Murderer!

Tears mingled with the rain as she fought her way across the water and the howl of the wind resembled the cry of a young boy with dark, curly hair whose smile had reminded her that, once, she'd done something good.

She'd made him.

Please, Josh. Just drive the car as far as you can. It's the last thing I'll ever ask of you.

Get out! Get out, and don't come back. You're nothing to me, now.

A thousand memories rose up and fell before her eyes.

Josh as a tiny baby cradled in her arms.

Josh taking his first steps and then tumbling down again.

The first time she'd seen Kris.

The last time she'd seen Kris.

Josh kissing Daisy.

Josh looking at her with revulsion, as though she was nothing.

Gemma's hands loosened on the wheel and then let go for a second as she laughed, a hysterical sound, and waited for the wind and sea to do the rest.

But then she caught sight of the Coastguard's powerful beam shining across the water as it approached from the north.

Her hands clutched the wheel again.

It wasn't over yet.

CHAPTER 37

The Coastal Area Commander acted quickly, deploying a rib from the base at Holy Island as well as Seahouses, where Ryan, Phillips and Hutch joined him and his deputy at the boathouse. From there, it took only minutes before they were out on the water and motoring through the harbour into open sea.

"*Misty Morning* hasn't got its AIS switched on, either!" Alex Walker shouted, as rain and sea spray ran down his face. "Without any idea of its location, we'll have a devil of a job finding her around the Farnes in these conditions!"

Ryan nodded, gripping the safety handles as it flew over waves almost as tall as him.

"She doesn't have anywhere to go!" he called back.

"The Holy Island rib is already on the water," Alex said, bracing himself against the violent rocking of the boat. "It'll intercept her from the north and head her off in that direction."

"There!" Hutch shouted, over the deafening sound of the waves. "There's a light, there!"

"That's the rib!" Walker called back, recognising the sister boat immediately. "I can't see the *Misty Morning*, though."

Ryan leaned over to where Phillips clung to the safety rail like a limpet.

"You alright, Frank?" he shouted.

"Oh, aye!" came the queasy reply, as Phillips worked valiantly to keep hold of his lunch. "Can't wait to go 'round the block again!"

Ryan slapped a hand on his back in support and then braced himself against another strong wave that seemed to rear up like a wild animal in the darkness before thundering down again, the force of it sweeping against the sturdy lifeboat so that her prow tipped up for endless seconds before dipping down again, as if in slow motion.

"We'll take the southern end of the Farnes while the other boat heads north," Walker told them. "We've got twice the speed of the *Misty Morning*, so she can't outrun us!"

Hutch wasn't listening to the boat talk; he was thinking of Gemma and of where she might go. Ryan was right when he said there was nowhere for her to run to, nowhere to hide—at least not for long. He gripped the rubbery edge of the rib as it wound around the cliffs of Staple Island, the rocks jutting upward like silent soldiers all around them, guarding entry to a protected world. He thought of the times when they were young, when he, Kris and Gemma would head out on the water together, back when it was the three of them. They'd explored every inch of the place, whether they were supposed to or not, but Gemma had always preferred the diving to the east of the Farnes. The water was wilder there, she'd said. Untamed and dangerous, which had always seemed to draw her in.

"Further east!" he called out, with a heavy heart. "She'll head east."

As Alex Walker brought the boat around to starboard, Gemma started to make the turn to cut through Brownsman's Gut, a narrow channel of water separating Staple Island and Brownsman island, flanked by tall cliffs on both sides. As she did, she caught the flash of a coastguard beam approaching from the northern end of the Gut and brought her boat back around quickly, changing her mind at the last moment. Her stomach performed a violent somersault as the boat lurched to one side in response and she had a very near miss off the Pinnacles, fighting the tide as it urged her closer and closer to the rocks, pushing the throttle as far as it would go as she fought against the inevitable.

"There!" Ryan shouted.

He pointed towards the outline of a small white-and-green diving boat that was struggling against winds coming up from the south and threatening to toss her against the sheer cliff face of the Pinnacles on the underside of Brownsman island.

"Where's she going?" he shouted.

Hutch shook his head, trying to think clearly but experiencing a crippling fear as he watched the woman he'd loved—*still* loved—battling the power of the North Sea in her bid to escape.

He was ashamed to love her, to feel anything for a woman who had murdered three people, but he did.

"Harcar!" he called out. "She'll cut under Big Harcar and make for Longstone!"

Walker brought the boat around, avoiding the hazardous cliff edges and rocks so he could follow the tide rather than battle against it.

The light from Longstone lighthouse cut through the darkness and illuminated the tiny dive boat with its single passenger, an insignificant speck on the ocean landscape. The rocks loomed all around, beautiful and unthreatening by day but sinister and immortal at night.

"She's trying to skirt around the bottom of Big Harcar," Ryan said. "Get the other boat to cut her off at the Craford's Gut!"

"Stop talking about guts, for pity's sake!" Phillips shouted. "Mine's only just hanging on!"

"Better keep tight hold of it, then, Frank! We're coming in!"

With that, Walker performed a series of expert moves so that the rib appeared to dance across the waves, bobbing up and down but never tipping too far in the wrong direction as he moved in to close the net.

After three years of knowing Maxwell Charles Finley-Ryan, his wife, Anna, had developed a sixth sense for when something was amiss. Such as the time he borrowed a horse and gave chase to a serial killer through Kielder Forest. Or the time he'd commandeered a surveillance van and entered into a high-speed car chase with an insane vicar who was making 'angels' across Newcastle. And not forgetting the time he took a fishing boat and made his way across the water from Budle to Holy Island to save her from harm, endangering himself in the process. When news reports started to trickle in about two lifeboats being deployed by HM Coastguard to chase down a missing dive boat, it had raised a red flag in her mind and she grabbed her bag and coat without further ado.

She stepped inside the Coastguard's Office to find it heaving with police and coastguard staff but no Ryan or Philips. She had only to seek out MacKenzie to have her suspicions confirmed.

"Let me guess," she said, weaving through the crowd. "Shark attack?"

"Not yet," her friend replied. "Try again."

"Extreme fishing?"

MacKenzie snorted.

"He's on one of the coastguard ribs with Alex, Frank and a couple of others. Gemma Dawson took her son's boat and she's making a run for it. Or should that be a sail for it?"

"Gemma?"

MacKenzie nodded.

"Are you so surprised?"

"Now you mention it, no, I'm not. Ryan told me he suspected her, and I couldn't believe it at the time. But I suppose that anybody is capable of murder."

"I'll murder Frank, if he doesn't come back in one piece," MacKenzie grumbled. "We've only been married for six months and I'm too young to be a widow."

As the lifeboat drew closer to the channel separating the islands of Big and Little Harcar, and the larger island of Longstone to the east, the *Misty Morning* came fully into view.

She was in severe distress.

Those aboard the rib could make out Gemma's tiny figure as she wrestled with the wheel of the boat, begging the engine to work harder against the waves that pummelled her from the south and thrust her towards Big Harcar and its unyielding rock face. Nearly two hundred years before, the engines of the *Forfarshire* steamship had failed, and she'd raised her sails in a treacherous North-Eastern gale, the force of which had swept her crashing onto those rocks. As if history were repeating itself, they watched in horror as an enormous wave rose up against the *Misty Morning* and drove it against the rocks, wood splintering.

As they drew closer, Hutch let out a cry of panic and, a moment later, he was in the water.

"Man overboard!" Phillips shouted, and the remaining crew were galvanised as they watched him swim single-mindedly towards the wreck and to the tiny outcrop where Gemma clung, her body shaking with shock and exposure, ready to let go and allow the sea to claim her. Ryan spotted a winch tethered to the lifeboat and shouted across to the others.

"I'll go in after Hutch! Reel us in from here—it's too dangerous to go any closer!"

The others knew he was right. In the slick, icy-black water that hissed and roared, they saw Hutch was already tiring, his head only just managing to keep above water.

"Go steady!" Walker told him, and didn't bother to put up a token protest. He knew Ryan to be a strong swimmer and easily fit enough to be one of the lifeguard crew, whereas he needed to stay on board to steer.

It made sense.

Phillips clipped the back of the winch onto Ryan's life jacket and gave him a nod.

"Come back to us, lad."

"I will."

Moving like lightning, Ryan tucked an arm around the life ring and, with a nod for Phillips, dived cleanly into the water. The shock of the temperature hit him like a brick wall, sending his whole body into instant shock—and he'd watched *Titanic* enough times to know that wasn't a good thing. He began to pump his arms and legs, slicing through the water with a powerful front crawl to reach Hutch, who was fifty feet away and beginning to flounder in his desperation to reach Gemma.

The force of the waves was terrifying, unlike anything he'd ever experienced. The fear he felt was primeval, a deep-rooted animal urge to guard himself against ending up in situations such as these, but he couldn't let a man die. Not when he was almost within his grasp.

Ryan's arms and legs began to tire, shaking with the early stages of hypothermia and fatigue as he worked against the tide, his face going under as another wave swept over him. He surfaced again, gasping for air, blinking water from his eyes to orientate himself.

He spotted Hutch and made one last push to reach him before the man submerged.

As Ryan finally reached Paul Hutchinson's flailing body, he grabbed a fistful of the man's jacket and heaved him up and over the life ring with blue, shaking fingers before tugging on the line at his back.

Before they could be pulled to safety, Hutch began to shout, his body rising up and struggling against Ryan and the life ring.

"Gemma! No! No!"

When Ryan felt Paul's body go limp and nearly submerge for a second time, he knew that Gemma Dawson had fallen. The sea had claimed another soul for its underwater graveyard; soon to be another woman whose legend would outlive her, and although it pained him to think it, perhaps there were some that could not be saved.

Ryan believed that a life was a life—it was worth saving regardless of whether the person living it was 'good' or 'bad'. It was the same principle that led him to fight for the dead, no matter their walk of life or personal attributes, whether they cheated on their girlfriends, let down their families or taken bribes from salvage companies.

Life, in and of itself, was important.

EPILOGUE

Nine months later

Paul Hutchinson closed the inn for the afternoon, which was a glorious, picture-perfect summer's day. The village was packed with tourists, all waiting and eager to spend their hard-earned cash, but he wasn't thinking about business just now; he was thinking about family.

He wandered down towards the harbour, stopping to wave and say 'hello' to the people he knew before making his way down towards the slipway, where an events organiser asked for his name. He was ushered down to a large, brand new diving boat, designed for specialist archaeological excavations. During the past year, the excavation team had found and preserved countless artefacts carefully recovered from the Viking warship Iain Tucker had found. It had been established as the largest and oldest surviving example of early Nordic construction, dated to at least fifty years before the first recorded attack on Lindisfarne and had, after a nifty interview with Detective Chief Inspector Ryan, come to be known as the 'Tucker Hoard'.

Excavation of the site had been an enormous task and archaeologists and historians from around the world had expressed their interest in working on the project. But it had been a key goal of the project to use local talent, wherever possible, and that had included making use of some of the best divers in the region.

It had included Josh.

Somewhere amidst the grief of losing everything he'd known, Josh had been given a purpose. He'd put on his tanks each day and gone down with the rest of them, the underwater world providing the quiet, peaceful space he'd needed to heal. And, along the way, Josh had made new friends, including the coastguard, who'd suggested he might like to put his skills to a different use and become a part of another important community.

Each night, he came home to the little apartment at the inn, which he was slowly redecorating so that it no longer resembled his mother's space. Forgiveness was too much to ask, and Hutch understood that.

He was working on it, himself.

"Hutch!"

Josh waved him over to where he stood by the water's edge in his new uniform, ready to see the christening of the new boat he'd commissioned for his diving school, where he now employed two other local divers.

Walking towards the young man, Hutch was filled with pride, and tried to find the words as he came to shake the boy's hand.

"This—it's wonderful, Josh. I'm so proud of all you've achieved."

"I had a bit of help from my family and friends," Josh said, with a smile. "It's been a hard road, this past year, but we're starting to see light at the end of the tunnel, aren't we?"

Hutch nodded, looking around at all the people who had gathered to watch the boat launch.

"I'm your uncle," he said, gruffly. "I wouldn't have missed this for the world."

Josh put a hand on his arm.

"You've been a father to me, Hutch. I know that, now."

It took him several seconds until he could trust his own voice to speak, and then he tried out a word he hadn't dared to speak.

"Thanks, son."

Josh nodded towards the harbour wall, where most of the village and more besides had gathered.

"Daisy came, look."

She'd moved away to make a clean break of it, down to Newcastle. They hadn't heard from her for the first six months; it had been too painful. But then, something had shifted for her, too. She'd found someone new, someone who knew nothing of her old life in Seahouses, and she'd realised she had a brother and an uncle, if she wanted them.

It had been strange and uncomfortable, that first meeting, but it was getting easier each time.

A few minutes later, Josh's boat took to the water. 'The Kraken' had smooth, elegant lines even Viking shipbuilders would have been proud of, and a host of high-spec machinery to enable another generation of adventurers to explore the seas.

From his position on the harbour wall, Ryan clapped along with the rest of the crowd.

"Nice day for it," he said, and slung an arm around his wife's shoulders as they turned to walk back into the village.

"All's well that ends well," Anna agreed. "Where are Jack and Mel, today?"

"He's giving her a hand moving house," MacKenzie said, with a suggestive wriggle of her eyebrows.

Phillips waited until an acceptable amount of time had passed, then turned to his companions to ask the question that was uppermost in his mind.

"Anybody fancy fish 'n' chips?"

AUTHOR'S NOTE

It was a pleasure to write *Longstone*. It is based around the little village of Seahouses, a place I've visited many times over the years and particularly during my childhood when, like Phillips, I'd stop in for fish and chips with my family and walk along the beach from there to Bamburgh. It's the best place to catch a boat trip to the Farne Islands, which are a beautiful example of the natural world and I'd advise anyone to go across to see the puffins and seals or the sea birds. If you're a diver, I can't promise that you'll find the fictional ships on these pages, but there are still many incredible wrecks to explore and more still to be discovered.

Longstone lighthouse is an architectural feat, an impressive structure that performs an important purpose and has done ever since it was first erected. It was made famous by the heroic actions of Grace Darling in 1838 and, nowadays, it is run remotely by the Trinity House charity and looked after by the very capable hands of its keeper,

George, who runs tours if you'd like to see the interior and get a feel for where Grace Darling spent her life.

Viking history in Northumberland is very well established but there is, in fact, some evidence to suggest their longships landed on the south coast of England prior to their invasion of Lindisfarne in 793 AD. This provided me with the inspiration for part of this story, allowing me to imagine the possibility of other ships having tried to land before. The recent, real-life discovery of a 2,400-year-old preserved Greek ship in the Black Sea also proves that it is possible for timber wrecks to survive, if the conditions are right. In that example, the water depth was much deeper than those I have discussed in this book, but that's the beauty of fiction.

I hope you enjoy this sea-faring mystery: happy reading!

LJ Ross
December 2018

ACKNOWLEDGEMENTS

Unbelievably, *Longstone* is my tenth novel. Back when I was writing my fourth and fifth books in the DCI Ryan series, many people warned me it was an established phenomenon that readers tended to lose interest in a series of books over time. However, this has not turned out to be the case, and *Longstone* went straight into the charts in the number one position on its very first day available to pre-order, making it the seventh DCI Ryan novel to claim the UK top spot in the space of three and a half years of writing. I owe all this to my readers, who seem to like the same silly humour that I do and who value the same things I and my characters do: friendship, loyalty and a bit of healthy banter—not to mention an appreciation of the humble bacon stottie.

Nothing in life is ever achieved without the support of a great many people and this is very much the case for me, too. I'm often asked why I write under the pen name 'LJ' and I'm always happy to explain that the 'J' in that moniker stands for 'James', my husband and best friend in life. I may write the stories but that is only made possible with his boundless help in other areas of our life together, his good humour and willingness to listen to story ideas for hours on end. For this story in particular, I want to thank: all the diving and boat tour companies in Seahouses, who enable ordinary people like me to glimpse another world; English Heritage, who care for and preserve the habitat of thousands of birds and other species on the Farnes, for all of us to enjoy; Kristopher Reid, whose generous charitable donation earned a starring named character role in this book; Paul Hutchinson, whose joinery, carpentry and building skills are second to none and whose love for his daughter inspired a character in this story.

Finally, thanks to all of my family and friends, to all the book bloggers and reviewers who have taken the time to read my stories—you're all fantastic!

ABOUT THE AUTHOR

LJ Ross is an international bestselling author, best known for creating atmospheric mystery and thriller novels, including the DCI Ryan series of Northumbrian murder mysteries which have sold over five million copies worldwide.

Her debut, *Holy Island*, was released in January 2015 and reached number one in the UK and Australian charts. Since then, she has released a further eighteen novels, all of which have been top three global bestsellers and fifteen of which have been UK #1 bestsellers. Louise has garnered an army of loyal readers through her storytelling and, thanks to them, several of her books reached the coveted #1 spot whilst only available to pre-order ahead of release.

Louise was born in Northumberland, England. She studied undergraduate and postgraduate Law at King's College, University of London and then abroad in Paris and Florence. She spent much of her working life in London, where she was a lawyer for a number of years until taking the decision to change career and pursue her dream to write. Now, she writes full time and lives with her husband and son in Northumberland. She enjoys reading all manner of books, travelling and spending time with family and friends.

If you enjoyed reading *Longstone*, please consider leaving a review online.

THE INFIRMARY

A DCI RYAN MYSTERY

—PREQUEL—

LJ ROSS

CHAPTER 1

Sunday 6th July 2014

The Sunday Market on Newcastle's Quayside was bustling. Traders touted everything from chocolates to knitted tea caddies, and the air was heavy with the scent of fudge and fried onions as John Dobbs fought his way through the crowd.

He walked with his head bent, avoiding the faces of those who jostled him along with impatient nudges and irritable sighs.

"'scuse me, mate."

A meaty hand thrust him aside and Dobbs stumbled backwards into the path of an oncoming buggy laden with children.

"Mind out o' the way, man!"

A rake-thin woman raced towards him, shoving the buggy out in front of her like a battering ram.

"Sorry," he muttered, ducking between the stalls.

Dobbs risked a glance between the flaps of colourful tarpaulin and waited. He searched the passing faces of the crowd and began to think he had imagined the creeping, paranoid feeling of being followed.

Then he spotted them.

A man and woman weaved purposefully through the stream of people and came to a standstill, craning their necks as they searched the faces with hard, focused eyes that set them apart from the common herd. It was the same pair he'd seen yesterday, and the day before that.

It could mean only one thing.

Police.

He felt his stomach jitter, one slow flip that brought bile to his throat. They had come for him.

"Oh, God," he whispered, and shuffled backwards, trying to make himself invisible. His chest shuddered in and out as he battled to remain calm, sucking in deep breaths of sickly-sweet summer air.

The policeman must have sensed him, because he turned suddenly and their eyes locked. Time slowed, the crowd became a blur and, in the second that PC Steve Jessop hesitated, Dobbs took his chance.

He spun around and burst through the brightly coloured canopies that billowed on the air, running along the quayside without any idea of where to go, driven only by the need to get away, to find somewhere safe.

"Hitchins! He's leggin' it!"

Dobbs heard the man shouting to his partner and knew they wouldn't be far behind. His feet slapped against the pavement and he'd barely gone a hundred yards before he began to tire, muscles screaming as he urged his useless body to go faster.

"*We're in pursuit of subject heading west along the Quayside! Surveillance is blown. Request further instructions. I repeat, request immediate instructions!*"

Dobbs cast a glance over his shoulder and saw the pair of them shouting into their radios as they gave chase. When he turned back, he lost his footing and careened into a group of teenagers, falling awkwardly to the sound of jeers.

He didn't stop to listen but scrambled up again, the pads of his fingers tearing at the rough paving stones as he fought to stay ahead. There was a buzzing in his ears as he leaped into the road.

Horns blared, brakes screeched as he ran beneath the enormous bridge connecting Newcastle and Gateshead. It towered high above his head in a graceful arch of painted green steel, its underbelly spattered with the faeces of a thousand birds who nested in its nooks and crannies. Their noise was deafening, a cacophony of squawks and cries as he searched for a way to escape, a quiet hollow where he could breathe and think clearly. He pressed his hands to his ears.

"Please, God," he muttered. "Make them stop."

Beneath the wide arches was a granite tower supporting the north side of the bridge. Usually, its doors were kept firmly locked to the public, but vandals seeking a new dumping ground had tampered with the chain and it lay in a heap of rusted metal on the floor, leaving the door tantalisingly ajar. Dobbs squeezed behind the barrier railing, yanked the door open with a creak of hinges, and hurried inside.

He blinked as his eyes adjusted to sudden darkness, retching at the overpowering smell of birds and mildew. Ahead of him, a staircase beckoned, and he followed it up to an enormous tower room. Its steel framework was still visible from the days when it had been used as a warehouse in the 1920s and, as the sun broke through the dusty window panes, he looked up to its high rafters in a kind of wonder. Tiny pigeon feathers and a haze of dust motes floated on the air and, to his fevered mind, it was a kind of cathedral, a place of sanctuary.

But not for long.

The sound of running footsteps followed him upstairs, and Dobbs flew up another staircase leading to the upper level. In the distance, he heard the long wail of police sirens outside and knew they were for him.

Sweat coursed down his face and into his eyes as he hurried upward. His legs burned, and his gasping breaths echoed around the high walls as he clambered higher.

"*Up there!*"

He heard them in the tower below, then the crackle of a police radio.

"Subject is inside north tower of the bridge and heading for the roadway exit on the top level. Requesting immediate support!"

"Where the hell is Cooper?"

Dobbs didn't stop to wonder who Cooper was. His lungs laboured, dragging stale air into his exhausted body. Clammy hands pushed against the crumbling wall as he struggled to reach the top of the stairs and whatever fate awaited him there.

"John!"

He heard the woman calling out to him, warning him to stop, to stay calm. All the things he couldn't do even if he wanted to.

He emerged from the stairwell onto a precarious gangway wrapping around the topmost level of steel frame and the height was enough to make him dizzy. His legs were shaking with fatigue and black dots swam in front of his eyes as he clung to the wall. He heard the rattle of metal as they climbed the stairs below and he searched desperately for a way out.

Dobbs spotted a door halfway along the gangway and began to edge forward, sweating as his feet slid against bird excrement and the gangway creaked beneath his weight. The birds were all around now, cooing and crying like the pealing of bells.

"John! Stay where you are!"

He clasped a hand around the heavy door handle that would lead him out onto the top of the bridge. On the other side, he could hear the thrum of traffic and he tugged harder, desperate to get out.

The door was locked.

A sob escaped him, echoing around the cavernous tower.

Frantic now, he put his weight behind it and kicked out at the old chain lock, but it wouldn't budge. He was almost beaten when he spotted a small hook to the side of the door with a set of old keys, coated in cobwebs and grime. His hands shook as he tried each of them in the lock until, miraculously, the chain fell away.

The police were only metres away by the time he prised the door open. When he burst onto the bridge, a gust of strong wind hit him like a fist to the face so that he almost fell backwards again. Cold air rolled in from the North Sea and whipped through the high arches, the metal screeching and moaning like a woman in torment. He shook his head to clear the sound, pressing the heels of his hands to the sides of his head to relieve the pressure.

"John?"

He backed away from the door as the two police officers joined him, red-faced and out of breath.

"John," the woman repeated, palms outstretched. "I'm Detective Constable Hitchins and this is Police Constable Jessop. All we want to do"—she paused to catch her breath—"all we want to do is talk to you."

But he heard fear and mistrust buried beneath the empty platitude.

"I don't believe you," he whispered and began to cry.

Jessop and Hitchins glanced at each other, neither sure how to handle a situation that was escalating rapidly out of their control.

Where was Cooper?

Vehicles and pedestrians moving in both directions across the bridge had come to a standstill and the road was blocked by the shrieking arrival of several squad cars. In his peripheral vision, Dobbs watched as more police officers swarmed out of their cars and began to set up makeshift barriers to protect the public from the madman on the bridge.

Tears spilled over his face. Small, salty rivers that pooled in the lines on his cheeks as he continued to edge backwards.

"John, listen to me," Hitchins began.

"It's all over!" Jessop cut across her, adopting the kind of aggressive stance he thought would help him get ahead in life. "Give yourself up, man!"

But he wasn't listening to either of them. He watched a seagull weave through the metal struts overhead with an elegant flap of wings, then dive towards the water somewhere below.

"...John Edward Dobbs, I am arresting you on suspicion of murder. You do not have to say anything. But it may harm your defence if you do not mention when questioned something which you later rely on in court. Anything you do say may be given in evidence."

As they surged forward to restrain him, Dobbs grasped the thick safety rail on the edge of the bridge. Drawing on the last drop of strength he had left, he heaved himself over the barrier and clung to the top, his knuckles glowing white as he held tight. He pressed his cheek against the cold metal and closed his eyes, mouthing a silent prayer.

"John, come down from the railing," he heard one of them say.

"Stay back!" he muttered, and opened his eyes. Far below, the river glistened diamond-bright in the early afternoon sunshine as it undulated gently towards the sea.

"John!" Hitchins' voice sounded urgent. "Don't do anything stupid. You don't want to do anything final."

But he knew she didn't care. She couldn't; not if he was a killer.

Another radio crackle.

"*Subject is volatile, there's a strong suicide risk. We need a crisis negotiator here, now!*"

Slowly, Dobbs began to relax his grip on the metal railing.

"John, there's still time to come down and talk about things," the woman tried again, her voice wobbling.

How strange, he thought, that it was they who were frightened in the end.

He watched the river, mesmerised by the ebb and flow of the waves as the police continued to talk, to cajole, and finally to threaten. New officers came and went, more sirens and more noise while Dobbs retreated to the recesses of his own mind.

"*John*! Tell us why, John! At least tell us whether there are any more! You owe us that!"

In his last moments, he thought of his life, and of the people he had known. He couldn't recall ever feeling truly happy; there might have been flashes over the years, but they had been outweighed by crushing loneliness. He thought of all the stupid, desperate actions he had taken to quell it. He thought of the dead woman, and started to laugh through his tears, a hysterical, maniacal sound that jarred in the surrounding silence.

And then, sweet oblivion as the water rose up to meet him.

LOVE READING?

JOIN THE CLUB...

Join the LJ Ross Book Club to connect with a thriving community of fellow book lovers! To receive a free monthly newsletter with exclusive author interviews and giveaways, sign up at www.ljrossauthor.com or follow the LJ Ross Book Club on social media:

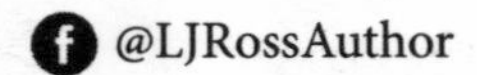

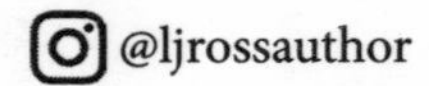